REPRESENTING SHAKESPEAREAN TRAGEDY

Reiko Oya explores theatrical expressions of Shakespearean tragedy in Georgian London and the relations between the representative players of the time – David Garrick, John Philip Kemble and his sister Sarah Siddons, and Edmund Kean – and their close circle of friends. The book begins by analysing the tragic emotion that Garrick conveyed through his performance of *King Lear*, and the responses to it from such critics as Samuel Johnson and Elizabeth Montagu. The second chapter examines the concept of sublimity in Kemble and Siddons's interpretations of *Macbeth*, and compares their legendary 1794 staging of the tragedy with parallel attempts at sublime expression in the works of Joshua Reynolds and Edmund Burke. The final chapter studies the disparity between the literary and the theatrical *Hamlet* in Kean's impersonation and William Hazlitt's response to it, before examining two offshoots of the tragedy: Samuel Taylor Coleridge's *Remorse* and John Keats's *Otho the Great*. With subjects ranging from Shakespearean promptbooks to paintings and the poetics of Romanticism, the book offers fascinating insights into the exchange of ideas and inspirations among the cultural luminaries who surrounded the Georgian London stage.

REIKO OYA is Associate Professor in the Faculty of Business and Commerce at Keio University, Japan. This is her first book.

REPRESENTING SHAKESPEAREAN TRAGEDY

Garrick, the Kembles, and Kean

By
REIKO OYA

CAMBRIDGE UNIVERSITY PRESS
Cambridge, New York, Melbourne, Madrid, Cape Town, Singapore, São Paulo

Cambridge University Press
The Edinburgh Building, Cambridge CB2 8RU, UK

Published in the United States of America by Cambridge University Press, New York

www.cambridge.org
Information on this title: www.cambridge.org/9780521879859

© Reiko Oya 2007

This publication is in copyright. Subject to statutory exception
and to the provisions of relevant collective licensing agreements,
no reproduction of any part may take place without
the written permission of Cambridge University Press.

First published 2007

Printed in the United Kingdom at the University Press, Cambridge

A catalogue record for this publication is available from the British Library

Library of Congress Cataloging in Publication Data

Oya, Reiko, 1965–
Representing Shakespearean tragedy : Garrick, the Kembles, and Kean / by Reiko Oya.
p. cm.
Includes bibliographical references and index.
ISBN-13: 978-0-521-87985-9 (hardback)
ISBN-10: 0-521-87985-X (hardback)
1. Shakespeare, William, 1564–1616 – Stage history – England – London. 2. Shakespeare, William, 1564–1616 – Stage history – 1625–1800. 3. Shakespeare, William, 1564–1616 – Stage history – 1800–1950. 4. Garrick, David, 1717–1779 – Performances. 5. Kemble, John Philip, 1757–1823 – Performances. 6. Siddons, Sarah, 1755–1831 – Performances. 7. Kean, Edmund, 1787–1833 – Performances. 8. Dramatic criticism – England – London – History. I. Title.
PR3106.093   2007
792.9'5–dc22   2007016471

ISBN 978-0-521-87985-9 hardback

Cambridge University Press has no responsibility for
the persistence or accuracy of URLs for external or
third-party internet websites referred to in this book,
and does not guarantee that any content on such
websites is, or will remain, accurate or appropriate.

To Ann and Akiko
'like twin-stars shall shine'

Contents

Acknowledgements	*page* viii
List of illustrations	x
Note on references	xii

	Introduction: Garrick's prologue	1
1	Winding up 'th'untuned and jarring senses': Garrick, *King Lear* and contemporary theatrical/literary criticism	8
	1 Adaptation and impersonation: Garrick's *King Lear*	8
	2 The mad monarch and critical reason: periodical writers	19
	3 Resisting Garrick: Samuel Johnson on Shakespeare	28
	4 Confrontation and evasion: Elizabeth Montagu's Bluestocking viewpoint	37
	5 The use of (hyper)criticism: Garrick's postscripts	46
2	'Who dares do more': Kemble, Siddons and the question of sublimity in *Macbeth*	59
	1 Encountering a stage ghost: Sir Roger, Mr Partridge and Sir Joshua	59
	2 Kemble, Siddons and *Macbeth*	67
	3 Materialising the immaterial: the 1794 performance	77
	4 'Ask Reynolds': the way to paint tragedy	84
	5 Punch and the madman: the theatrical career of Edmund Burke	108
3	'Speak the speech, I pray you': Kean, *Hamlet* and the Romantic 'playwrights'	122
	1 Several mirrors up to nature: Reynolds and Johnson, Blake and Hazlitt	122
	2 Readers' *Hamlet*, actors' *Hamlet*	131
	3 In the theatre of remorse: Coleridge, his friend and his tragedy	146
	4 Fables of identity: Keats, Kean and *Otho the Great*	161
	Conclusion: Kean's farewell	185

Notes	191
Bibliography	215
Index	238

Acknowledgements

The work has passed through several stages and at each I have incurred debts, which I now take pleasure in acknowledging. Ann Thompson, my supervisor at King's College London, watched over this book from start to finish and guided me with wisdom and kindness at many turns, putting her encyclopaedic knowledge at my disposal. Akiko Kusunoki inspired my interest in Shakespeare and taught me more than she probably realised through conversations over many a lunch at the British Library as well as through her excellent publications. Michael Dobson and Thomas Healy examined my PhD dissertation and kindly suggested the possibility of putting together a monograph out of it.

My profound indebtedness to the Midgleys must be registered here. My good friend Nick Midgley, psychoanalyst, braved both a very early draft and the final version of my dissertation and believed in the book. His father, the theatre director Robin Midgley, commented insightfully on the final manuscript and patiently and politely noted errors.

Many people have commented helpfully and critically on the manuscript. Yuji Kaneko, one of the earliest instigators of this project, read the whole piece with rigour and generosity. I have appreciated advice about particular chapters from Yeeyon Im, Nahoko Miyamoto Alvey and David Shea. Matthew Hanley provided a much-needed additional pair of sharp eyes to check part of the manuscript during the final stages. Bibliographer Noriko Sumimoto helped me to gain access to the splendid Shakespeare collection of Meisei University Library and to make arrangements for reproduction of some of the figures.

I should also like to thank Akihiro Yamada, whose lofty academic standards are an inspiration in themselves, John Thompson, who helped me to develop some key ideas underlying my discussion, and my teachers at Tokyo University, George Hughes, Susumu Kawanishi, Atsuhiko Narita and Yuichi Takamatsu in particular, who together have constituted my rock. The passing of Yasunari Takahashi and Hiroshi Izubuchi is mourned with special poignancy. Their erudition and dedication to literary criticism have inspired generations of researchers, myself included.

Keio University, Tokyo, has been generous in support of this project through a Keio Gijuku research grant (2001) and sabbatical extension grant (2002), which enabled me to complete the dissertation on which the current book is based, as well as through a grant from the Keio Gijuku Fukuzawa Memorial Fund for Advancement of Education and Research (2007). An early version of part of chapter 1 ('Poetic justice and madness') was read at the annual conference of The Shakespeare Society, Japan, in October 2000.

Cambridge University Press has given all that an author can hope for in the way of encouragement and support. I must particularly mention Sarah Stanton for her unfailingly sagacious advice and generosity to this clumsy first-time author, Rebecca Jones and Rosina Di Marzo for their expert supervision of the production process, and my copy-editor Libby Willis for her numerous improvements to my text. My anonymous CUP readers also merit special recognition. Their acute, insightful comments enabled me to restructure the thesis with more coherence.

My parents and my sister have been my most loyal supporters throughout this project, and to them I owe my dearest thanks.

Illustrations

1 Benjamin Wilson, *David Garrick as King Lear*. Engraved by James McArdell. By permission of the Folger Shakespeare Library. *page* 9
2 Francis Hayman, *King Lear* (Charles Jennen's 1770 edition of *King Lear*). Engraved by Ravenel. Courtesy of Meisei University Library, Tokyo. 17
3 Thomas Beach, *Kemble and Siddons in* Macbeth. The Art Archive/Garrick Club. 60
4 Henry Fuseli, *Lady Macbeth Seizing the Daggers*. © Tate, London 2006. 80
5 Joshua Reynolds, *Count Ugolino and His Children*. The Sackville Collection (The National Trust), (c) NTPL/Brian Tremain. 85
6 Joshua Reynolds, *Puck (Robin Goodfellow)*. Engraved by Luigi Schiavonetti. © Copyright the Trustees of The British Museum. 89
7 Henry Fuseli, *Robin Goodfellow-Puck*. By permission of the Folger Shakespeare Library. 90
8 Joshua Reynolds, *The Death of Cardinal Beaufort*. Engraved by S. W. Reynolds. © Copyright the Trustees of The British Museum. 91
9 Henry Fuseli, *The Nightmare*. Founders Society Purchase with funds from Mr and Mrs Bert L. Smokler and Mr and Mrs Lawrence A. Fleischman. Photograph © 2005 The Detroit Institute of Arts. 94

List of illustrations   xi

10 [François Boitard], *Henry VI Part 2* (Nicholas Rowe's 1709 edition of Shakespeare). Engraved by Elijah Kirkall (?). Courtesy of Meisei University Library, Tokyo. 95

11 H. François Gravelot, *Henry VI Part 2* (Thomas Hanmer's 1744 edition of Shakespeare). Courtesy of Meisei University Library, Tokyo. 96

12 Henry Fuseli, *The Death of Cardinal Beaufort*. Engraved by Moses Haughton. © Copyright the Trustees of The British Museum. 97

13 Joshua Reynolds, *The Death of Cardinal Beaufort*. Engraved by Caroline Watson. © Copyright the Trustees of The British Museum. 98

14 Joshua Reynolds, *Macbeth and the Witches*. Engraved by Robert Thew. © Copyright the Trustees of The British Museum. 99

15 [François Boitard], *Macbeth* (Nicholas Rowe's 1709 edition of Shakespeare). Engraved by Elijah Kirkall (?). Courtesy of Meisei University Library, Tokyo. 100

16 Henry Fuseli, *Macbeth Consulting the Vision of an Armed Head*. By permission of the Folger Shakespeare Library. 102

17 Joshua Reynolds, *Sarah Siddons as the Tragic Muse*. Courtesy of the Huntington Library, Art Collections, and Botanical Gardens, San Marino, California. 104

18 Michelangelo, *Isaiah*. Alinari Archive, Florence. 106

19 Daniel Maclise, *The Play Scene in* Hamlet *exhibited 1842*. © Tate, London 2006. 123

20 John Constable, *The Cenotaph*. Photograph © The National Gallery, London. 187

Note on references

References to Shakespearean editions, acting versions and adaptations are keyed to the abbreviations listed in section 1 of the Bibliography. For ease of consultation Shakespearean quotations are followed by line reference to *The Arden Shakespeare Complete Works*, general editors Richard Proudfoot, Ann Thompson and David Kastan, 2nd edn (London: Arden Shakespeare, 2001). Exceptions are cited individually in the notes. All quotations follow the typography and orthography of the sources from which they are taken.

Introduction: Garrick's prologue

> When Learning's triumph o'er her barb'rous foes
> First rear'd the stage, immortal SHAKESPEAR rose . . .

On 15 September 1747 David Garrick (1717–79) was hoping for yet another evening of triumph to ornament his distinguished theatrical career. After making his sensational London debut as Richard III at Goodman's Fields in 1741, the talented actor successfully transferred to Drury Lane the next year and went on to contract with James Lacy as its joint patentee in April 1747. Garrick was opening the first theatrical season under his management that evening and was to deliver a special prologue to mark the occasion. The majestic first stanza of the poem traced the history of the London stage, with William Shakespeare at its glorious root:

> When Learning's triumph o'er her barb'rous foes
> First rear'd the stage, immortal SHAKESPEAR rose;
> Each change of many-colour'd life he drew,
> Exhausted worlds, and then imagin'd new:
> Existence saw him spurn her bounded reign,
> And panting Time toil'd after him in vain:
> His pow'rful strokes presiding truth impress'd,
> And unresisted passion storm'd the breast.[1]

This was a perfect inaugural statement for Garrick, whose ingenious impersonation of the Shakespearean characters, together with his professed 'idolatry' of the playwright himself, was soon to establish him as the 'high priest' of the great Elizabethan. The prologue, however, was not of his own composing. The sweeping couplets had been penned by a struggling literary hack, one Samuel Johnson, who, after unsuccessfully proposing a new Shakespeare edition in 1745, was now launching a project of a new English dictionary. It was uncharacteristically generous of Johnson to let Garrick mouth his excellent prologue. The real author was not going to be mentioned on that evening's stage (in fact, Johnson's authorship would not be acknowledged until the publication of Robert Dodsley's *Collection of Poems by Several Hands* in 1748) and the audience would naturally assume the prologue to be Garrick's. This normally uncompromising lexicographer-to-be had even made a textual alteration 'at the remonstrance of Garrick' ('I did not think his criticism just; but it was necessary he should be satisfied with what he was to utter').²

From the next stanza, the prologue charted the general decline of the London stage. After Shakespeare came Ben Jonson (stanza 2), who lacked his predecessor's natural inspiration and made do with 'studious patience, and laborious art'. Predictably, although his reputation endured, the plays themselves were of only temporary interest:

> A mortal born he met the general doom,
> But left, like Egypt's kings, a lasting tomb. (ll. 15–16)

After the intermission caused by the Civil War, immorality and obscenity dominated the Restoration stage (stanza 3). The playwrights did not aspire to 'JOHNSON's art, or SHAKESPEAR's flame' but indulged in the decadent cultural climate and shamelessly catered for the pleasure-seeking audience:

> Themselves they studied, as they felt, they writ,
> Intrigue was plot, obscenity was wit.
> Vice always found a sympathetick friend;
> They pleas'd their age, and did not aim to mend. (ll. 19–22)

Finally, 'Virtue' banished the lewd shows and the age of neoclassicism arrived (stanza 4). Knowledgeable rules and regular declamations were, however, not a recipe for a true tragedy:

> Then crush'd by rules, and weaken'd as refin'd,
> For years the pow'r of tragedy declin'd;
> From bard, to bard, the frigid caution crept,
> Till declamation roar'd, while passion slept. (ll. 29–32)

The mindlessly regular drama eventually gave way to 'Pantomime, and Song' that were entertaining in a more obvious manner.

What would happen on the London stage under Garrick's new management? Johnson did not give any definite answer (stanza 5), as nobody 'the coming changes can presage, / And mark the future periods of the stage':

> Perhaps if skill could distant times explore,
> New Behns, new Durfeys, yet remain in store.
> Perhaps, where Lear has rav'd, and Hamlet dy'd,
> On flying cars new sorcerers may ride.
> Perhaps, for who can guess th'effects of chance?
> Here Hunt may box, or Mahomet may dance. (ll. 41–6)

Introduction: *Garrick's prologue*

As will be surveyed in the following chapters, all these possibilities were to become a reality. Writers at least as talented as Aphra Behn and Thomas D'Urfey, if not quite Shakespeare, would try their hands at playwriting. Flying witches would stay as popular as ever, while Lear and Hamlet would not stop raving and dying. Edward Hunt's boxing and Mahomet Mussulmo's rope-dancing might not actually reach Drury Lane, but one of the four tragedians I shall discuss would certainly resort to these light entertainments in his strolling days.

The new manager and leading actor could not tell the future of the stage, as it was the audience that had the casting vote on it. Johnson's prologue continued (stanza 6):

> Hard is his lot, that here by fortune plac'd,
> Must watch the wild vicissitude of taste;
> With ev'ry meteor of caprice must play,
> And chase the new-blown bubbles of the day.
> Ah! let not censure term our fate our choice,
> The stage but echoes back the publick voice.
> The drama's laws the drama's patrons give,
> For we that live to please, must please to live. (ll. 47–54)

This was a drastically pessimistic rereading of Hamlet's famous definition of 'the purpose of playing, whose end, both at the first and now, was and is to hold as 'twere the mirror up to nature; to show virtue her feature, scorn her own image, and the very age and body of the time his form and pressure' (3.2.21–5). While Hamlet emphasised the purposefulness of the theatrical mirroring, Johnson lamented the helplessness and passiveness of players and managers in the face of the frivolous public. Hamlet's theatre taught the world, while Johnson's counterpart was taught by it. As was customary in a theatrical prologue, Johnson's 'drama's patrons' primarily referred to the immediate audience rather than Hamlet's 'nature' or 'the very age and body of the time' at large: the new manager needed to gesture deferentially to the spectators in front of him and plead for their support. Nevertheless, the two formulations did point to the same complicity of the stage, the audience and contemporary cultural climate.

The ensuing chapters are an attempt to delineate the theatrical future that Johnson refrained from foretelling, with special reference to the four great Shakespearean tragedians who adorned the eighteenth- and early nineteenth-century London stage: David Garrick, John Philip Kemble and his sister Sarah Siddons, and Edmund Kean. The premise throughout is that their performance can be appraised correctly only when placed alongside contemporary criticism, playwriting, painting and other art forms. The players gave daring expression to Shakespeare's tragedies by modifying the scripts and sophisticating their acting, and their interest in strong tragic emotion and characterisation facilitated, and was facilitated by, theatrical and literary critics, playwrights and painters. The dialogic relations between the four tragedians and their contemporaries constitute the topic, or even the contention, of this study, which needs to be defined further against a recent critical trend.

From the 1980s, the post-Restoration afterlives of Shakespeare came to be investigated in broader cultural contexts than in traditional literary scholarship and (to use the dominant metaphor) the processes of 'appropriation' of his plays and his authorial image have been brought to light. Studies into theatrical adaptations,[3] scholarly editions[4] and Shakespearean allusions and quotations in political propaganda and Romantic poetry[5] have illuminated the ways in which Shakespeare and his posterities have utilised each other's contemporary political and ideological relevance. Michael Bristol's provocative discussion of the phenomenal celebrity of the Bard and Gary Taylor's spirited overview of what he called 'Shakesperotics' epitomised the new cultural interest,[6] while studies in more particularised problems of Shakespeare's reception have been collected in several anthologies.[7]

While successfully revising the 'deadening historicism' of the old philologists and their avowedly neutral (but in fact very judgemental) literary studies, the new cultural approaches entail their own theoretical difficulties. First, many of the recent researchers share an interest in the history, politics and ideology that presumably dictated Shakespeare's afterlife and, all too often, regard the specific personalities involved in the appropriations as part of a larger historical process that is predominantly anonymous, impersonal and inexorable. Shakespeare's posthumous destiny was allegedly controlled by 'paradigm', 'a certain historical juncture known as the Enlightenment', 'England's own transition from the aristocratic regime of the Stuarts to the commercial empire presided over by the Hanoverians', 'politics in Georgian England', and 'our culture, as well as that of generations before us'.[8] The preoccupations of these critics are typically to chart 'a *shared* sense of the *national* importance of Shakespeare and a *general* agreement about the *broader* contours of his authorial image',[9] rather than particular manifestations of the playwright and his plays as such.

The impersonal perception of history shared by these critics obviously owes much to such Marxist sponsors of reception studies as Walter Benjamin, Robert Weimann and Raymond Williams. In an influential formulation of the concept of history, Benjamin for one states that the 'products of art and science owe their existence not merely to the effort of the great geniuses who created them, but also, in one degree or another, to the anonymous toil of their contemporaries'.[10] The exiled thinker's acute awareness of the violent historical process and sympathy with the oppressed multitude notwithstanding, I find this dichotomy between great geniuses and their anonymous contemporaries highly problematic. My work will register many individuals who, strictly speaking, were not prodigies but would strenuously resist being categorised into the nameless, uninterested and uninteresting group of 'contemporaries'. Being less talented than Shakespeare did not stop them being men and women of great enterprise, and their undertakings were too ambitious and daring, if ultimately unsuccessful, to be described as mere toil. Benjamin's 'great geniuses' themselves are little more than impersonal abstractions, in that they supposedly create masterpieces outside the sphere of everyday human intercourse. Some of the personalities I will survey (David Garrick, for example) did have a fair claim to the rank of genius, but even their works came into being through vivid interactions with their colleagues, rivals and predecessors. Shakespeare's cultural relevance in eighteenth- and nineteenth-century London can, and indeed should, be illustrated in more intimate, personal terms through analyses of the incessant dialogues between the players and their friends.

The second difficulty is closely related to the first. The concept of 'appropriation' postulates a certain strategy and purposefulness on the part of the appropriater, and the most significant achievement of the recent cultural scholarship has been the discovery of the immediate political and ideological objectives that Shakespeare's seemingly frivolous afterlife has served. Defying the critical tradition (numbering the authoritative George C. D. Odell, Hazelton Spencer and Brian Vickers among its advocates) that dismissed the post-Restoration theatrical adaptations as sheer artistic blunders, researchers have proved Nahum Tate, for example, to have been no fool in creating his happy-ending *King Lear* in 1681 but on the contrary an efficient propagandist of the Tory cause at the time of the Exclusion Crisis.[11] Cultural approaches, on the other hand, tend to turn a blind eye to what was left *un*appropriated. An interesting case in point is the following passage from Tate's preface to his *King Lear*:

> *Lear's real, and* Edgar's *pretended Madness have so much of extravagant* Nature *(I know not how else to express it) as cou'd never have started but from our* Shakespear's *Creating Fancy. The Images and Language are so odd and surprising, and yet so agreeable and proper, that whilst we grant that none but* Shakespear *cou'd have form'd such Conceptions, yet we are satisfied that they were the only Things in the World that ought to be said on those Occasions.*[12]

This remarkable statement, which has been largely overlooked by the researchers of appropriation, vividly conveys how the frenzied characters' effusion of tragic sentiments surprised the adapter and even baffled his enterprise in part. According to the same preface, Tate intended to add 'Probability and Regularity' to the original tragedy and would have fared better if he had dropped Shakespeare's 'odd and surprizing' lines, which actually create the feeling of 'there being two different plays uneasily combined' in the adaptation.[13] Along with his appropriative strategies, Tate's inability either to cut or to replace the raging language, his amazement and bewilderment – in other words, the adapter's failed appropriation – must be carefully attended to, as they shed light on the immense potential of the Shakespearean tragedy that has survived political and ideological contingencies for more than four hundred years.

My first chapter, on David Garrick and his *King Lear*, addresses this province of the irrational by tracing the attempts of the talented actor and his close circle of friends to portray, and explain, the protagonist's madness on stage and on page, with various degrees of success. It studies the tragic emotions that Garrick conveyed through (and sometimes in spite of) the promptbooks he used, and maps out the theatrical and literary responses that his impersonation occasioned. The second chapter, on the Kemble siblings and *Macbeth*, discusses the two essays on the tragedy written by the actor and actress respectively and their partnership on stage as the regicide couple. Their compelling representation of terror and supernaturalism in the legendary 1794 staging of *Macbeth* is subsequently compared with parallel attempts at sublime expression in the works of Joshua Reynolds and Edmund Burke. The third chapter, on Edmund Kean and *Hamlet*, studies the disparity between the theatrical and literary lives of the Danish prince in Kean's performance and the critic William Hazlitt's response to it. The compositional processes of Samuel Taylor Coleridge's *Remorse* (1813) and John Keats's *Otho the Great* (1819) are also examined in detail, as they are rather unlooked-for offshoots of the literary and theatrical *Hamlet*.

Encompassing various cultural interests over many decades, my discussion is necessarily eclectic. The chosen materials, however, are analysed in textual as well as intimate and personal details. Much attention is paid to the many theatrical anecdotes recorded in popular biographies and in personal letters. Admittedly, their testimonies are inconsistent, incomplete and openly prejudiced, and hardly qualify as records of historical truth. Their unrestrained narratives, on the other hand, capture the haunting memories and emotions of the Shakespearean stage in a way not possible in other types of writing. These documents record the ongoing dialogues between the individuals concerned and, as seen in Tate's dedicatory letter, their very incoherence often reveals their innermost concerns. The concept of 'truth' may not be particularly valid in theatrical studies to begin with, when a performance is no doubt experienced differently by every one of the few thousand spectators each night.

Human intercourse is liable to coincidences and accidents, another fact that has been neglected by cultural critics. For instance, the generous gesture that Johnson displayed in letting Garrick use his prologue is understandable only when we go back to Lichfield in 1736 when a small boarding school was launched and advertised in the *Gentleman's Magazine*: 'At Edial, near Lichfield, in Staffordshire, young gentlemen are boarded and taught the Latin and Greek languages, by SAMUEL JOHNSON'. The only pupils enrolled were an eighteen-year-old neighbour David Garrick, his brother George, and one Mr Offely, and the school collapsed in no time. Johnson and Garrick soon left their hometown together to try their fortunes in London.[14]

Or we must go further back to 1727, when the ten-year-old Garrick put on the very first performance of his life at the house of his mentor Gilbert Walmesley. The play was George Farquhar's *The Recruiting Officer* (1706). Garrick not only took the role of Sergeant Kite himself but also tried out various 'young gentlemen and ladies' and distributed the parts very carefully. Johnson, who was also a frequent visitor at Walmesley's, 'was applied to by the little manager for a prologue to be spoken on the occasion'. Johnson was 'willing enough to oblige his young friend' but somehow failed to compose one in time for the performance. As W. Jackson Bate points out, Johnson probably decided to make up for the past failure by writing the Drury Lane prologue twenty years later.[15]

Johnson's great prologue challenges cultural determinism even further by having remained unspoken by Garrick after all. He was indisposed on that opening night. By terrible misfortune, Garrick missed the very first show under his management and was replaced by an understudy.[16] The prologue which the feverish manager failed to deliver concluded:

> Then prompt no more the follies you decry,
> As tyrants doom their tools of guilt to die;
> 'Tis yours this night to bid the reign commence
> Of rescu'd Nature, and reviving Sense;
> To chase the charms of sound, the pomp of show,
> For useful mirth, and salutary woe;
> Bid scenic virtue from the rising age,
> And Truth diffuse her radiance from the stage. (ll. 55–62)

Now we are ready to explore Garrick's, Kemble and Siddons's, and Kean's Shakespearean enterprises, along with all the individuals and happenings that surround them.

I

Winding up 'th'untuned and jarring senses': Garrick, King Lear *and contemporary theatrical/literary criticism*

I ADAPTATION AND IMPERSONATION: GARRICK'S *KING LEAR*

A controversy

From the end of 1753, a series of journal articles attracted the attention of the literati and theatregoers of London. In the three instalments from 4 December of the *Adventurer*, Joseph Warton analysed the madness of King Lear and identified his misguided resignation of the crown as its cause. Warton's proposition was instantly contradicted in the *Gray's-Inn Journal* by Arthur Murphy (alias Charles Ranger), who held the ingrate Goneril and Regan, not the lost kingship, responsible for Lear's madness. An anonymous third writer then joined the discussion and imputed the insanity, rather predictably, to the combination of the political and domestic factors.[1]

Their different conclusions notwithstanding, the three critics shared an important critical inspiration: their essays followed the plot and language of the contemporary literary editions, rather than the happy-ending stage versions, of *King Lear*, but their appreciation of the tragedy was deepened by David Garrick's acting in the title role. Referring to Lear's 'O me, my heart! My rising heart! But down!' (2.2.313), Warton commented:

> I SHOULD be guilty of insensibility and injustice, if I did not take this occasion to acknowledge, that I have been more moved and delighted, by hearing this single line spoken by the only actor of the age who understands and relishes these little touches of nature, and therefore the only one qualified to personate this most difficult character of LEAR, than by the most pompous declaimer of the most pompous speeches in CATO or TAMERLANE. (*Adventurer* 2:256)

Murphy's acknowledgement was more comprehensive. Republishing the *Gray's-Inn Journal* essays in two volumes in 1756, Murphy revised this article and inserted a new introductory statement (using the persona of

8

1 Benjamin Wilson, *David Garrick as King Lear*. Engraved by James McArdell.

'Mr. Candid') specifically to inform the reader how Garrick had stimulated his criticism:

> At the last Meeting of our Club, my Friend, Mr. *Candid*, informed us, that he had lately seen the Character of King *Lear* admirably performed by Mr. *Garrick*, and that he had since thrown together some Remarks upon that excellent Tragedy, which he desired I would this Day communicate to the Readers of the *Gray's-Inn-Journal*. (*Gray's-Inn Journal* 2:73)

The third anonymous writer complained about 'the several Attempts that have been made by different Commentators from the Time of Mr. *Rowe*' that had led 'to the mutilated Condition our Poet was thrown into by subsequent Editors'. In fact, the best annotation on Shakespeare could be found on the stage:

> I can't forbear mentioning the Obligation which the Public has to the Genius of Mr. *Garrick*, who has exhibited with great Lustre many of the most shining Strokes of *Shakespear*'s amazing Art; and may be justly stiled (as he was once called by you) his best Commentator: For 'tis certain, he has done our Poet more Justice by his Manner of playing his principal Characters, than any Editor has yet done by a Publication. (*Gray's-Inn Journal* 2:88)

In his reply to the third critic, Murphy complimented the actor once again by referring the readers to 'the noblest Commentary this, or any Poet ever had':

> I mean Mr. *Garrick*'s Performance of *Lear*, in which there is displayed in so just a Knowledge of the human Mind under a State of Madness, together with such exquisite Feelings of the various Shiftings of the Passions, so finely at the same Time enfeebled with the Debility of Age, that I believe, whenever this admirable Actor ceases to play this Part, the unhappy Monarch will lose more than *fifty of his Followers at a Clap*. (*Gray's-Inn Journal* 2:222)[2]

Before going into the details of their theatre-inspired literary analyses, and the impact they were to have on Samuel Johnson's edition of Shakespeare, some reference to the mid-century *King Lear* on stage, with the charismatic Garrick in the title role, is due.

Poetic justice and madness: Tate and Garrick

Immediately after the Restoration, Nahum Tate drastically rewrote Shakespeare's *King Lear* at the instigation of one Thomas Boteler.[3] According to Tate's dedicatory letter to this obscure gentleman, the original tragedy was '*a Heap of Jewels, unstrung and unpolisht*' that needed to be supplied with '*what was wanting in the Regularity and Probability of the Tale*'; two qualities the absence of which adds to, rather than detracts from, the greatness of the tragedy for today's audience. While 'Tatifying' Shakespeare's language, the adapter simplified the characters and made the plot both understandable and overtly entertaining.[4] Cordelia was provided with a lover (Edgar) and her blunt rejection of an oath to Lear, which was an 'unjustified roughness' in a dutiful daughter,[5] was rationalised as an emergency measure for her to avoid marriage to Burgundy. In a new aside Tate's Cordelia explained her straits to the audience and secured her moral integrity:

> Now comes my Trial, how am I distrest,
> That must with cold speech tempt the chol'rick King
> Rather to leave me Dowerless, than condemn me
> To loath'd Embraces! ('Tate', 1.1.92–5)

Edgar's disguise as Mad Tom, which was originally a way to save his own life, was likewise dignified as a decision secretly to help Cordelia. Tate's Edmund ('Bastard'), on the other hand, was wicked in a far less excusable manner than in Shakespeare and his illicit love affairs with the two elder daughters and lust after Cordelia were portrayed emphatically.

Most of all, Tate transformed the denouement by sparing the lives of Lear and Cordelia and crowning the good daughter jointly with Edgar.

With virtue rewarded and vice punished, the poetically justified tragedy ended in triumph with Edgar's declaration:

> Our drooping Country now erects her Head,
> Peace spreads her balmy Wings, and Plenty Blooms.
> Divine *Cordelia*, all the Gods can witness
> How much thy Love to Empire I prefer!
> Thy bright Example shall convince the World
> (Whatever Storms of Fortune are decreed)
> That Truth and Vertue shall at last succeed. ('Tate', 5.4.155–61)

Tate's objectives were certainly achieved and 'Regularity and Probability' were abundantly supplied. However, as noted in the Introduction, Tate retained a considerable portion of 'the Images and Language' of Mad Tom and the deranged Lear and thereby put a strain on the optimistic drive of his version. This tension between Shakespeare's tragedy and Tate's adaptation only increased when Garrick modified the script further for his own performance.

Lear was among Garrick's most successful roles throughout the three decades of his theatrical career. He exerted his talent not only as a performer but also as a 'restorer' of the tragedy and, while retaining Tate's plot, gradually replaced the adapter's wording with Shakespeare's poetry.[6] Critics disagree as to the historical significance of Garrick's editorial efforts. George W. Stone regards the actor as the first pioneer, arguing that he had revised the promptbook substantially by 1756, when a *King Lear* 'with restorations from Shakespeare' was advertised.[7] Arthur John Harris argues that George Colman's 1768 version, which expelled Tate's love plots, was the real step forward, and that Garrick only regressed from Colman to Tate regarding the storyline.[8] In the meantime, the two camps do agree that Garrick's restoration of Shakespearean verse was laudable in itself. It was 'as good as a false start [of Tate] allowed it to be', and it was 'as if one looked again through recently polished windows, after for a long time having viewed the scene through very dirty glass'.[9] Recent writers are certainly more careful about the political and cultural implications of both the adaptation and the restoration, but have not quite noted that, in terms of dramatic coherence, Garrick's partial restoration made the play even 'worse' than either Shakespeare or Tate. For example, Garrick's Cordelia was still romantically linked to Edgar, but Tate's rationalisation of her refusal of the oath was discarded and replaced with the original aside:

> What shall Cordelia do? Love and be silent.
> . . .
> Then poor Cordelia!

> And yet not so, since I am sure my love's
> More pond'rous than my tongue.[10]

Garrick kept Tate's love interest but disconnected it from the central question of the division of the kingdom. Likewise, after reuniting Edgar with Cordelia on the heath after Tate, Garrick restored Shakespeare's gloomy lines to the supposedly blissful lover on his reentrance immediately afterwards ('Yet better thus, and known to be condemned, / Than still condemned and flattered...', 'Garrick', 4.1.1–9). The romance between the two virtuous characters was supposed to tidy up the 'Heap of Jewels, unstrung and unpolisht' of the original tragedy. Yet by combining Tate's love plot with Shakespeare's poetry, Garrick's version became even less unified than either the Jacobean or the Restoration *Lear*.

Garrick's restoration even jeopardised the emotional coherence of the tragedy as a whole. Opening the so-called heath scene (3.2.1–9), Tate had supplied a feeble substitute verse:

> Blow Winds and burst your Cheeks, rage louder yet,
> Fantastick Lightning singe, singe my white Head;
> Spout Cataracts, and Hurricanos fall
> Till you have drown'd the Towns and Palaces
> Of proud ingratefull Man. ('Tate', 3.1.1–5)

Garrick restored Shakespeare's awe-inspiring exclamation:

> Blow, winds, and crack your cheeks! rage, blow!
> You cataracts and hurricanoes, spout
> Till you have drenched our steeples, drowned the cocks!
> You sulph'rous and thought-executing fires,
> Vaunt-couriers of oak-cleaving thunderbolts,
> Singe my white head. And thou, all-shaking thunder,
> Strike flat the thick rotundity o'th'world,
> Crack nature's mold, all germins spill at once,
> That make ingrateful man. ('Garrick', 3.1.1–9)

It seems unlikely that this frenzied monarch should be happy again within the remaining two acts, make a euphoric announcement ('Cordelia then shall be a queen, mark that!', 'Garrick', 5.4.116) and then 'calmly pass our short reserves of time / In cool reflections on our fortunes past, / Cheered with relation of the prosp'rous reign / Of this celestial pair' with Kent in tow ('Garrick', 5.4.156–60). As a matter of fact, Shakespeare's tragic verse and Tate's storyline would disintegrate further when the incomparable actor put this text on stage.

Enacting strong feelings

Garrick attempted the excruciating impersonation of King Lear in his debut season at Goodman's Field, when he was still in his mid-twenties. He asked the veteran actor Charles Macklin and Dr William Barrowby to attend the first performance and give him advice afterwards. The performance satisfied 'the generality of the audience' but the two connoisseurs picked up several problems. Garrick dressed himself up suitably as Lear but did not enter into the infirmities of a 'man fourscore and upwards'. Garrick 'began too low, and ended it too high' in cursing Goneril at the close of Act 1, and 'he had not dignity enough for a King' when imprisoned with Cordelia. Garrick's delivery of the murderous flights of frenzy was found particularly defective. The passage in Tate's adaptation, which was still in use at this first performance, read as follows: 'It were an excellent Stratagem to Shoe a Troop of Horse with Felt, I'll put't in proof – no Noise, no Noise – now will we steal upon these Sons in Law, and then – Kill, kill, kill, kill!' ('Tate', 4.4.168–70). According to their judgement, Garrick raised his voice 'too high in the first part ... letting it down too much in the last line', when the text cued the actor to be low at first ('no Noise, no Noise') and express 'all the loud-toned fury of revenge' at 'Kill, kill, kill, kill!'.[11]

The three scenes thus scrutinised are the emotional climaxes of the tragedy: they are moments of extreme anger at a daughter's ingratitude, indignation against injustice and violence (in Tate's final scene set in 'A Prison'), and raging madness. We can imagine the difficulty that an inexperienced young actor, even with Garrick's precocious mastery of voice and gesture, would have had in portraying these extreme passions. Much to our (and the tutors') surprise, Garrick quickly refurbished the faulty impersonation into a real triumph:

> [The] curse he [Macklin] particularly admired; he said it exceeded all his imagination; and had such an effect, that it seemed to electrify the audience with horror. The words, 'Kill – kill – kill – ', echoed all the revenge of the frantic King; whilst he exhibited such a scene of the pathetic on discovering his daughter Cordelia, as drew tears of commiseration from the whole house.[12]

'In short, Sir,' added Macklin, 'the little dog made it a *chef d'oeuvre*, and a *chef d'oeuvre* it continued to the end of his life.'

Garrick's success as Lear was no doubt attributable to his innovative acting style. Arriving in London in the late 1730s, the actor witnessed the 'conventional' acting that communicated human emotions in 'stylized and often symbolic fashion', on the assumption that every passion 'has its peculiar and appropriate look, and every look its adopted and peculiar gesture' and that no human is apt to 'laugh in anger, grind his teeth in tender love, or smile in rage'. Also, owing to weak ensemble performance and noisy audiences, star actors customarily resorted to arialike declamation to keep the show going.[13] It seems that the audience was aware that this smooth, formalised delivery hardly did justice to a strong, tempestuous, agonised tragic character such as Lear. Resenting 'the unquicken'd Serenity' of an unnamed 'popular Player' (almost certainly James Quin, who was known for his regular declamation) in Lear, Aaron Hill expressed his dissatisfaction: 'He shou'd be turbulent in his *Passions*, – sharp, and troubled, in his *Voice*; – torn, and anguished, in his *Looks*, – majestically broken in his *Air* – and discompos'd, interrupted, and restless, in his *Motions*.'[14]

While mastering the merits of the conventional acting, Garrick expressed tragic passions by discarding regular declamation and pursuing psychological realism. Alan S. Downer's insistence that Garrick was more 'a refiner' than 'a reformer' of the traditional style is certainly right in that tragedians had always aimed at correct delineation of passions.[15] It is, however, also true that eyewitnesses of the actor emphasised discordance, not continuity, when they reported their Drury Lane experience. Garrick's acting *felt* like a revolution. Richard Cumberland recalled seeing Garrick (as Lothario) and Quin (as Horatio) in Nicholas Rowe's *The Fair Penitent* (1703):

– heavens, what a transition! – it seemed as if a whole century had been swept over in the transition of a single scene; old things were done away with, and a new order at once brought forward, bright and luminous; and clearly destined to dispel ... the illusions of imposing declamation ... It is difficult to give Garrick his due as the foremost actor of the age.[16]

Quin himself reportedly growled at Garrick's London debut: 'If this young fellow is right, I, and the rest of the players, must have been all wrong.'[17] Joseph Roach regards Garrick's departure from the traditional style as 'a theatrical version of what historians of science would term a revolutionary paradigm shift', where the singsong smoothness was crucially abandoned in favour of psychological realism.[18] While various opera and *kabuki* performances suggest that formal delivery and emotional immediacy are not necessarily incompatible, there is no denying that Garrick 'shone forth like a theatrical Newton' to his contemporaries, outdating his predecessors once and for all.[19]

Garrick also believed in his own role in a revolution in acting. '[At] my first setting out in the Business of an Actor,' he recalled, 'I endeavour'd to shake off the Fetters of Numbers, and have been often accus'd of neglecting the Harmony of the Versification, from a too close Regard to the Passion, and the Meaning of the Author.'[20] He would suppress his voice, even in the middle of a line, to portray the psychology of his dramatic persona. Thus his Hamlet would speak to Horatio: 'I think it was to see – [voice suppressed] – my mother's wedding.'[21] His swift transition from one facial expression to another also proved invaluable in delineating the multifaceted Shakespearean characters or, as Garrick's biographer put it regarding Hamlet: 'To do justice to such a character, it was necessary that the talents of the actor should be as various as those of his great master.'[22]

Indeed, Garrick's acting of Lear went well beyond the half-Tatified, half-Shakespearean state of his own script, and realised the intensity and complexity of the original tragedy. Another contemporary controversy bears testimony to this. In 1747 Samuel Foote censured Garrick for infusing a sense of pathos into Lear's imprecation upon Goneril ('nor can I easily pardon the Tears shed at the Conclusion; the whole Passage is a Climax of Rage; that strange Mixture of Anger and Grief is to me highly unnatural'). Foote sided with the older acting school and, in defiance of 'the ill-judged Applause of the Multitude', attacked Garrick's virtuoso portrayal of the changing emotions.[23] An anonymous writer defended the tragedian later the same year by invoking the authority of Shakespeare's text, arguing that had Foote 'look'd into *Shakespear*, he would not have been so severe upon *your Tears shed at the Conclusion*, or have said that the *strange Mixture of Grief and Passion was highly unnatural*; for this Speech immediately following the Curse, is your Direction and Authority'.[24]

Under discussion is the passage beginning: 'Hear, Nature, hear, dear goddess, hear' (1.4.267–81). Tate had replaced difficult words with easier ones ('the barren Curse' for 'stirrility', and 'blasted Body' for 'derogate body') in these lines and concluded Act 1 with a short exchange between Goneril and Albany immediately afterwards, omitting the rest of scene 4 and the whole scene 5. Garrick recovered Lear's original verse and ended the Act with his exclamation, 'How sharper than a serpent's tooth it is / To have a thankless child! Away, away' (1.4.280–1). Even more importantly, Garrick restored the sentiments of Shakespeare's Lear when he mixed tears and anger. As the anonymous writer rightly pointed out, the actor's 'Tears shed at the Conclusion' were based on the lines that were actually omitted from his own acting texts:

> Life and death, I am ashamed
> That thou hast power to shake my manhood thus,
> That these hot tears, which break from me perforce,

> Should make thee worth them. Blasts and fogs upon thee!
> Th'untented woundings of a father's curse
> Pierce every sense about thee. Old fond eyes,
> Beweep this cause again, I'll pluck ye out,
> And cast you with the waters that you loose
> To temper clay. (1.4.288–96)

The handling of this scene was characteristic of Garrick, who retained most of Tate's storyline but filled it with Shakespeare's poetry as applicable and with even more of Shakespearean sentiment as gleaned from elsewhere in the original.

Garrick's treatment of Lear's madness in Act 3 was similarly oriented. Like Tate before him, he expelled the Fool, cut and reassigned the lines to the remaining characters, and merged scene 4 with scene 6. He then substituted Tate's wording with Shakespeare's verse and restored, as noted earlier, the brilliant exclamation to his Act 3 scene 1 ('Blow, winds, and crack your cheeks! . . .'). Garrick's conception of the Act was in fact even closer to Shakespeare's original than his revised promptbook would suggest. At a request from the illustrator Francis Hayman for an idea for a frontispiece to Charles Jennen's 1770 edition of *King Lear*, Garrick suggested the following composition:

> Suppose Lear Mad upon the Ground with Edgar by him; His Attitude Should be leaning upon one hand & pointing Wildly towards the Heavens with his Other, Kent & Fool attend him & Glocester comes to him with a Torch; the real Madness of Lear, the Frantick Affectation of Edgar, and the different looks of Concern in the three other Characters will have a fine Effect; Suppose You express Kent's particular Care & distress by putting him upon one Knee begging & entreating him to rise & go with Gloster.[25]

The actor obviously regarded this scene of madness and agony as the epitome of the tragedy, and incorporated not only his own stage business of lying upon the heath but also the Fool in the imaginary picture, if not in the promptbook.[26]

Garrick's portrayal of madness in this scene was indebted to a curious incident that he witnessed 'when he began to study this great and difficult part'. As the *Gray's-Inn Journal*'s Murphy recorded:

> [Garrick] was acquainted with a worthy man, who lived in Leman-street, Goodman's Fields; this friend had an only daughter, about two years old; he stood at his dining-room window, fondling the child, and dangling it in his arms, when it was his misfortune to drop the infant into the flagged area, and killed it on the spot. He remained at his window screaming in agonies of grief.

Garrick, King Lear *and contemporary criticism*

2 Francis Hayman, *King Lear* (Charles Jennen's 1770 edition of *King Lear*). Engraved by Ravenel.

The neighbours flocked to the house, took up the child, and delivered it dead to the unhappy father, who wept bitterly, and filled the street with lamentations. He lost his senses, and from that moment never recovered his understanding.[27]

Garrick often visited this distracted gentleman, who would repeat a series of gestures by the fatal window, 'there playing in fancy with his child': 'After some dalliance, he dropped it, and, bursting into a flood of tears, filled the house with shrieks of grief and bitter anguish. He then sat down, in a pensive mood, his eyes fixed on one object, at times looking slowly round him, as if to implore compassion.' Garrick studied this painful spectacle closely, and 'it gave him the first idea of *King Lear*'s madness'. 'There it was', said the actor, *'that I learned to imitate madness*; I copied nature, and to that owed my success in *King Lear*.'²⁸

Garrick often mimed the unfortunate father as a party piece, in which Murphy saw an unmistakable connection with his acclaimed Lear:

[Garrick's Lear] had no sudden starts, no violent gesticulation; his movements were slow and feeble; misery was depicted in his countenance; he moved his head in the most deliberate manner; his eyes were fixed, or, if they turned to any one near him, he made a pause, and fixed his look on the person after much delay; his features at the same time telling what he was going to say, before he uttered a word. During the whole time he presented a sight of woe and misery, and a total alienation of mind from every idea, but that of his unkind daughters.²⁹

We probably should not take Garrick's explanation of his histrionic inspiration ('I copied nature') quite as literally as Murphy did: his acting might have owed more to rival actors and their styles than he was willing to admit. What is truly noteworthy is that, his emphatic acknowledgement of indebtedness notwithstanding, this piece of real-life domestic tragedy did not quite fit in Garrick's promptbook, which still retained the 'probable', 'regular' and ultimately happy storyline. What happened to the unfortunate father is comparable in its sheer tragic intensity only to what Shakespeare's Lear experiences when Cordelia is strangled to death:

> Howl, howl, howl, howl! O, you are men of stones!
> Had I your tongues and eyes, I'd use them so
> That heaven's vault should crack: she's gone for ever.
> I know when one is dead and when one lives;
> She's dead as earth. (5.3.255–9)

In this way Garrick crammed Tate's happy-ending tragedy with not only the verses but also the sentiments of Shakespeare's *King Lear* and, for all the textual and emotional inconsistencies it entailed, overwhelmed the audience without fail. A Mr G. Tighe reported his companions' appreciation of the show to the thespian:

Miss Montgomerys sat just before us, and (in spite of your admirable performance) it was impossible not to watch their countenances.

The expression of the eldest was wonderful, and *such as the mighty master would have smiled to see*. She gazed, she panted, she grew pale, then again the blood rose in her cheeks, she was elevated, she almost started out of her seat, and tears began to flow, &c. &c.³⁰

It seems that, with the help of Garrick's virtuoso acting, spectators would relish even a most incoherent script, growing red and white as it goes along. They would be engrossed and entertained by the overriding sorrow, anger, pathos, sympathy, joy and so on, as they are presented on stage. What would happen, then, when they come back home from the theatre and begin to think again, to examine the details of what they have just seen, and to try to form a coherent picture of it? To answer this question, we would have to go back to the 1753–4 controversy.

2 THE MAD MONARCH AND CRITICAL REASON: PERIODICAL WRITERS

Joseph Warton and the discourse of madness

In March 1753 Joseph Warton, poet and editor of Virgil, was invited to contribute to the *Adventurer*, a highly successful periodical that Samuel Johnson and John Hawkesworth had started a year earlier.[31] Johnson proposed that the 'Province of Criticism and Literature' be covered by Warton, who graciously agreed and went on to publish some twenty-four essays, of which three dealt with the madness of King Lear.[32]

The first essay (no. 113, 4 December 1753) began by criticising 'the prevailing custom of describing only those distresses that are occasioned by the passion of love' (2:253). Shakespeare wrote masterly tragedies without relying on love interests and proved that 'BOILEAU was mistaken' when he affirmed: '– *de l'amour la sensible peinture, / Est pour aller au coeur la route la plus sûre* [sic]' (2:254). While retaliating on French classicists, here represented by Nicholas Boileau-Despréaux, who often faulted Shakespeare as lacking in stylistic sophistication, Warton in effect disapproved the 'Tatified' theatrical *King Lear* featuring many additional love affairs. Accordingly, Warton's criticism was based on a contemporary literary edition and traced the process through which the 'unnatural ingratitude, the intolerable affronts, indignities, and cruelties' of the two elder daughters at first 'inflame him [Lear] with the most violent rage', and 'by degrees drive him to madness and death' (2:254). Except for three isolated instances (Mad Tom's exclamation, 3.4.50–7; Cordelia's reflection on her sisters' ingratitude, 4.7.30–2; two lines from Lucretius), Warton's quotations, which occupy roughly half of each printed page, were exclusively from Lear's lines. By precluding other dramatic characters, the critic searched deep into Lear's disturbed mind, reading not only into what the king actually says but, more often, into the gaps between the lines, or even within a single line.

Charles Harold Gray notes the paucity of theatrical discussion in the *Adventurer* and its predecessor the *Rambler*, no doubt thanks to 'Johnson's lack of interest in the contemporary drama and his often expressed contempt for the art of acting', and states that Warton 'gave his attention to literary problems not associated with the theatre, even in his discussions of Shakespeare's plays'.[33] Warton's *King Lear* essays, however, point to a subtle interaction between the book and the stage in the critic's mind. David Garrick's rendition of Lear's 'O me, my heart! My rising heart! But down!' not only deepened Warton's understanding of the play but, indeed, defined his critical stand:

> By which single line, the inexpressible anguish of his mind, and the dreadful conflict of opposite passions with which it is agitated, are most forcibly expressed, than by the long and laboured speech, enumerating the causes of his anguish, that ROWE and other modern tragic writers would certainly have put into his mouth. But NATURE, SOPHOCLES, and SHAKESPEARE, represent the feelings of the heart in a different manner; by a broken hint, a short exclamation, a word, or a look. (2:255)

Rather than 'long and laboured' eloquence, Warton was interested in the monarch's 'inexpressible anguish' that his 'broken' and 'short' words, or even a look without a word, represent.

Garrick was a master of strong passions. As impressed contemporaries testified, he 'studied the characters of his personages, and still more their passions' and '[t]ill this excellent performer play'd this part [of Archer in George Farquhar's *The Beaux' Stratagem* (1707)] we never knew what beauties it was capable of in the sudden transitions from passion to passion in the last act'.[34] Warton shared this preoccupation with strong emotions with the foremost tragedian of Drury Lane. While Garrick portrayed Lear's psychology even at the expense of eloquence and dramatic coherence, Warton was interested in the gaps in Lear's lines and in the emotion behind them. He analysed Lear's imprecation to Goneril (1.4.288–302):

> WHEN ALBANY demands the cause of this passion, LEAR answers, 'I'll tell thee!' but immediately cries out to GONERILL,
>
>> – Life and death! I am asham'd,
>> That thou hast power to shake my manhood thus.
>>   – Blasts and fogs upon thee!
>> Th'untented woundings of a father's curse,
>> Pierce every sense about thee!
>
> He stops a little and reflects:
>
>> Ha! is it come to this?
>> Let it be so! I have another daughter,
>> Who, I am sure, is kind and comfortable. (2:255)

Warton's reading of Lear's confrontation with Goneril and Regan in Act 2 scene 2, which 'abounds with many noble turns of passion; or rather conflicts of very different passions' (2:257), was similarly oriented. Being urged by the two daughters to give up his attendants, Lear at first appeals to heavens ('You see me here, you gods . . . To bear it tamely', 2.2.464–8) but then 'suddenly he addresses GONERILL and REGAN in the severest terms and with the bitterest threats':

> No, you unnatural hags,
> I will have such revenges on you both
> That all the world shall – I will do such things –
> What they are yet I know not. (2.2.470–3)

According to Warton, Lear's inability to come up with any specific infliction eloquently delivers the enormity of his anger and agony: 'Nothing occurs to his mind severe enough for them to suffer, or him to inflict. His passion rises to a height that deprives him of articulation' (2:258).

Lear's verbal slips and silences culminate on the stormy heath of Act 3, to the analysis of which Warton's second essay (no. 116, 15 December 1753) was devoted. For example, when Kent entreats him to enter a hovel and avoid the storm, Lear rather irrelevantly interrogates, 'Wilt break my heart?' (3.4.4). Warton paraphrased the four words with recourse to Lear's psychology:

Much is contained in these four words; as if he had said, 'the kindness and the gratitude of this servant exceeds that of my own children. Tho' I have given them a kingdom, yet have they basely discarded me, and suffered a head so old and white as mine to be exposed to this terrible tempest, while this fellow pities and would protect me from its rage. I cannot bear this kindness from a perfect stranger; it breaks my heart.' (2:272)

'All this [paraphrased meaning] seems to be included in that short exclamation', admired Warton, who learnt to distinguish between explanatory description and truly tragic expression (2:272–3).

In answer to Garrick's midline suppressions of voice, Warton divided Lear's next speech (3.4.11–22) into five sections and inserted his interpretations:

> When the mind's free,
> The body's delicate: the tempest in my mind
> Doth from my senses take all feeling else,
> Save what beats there. –

Here the remembrance of his daughters['] behaviour rushes upon him, and he exclaims, full of the idea of its unparalleled cruelty

> – Filial ingratitude!
> Is it not, as this mouth should tear this hand
> For lifting food to't! –

He then changes his stile, and vows with impotent menaces, as if still in possession of the power he had resigned, to revenge himself on his oppressors, and to steel his breast with fortitude:

> – But I'll punish home.
> No, I will weep no more! –

But the sense of his sufferings returns again, and he forgets the resolution he had formed the moment before;

> – In such a night,
> To shut me out? – Pour on, I will endure! –
> In such a night as this? –

At which, with a beautiful apostrophe, he suddenly addresses himself to his absent daughters, tenderly reminding them of the favours he had so lately and so liberally conferred upon them:

> – O Regan, Gonerill,
> Your old kind father; whose frank heart gave all! –
> O that way madness lies; let me shun that;
> No more of that! – (2:273)

Warton's attention was to Lear's involuntary remembering and forgetting, meaningless menaces and imaginary conversation with the absent daughters. Under examination was not what Lear means but what disrupts his speech, or as the critic himself put it, 'The turns of passion in these few lines, are so quick and so various, that I thought they merited to be minutely pointed out by a kind of perpetual commentary' (2:273).

Throughout the first two essays, Warton carefully avoided such abstract statements as 'the madness of LEAR was very natural and pathetic', in the belief that 'GENERAL criticism is on all subjects useless and unentertaining; but is more than commonly absurd with respect to SHAKESPEARE', whose 'gradual *developements* of characters and passions' escape any generalisation (2:276). However, the third essay (no. 122, 5 January 1754) struck a noticeably different note. Instead of tracing 'the origin and progress' of insanity as in the earlier instalments, Warton attended to the 'single object' underlying Lear's inconsistent utterances and identified it as the loss of kingship ('MADNESS being occasioned by a close and continued attention of the mind to a single object, SHAKESPEARE judiciously represents the loss of royalty, as the particular idea which has brought on the distraction of LEAR, and which perpetually recurs to his imagination, and mixes itself with all his ramblings,' 2:307).³⁵ In demonstrating this thesis, the critic suddenly lost his grip on the text before him. His interpretation of the poignant passage (4.6.96–104) where Lear mistakes Gloucester for Goneril (and Regan, as in Q1 and the eighteenth-century reading texts), was symptomatic of his new approach. Warton's quotation ran as follows:

Ha! Goneril, ha! Regan! They flattered me like a dog, and told me, I had white hairs on my beard, ere the black ones were there. To say ay, and no, to every thing that I said – ay and no too, was no good divinity. When the rain came to wet me once, and the wind to make me chatter; when the thunder would not peace at my bidding; there I found 'em, there I smelt 'em out. Go to, they're not men of their words; they told me I was every thing: 'tis a lie, I am not ague-proof. (2:308)

From this, Warton merely deduced Lear's awareness of the 'impotence of royalty to exempt its possessor, more than the meanest subject, from suffering natural evils' (2:308) and his regret over the lost crown. However, these richly equivocal lines point not only to the question of royalty, but rather to the incessant shifting and slipping in Lear's thinking, of which filial ingratitude constitutes an unmistakable part. Lear associates the white-bearded Gloucester simultaneously with his ingrate daughters and courtiers in terms of flattery and deceit, and with his own old age. In Warton's quotation 'they' from the second sentence onwards primarily refers to the courtiers (and thus indicates the issue of kingship), but also reminds us of the two daughters' flattering remarks to the father at the outset of the play. The courtiers' compliment on the young Lear's precocious wisdom ('I had white hairs on my beard, ere the black ones were there') ironically reverberates the Fool's 'Thou shouldst not have been old till thou hadst been wise' (1.5.41–2). In an effort to rationalise Lear's madness, Warton's analysis lost the exhilarating power it had had in the previous two essays, where inconsistency was appreciated as inconsistency.

Just as weak was the concluding paragraph, where the critic hastily and insufficiently reviewed the topics that were not covered in the main body of the discussion, and disparaged the play from the typical neoclassical standards of double plot, stage cruelty and probability:

I SHALL transiently observe, in conclusion of these remarks, that this drama is chargeable with considerable imperfections. The plot of EDMUND against his brother, which distracts the attention, and destroys the unity of the fable; the cruel and horrid extinction of GLO'STER's eyes, which ought not to be exhibited on the stage; the utter improbability of GLO'STER's imagining, though blind, that he had leaped down Dover Cliff; and some passages that are too turgid and full of strained metaphors; are faults which the warmest admirers of SHAKESPEARE will find it difficult to excuse. I know not, also, whether the cruelty of the daughters is not painted with circumstances too savage and unnatural: for it is not sufficient to say, that this monstrous barbarity is founded on historical truth, if we recollect the just observation of BOILEAU,

> Le vrai peut quelquefois n'etre pas vraisemblable. (2:312)

The classicist Boileau-Despréaux had been roundly refuted at the beginning of the first essay but was now styled as a 'just' observer, signalling Warton's change of mind.

When the *Adventurer* ceased in 1754, Johnson wrote to Warton to 'congratulate you upon the conclusion of a work in which you have born so great a part with so much reputation', noting that Hawkesworth and 'every other man' mentioned his essays 'with great commendation, though not with greater than they deserve'.[36] It does seem, however, that Warton's true critical virtue was lost upon his readers. It was the unconvincing thematic discussion of the third essay that was to prompt Arthur Murphy's response in the *Gray's-Inn Journal* and consequently to become widely known, while Johnson in his turn would make a glaringly wrong use of Warton's criticism in his edition of Shakespeare. Let us turn to what Murphy made out of Warton's insights first.

Making sense out of frenzy: the Gray's-Inn Journal *essays*

Murphy was an avid theatregoer and friend of Henry Fielding, Samuel Foote and Garrick. He published the *Gray's-Inn Journal* from 21 October 1752 to 12 October 1754, when he suspended his journalistic career to turn actor and playwright. Little wonder that his journal included many references to plays and players. Just a week after the final instalment of the *Adventurer* essays, Murphy set out to refute one of Warton's theses and to identify the filial ingratitude, not the loss of the crown, as the cause of Lear's derangement (no. 65, 12 January 1754).

Like Warton before him, Murphy preferred Shakespeare's emotional immediacy to ornate description and examined the 'artful Mixture of thwarting Passions' and 'frequent Transition and Shifting of Emotions' (2:75–6) in *King Lear* by quoting almost exclusively from the protagonist's lines. His conception of Shakespeare's creative process, however, crucially departed from Warton's and dictated his idiosyncratic interpretation. While Warton traced 'the origin and progress' of Lear's madness through close textual analyses and speculated on the cause of the derangement only in the final instalment, Murphy clarified his agenda at the outset of the essay:

> To be able to criticise a Poet with any Degree of Perspicuity, it is requisite to consider the Nature of his Fable; and the moral Use of the Work. This being sketched, we may then proceed to observe how he lays on his Colouring, the Disposition of each Personage, the Expression of the Passions, and which is the capital Figure in the Piece. (2:73)

Murphy's view of drama was clearly 'deductive' in the logical sense of the term, with the supposed dramatists (and therefore dramatic critics) establishing the fundamental 'Nature' and 'moral Use' of the work before applying the superficial 'Colouring' of characters and their speeches. According to him, Shakespeare 'intended to exhibit, in the most striking Colours, the horrid Crime of Filial Ingratitude' by composing *King Lear*, and it was to 'enforce' this moral that 'he represents an old Monarch tired with the Cares of State, and willing to distribute his Possessions among his Daughters, in Proportion to their Affections towards his Person'. 'Accordingly,' Murphy continued, 'the two that flatter him obtain all, the third Sister being disinherited for her Sincerity, and the King is at length driven by the Ingratitude of his two eldest Daughters, to an extreme of Madness, which produces the finest Tragic Distress ever seen on any Stage' (2:73). Murphy therefore was interested only in the 'cause', and not the 'origin and progress', of Lear's madness:

> As this is the Ground-work of the Play, I am surprized that any Critic should impute the Madness of *Lear* to the Loss of Royalty. The Behaviour of his Children is always uppermost in his Thoughts, and we perceive it working upon his Passions, till at Length his Mind settles into a fixed Attention to that single Object. This, I think, will appear in a critical Examination of the Play. (2:73–4)

Once again, Murphy's procedure was openly deductive. He established filial ingratitude as 'the Ground-work' even before analysing the play, and subsequently hunted after examples to enhance the credibility of his thesis. His reading of Lear's three queries to Mad Tom (3.4.62–3) was a case in point:

> *Lear*'s first Question is, 'have his Daughters brought him to this Pass? couldst thou save nothing? didst thou give them all?' – And this I take to be the first Touch of fixed Madness in the Play [, and might point out to any Man the Cause of his Destraction, without thinking of the Resignation of his Sceptre, or the mere Loss of regal Power]. (2:77)[37]

Murphy attended only to the 'Daughters' in Lear's first question and ignored what 'this Pass' signifies in relation to the lost royalty. The implications of 'saving nothing' and 'giving all' in the second and third enquiries were also neglected, though the reference was as much to Lear's loss of regal trappings as to the daughters' ingratitude. Likewise, Murphy insisted that 'there is not a Word said of his Royalty' in the mock trial scene. He was indeed aware that Lear's employment of Edgar 'for one of my hundred' (3.6.77) might sound suspiciously regal, but defended his stand (unpersuasively) by observing that the 'hundred was appointed after his Abdication' (2:78). Murphy's confidence was not shaken even when the mad monarch enters crowned with wild flowers, muttering things like 'No, they cannot touch me for coining. I am the King himself' (4.6.83–4) and 'Ay, every inch a king' (4.6.106). His comment on this scene shows how arbitrary and self-serving a critical interpretation could be:

> It was *Shakespear's* Art to reserve his being crowned with Straw for the last Scene of his Madness, as it is a Representation of human Nature reduced to the lowest Ebb. Had he lost his Reason on Account of his abdicated Throne, the Emotions of Pity would not be so intense, as they now are when we see him drove to that Extreme by the Cruelty of his own Children. (2:79)

Filial ingratitude is no doubt responsible for Lear's madness, but Murphy's deductive thinking and simplification of dramatic motive strained his discussion and distorted the text that he set out to elucidate. Murphy's quotation from John Locke ('*Madmen do not seem to have lost the Faculty of Reasoning; but having joined together some Ideas very wrongly, they mistake them for Truths*', 2:77) illustrates not only Lear's madness but, more aptly, the critic's own analytical procedure. Murphy concluded the essay with unswerving conviction:

> So that before his Madness, in it, and after it, *Lear* never loses Sight of the Ideas which had worn such Traces on his Brain; and he must be unfeeling to the great Art of our Poet, who can look for any other Cause of Distress, in Scenes which are drawn so forcibly and strong, and kept up with the most exquisite Skill to the very dying Words of the unhappy Monarch. (2:80)

The one-sidedness of Murphy's discussion did not remain unnoticed for long. The next number of the *Gray's-Inn Journal* (no. 66, 19 January 1754) already printed an anonymous reader's response to Murphy's essay. Balancing the viewpoints of his two predecessors, this third writer contended that *both* the loss of kingship *and* the ingratitude of the daughters cause Lear's insanity:

> The Critic in the *Adventurer* was somewhat wanting in Justice to the Poet, by mentioning the Loss of Royalty as the sole Cause of *Lear*'s Madness, without taking Notice at the same Time of the forcible Idea he must have of the Ingratitude of his two Daughters; and I think Mr. *Ranger* [i.e. Murphy] also wrong, in

excluding intirely his Opinion. What I purpose here is, to point out *both the Ideas* working strongly in his Mind, and what the Author intended as conductive to the Moral of his Play. (2:83)

Lear's madness is certainly attributable to these two factors but plausibility of this sort seldom illuminates the nature of a work of art. The third critic's contention was too true to mean anything, especially when he lacked insight into how the combination of the two elements is given dramatic expression in the lines of the mad monarch. The anonymous writer defined Lear's character as Goneril paints it to Regan ('a haughty passionate, inconstant, weak old Man') and treated Lear's lines only as something 'agreeable' to this definition. His commentary on the much-discussed three questions ('Have his daughters brought him to this pass? / Couldst thou save nothing? Wouldst thou give 'em all?') was exemplary:

This is agreeable to his Character – And from all that we hear in common Life (for there are many Stories) of old weak Parents, who have acted much in the Manner of *Lear*, and to the Reproach of human Nature, have met with Ingratitude and Disobedience; these, I say, in their Feeling-hours of Distress, are reported to have reproached themselves with their Folly in GIVING ALL, as well as exclaimed against the Ingratitude of their Children. (2:87)

This third critic even chose to 'FORBEAR making any Quotations from Lear's Speeches in his Madness' of Act 3 onwards, believing that Shakespeare 'had a perfect Knowledge of the Workings of the human Mind' and 'has drawn both the Ideas in Lear's Madness, agreeable to the Representation he has made of him in the first Act' (2:87). Here the controversy reached the farthest point from Warton's analyses in terms not only of the conclusion but also of the critical method: the third writer analysed Lear's madness with reference to 'his Character' rather than to his deranged lines.

Editing the 1756 collection of the periodical, Murphy composed another essay (falsely dated 'no. 87, 15 June 1754') to defend his theory once again, though his discussion ('had those Children not proved ungrateful ... there is no Reason to imagine, the King's Mind would have taken the fatal Turn it did [even without his crown]', 2:219) was rather a matter of rhetorical sophistry than literary criticism. Murphy also related Lear's madness to his innate character:

But the best Way of knowing, with any Degree of Certainty, the secret Causes of those Effects, which disclose themselves in sundry Appearances in human Life, is by gaining an Insight into the private Tempers of Men. *Lear*, considered in this Manner, soon discovers to us the latent Seeds, which are likely to kindle into a Blaze, upon the Revolt of his Daughters. (2:219–20)

Like the third anonymous critic before him, Murphy shifted his attention from the actual drama ('those Effects') to the 'private Tempers', or the character, of the protagonist that even precede 'the Revolt of his Daughters'.

In 1752 John Hill, with other members of the audience, experienced an incongruous mixture of feelings while watching Garrick's performance of Lear. They laughed at the madman and were unwittingly moved to tears at the same time:

> 'Tis an odd Effect of a Laugh to produce Tears; but I believe there was hardly a dry Eye in the House on his executing that first absolute Act of Madness in the Character. While I admired the Action, I was almost at a Loss to comprehend in what Manner it was performed: 'Twas not any thing like the Laugh of Mirth or Pleasantry, the Triumph of a happy Imagination; but seemed merely an Exertion of the Organs of the Body, without any Connection with the Soul; an involuntary Emotion of the Muscles, while the Mind was fixed on something else.

Through Garrick's accomplished portrayal of the conflicting passions (and conflicting script), this mysterious working of human mind, both of Lear and of the audience, came to the fore: 'Upon the whole, the other Lears I have seen, not excepting one, of whom the World supposes me too fond, must pardon me, if I declare, that the frantic Part of the Character seems never to have been rightly understood till this Gentleman studied it.'[38] Stimulated by Garrick's acting, the three critics studied Lear's disruptive lines, and the character supposedly underlying them, in a bid 'to comprehend in what Manner it was performed' on the page.[39] Their rationalisations might have been ultimately irrelevant to Lear's madness, but that did not prevent Johnson from distorting them further in his Shakespeare edition.

3 RESISTING GARRICK: SAMUEL JOHNSON ON SHAKESPEARE

In February 1737 Gilbert Walmesley, Lichfield's registrar of the Ecclesiastical Court and gentleman-scholar, wrote to the Rev. John Colson of London to ask him a favour:

> My neighbour, Captain Garrick, (who is an honest valuable man,) has a son, who is a very sensible young fellow, and a good scholar, and whom the Captain hopes, in some two or three years, he shall be able to send to the Temple, and breed to the Bar. But, at present, his pocket will not hold out for sending him to the University. I have proposed your taking him, if you think well of it, and your boarding him, and instructing him in mathematics, and philosophy, and human learning. He is now nineteen, of sober and good dispositions, and is as ingenious and promising a young man as ever I knew in my life.[40]

Colson agreed to give the young man boarding and education. Walmesley sent a second letter to thank him and to inform him of another Lichfieldian who would accompany the son of Captain Garrick. This man had been a teacher of the young boy but his boarding school had recently gone bankrupt:

> He and another neighbour of mine, one Mr. Johnson, set out this morning for London together: Davy Garrick to be with you early the next week; and Mr. Johnson to try his fate with a tragedy [i.e. *Irene*], and to see to get himself employed in some translation, either from the Latin or the French. Johnson is a very good scholar and poet, and I have great hopes will turn out a fine tragedy writer. If it should any ways lie in your way, I doubt not but you would be ready to recommend and assist your countryman.[41]

As it transpired, neither of them would achieve their initial objectives in London, as David Garrick would become the most illustrious actor of the century instead of a lawyer, while Samuel Johnson would fail as dramatist and eventually establish himself as lexicographer and editor of Shakespeare. The relationship between these two significant Shakespeareans, one on stage and the other on page, would also prove less than straightforward. Some twenty years later, Johnson was to perplex his friends by not mentioning Garrick in his Shakespeare edition, though the actor was by then a major celebrity, manager of Drury Lane, collector of antique play-books and, according to public opinion, the best commentator on Shakespeare's plays. Johnson's biographer, James Boswell, complained about this awkward omission and 'asked him [Johnson] if he did not admire him'.[42]

Before examining the doctor's answer to this intriguing question, let us look into two instances where he easily could, and indeed should, have referred to the actor but quite deliberately failed to do so. In both cases, by mistaking and misquoting the source materials and significantly neglecting the foremost Shakespearean actor of the age, the editor would formulate a highly idiosyncratic theory of the art of drama.

The King Lear *stricture*

While his contract stipulated that 'the work shall be published on or before Christmas 1757', it was not until 1765 that Johnson brought out his edition of Shakespeare. Along with the celebrated Preface and notes, the editor appended many of the plays with 'general observations', or 'strictures' as he liked to call them, 'containing a general censure of faults, or praise of excellence'.[43] In his stricture on *King Lear*, this critical intelligence surprises us by preferring Nahum Tate's version over Shakespeare's original and confessing to his sentimental response to the death of Cordelia ('I was many years ago so shocked by Cordelia's death, that I know not whether I ever endured to read again the last scenes of the play till I undertook to revise them as an editor'). His handling of 'the current opinion' of Joseph Warton and Arthur Murphy also strikes us as quite unexpected, though in a less obvious way. First, Johnson described the emotional hold that the tragic plot and characters exert over the reader's, and spectator's, imagination: 'The tragedy of Lear is deservedly celebrated among the dramas of Shakespeare. There is perhaps no play which keeps the attention so strongly fixed; which so much agitates our passions and interests our curiosity ... So powerful is the current of the poet's imagination, that the mind, which once ventures within it, is hurried irresistibly along' (702–3). The critic then defended the seeming improbability of Lear's conduct by remembering 'the barbarity and ignorance of the age to which this story is referred' and by reducing the character of the king, arguing that '[s]uch preference of one daughter to another, or resignation of dominion on such conditions, would be yet credible, if told of a petty prince of Guinea or Madagascar' (703).

As Arthur Sherbo emphasises, it was customary for an eighteenth-century critic to discuss Shakespeare's failings, and 'some knowledge of the wealth of adverse criticism of Shakespeare scattered throughout the books and periodicals of the eighteenth century is necessary before one can hope to realize the mildness of Johnson's statements on Shakespeare's faults'.[44] It is true that, unlike Tate, who changed the plot to increase the play's probability and regularity, Johnson defended Lear's behaviour as plausible on historical grounds and was apparently respectful of the original tragedy. But the tragedy, if anything, suffered in being defended by this commentator. His conception of Lear was patronising and belittling and clearly detracted from the haunting power of the tragedy that he himself attested to in the first paragraph. It was as if the critic had resisted the overwhelming 'current of the poet's imagination' by slighting the protagonist as a 'petty prince of Guinea or Madagascar'.

In this short stricture Johnson paid considerable attention to Warton and Murphy: three paragraphs out of the total eight were devoted to the examination of their theses. As for the cause of Lear's madness, Johnson sided with Murphy:

Mr. Murphy, a very judicious critick, has evinced by induction of particular passages, that the cruelty of his daughters is the primary source of his distress, and that the loss of royalty affects him only as a secondary and subordinate evil; he observes with great justness, that Lear would move our compassion but little, did we not rather consider the injured father than the degraded king. (705)

No wonder Murphy was flattered to find this reference.[45] We may just quickly note that Johnson mistook Murphy's method as inductive, and referred to the paragraph on Act 4 scene 6 where, as I pointed out in the previous section, his argument was particularly weak.

Johnson's treatment of Warton was even less satisfactory: 'My learned friend Mr. Warton, who has in the *Adventurer* very minutely criticised this play, remarks, that the instances of cruelty are too savage and shocking, and that the intervention of Edmund destroys the simplicity of the story' (703). Johnson neglected Warton's 'minute' analysis and speculations on the cause of Lear's madness altogether and picked up only the concluding paragraph of the final instalment, which was professedly 'transient' and uncharacteristically neoclassical. Even worse, this passage was cited only for the sake of refutation: 'These objections may, I think, be answered, by repeating, that the cruelty of the daughters is an historical fact, to which the poet has added little, having only drawn it into a series by dialogue and action' (703).

It is also noteworthy that, while countering Warton's criticism, Johnson himself did not show much appreciation of Shakespeare's compelling portrayal of the vicious characters: he simply apologised for, and explained away, the elder sisters in terms of the savagery of the age in which the tragedy is set. The editor likewise imputed the gory extrusion of Gloucester's eyes to the barbarity of Shakespeare's London: 'Yet let it be remembered that our authour well knew what would please the audience for which he wrote' (703). Johnson clearly missed not only the merit of his friend's essays but also the true tragic power of *King Lear*.

Warton was understandably mortified to find his discussion distorted in the Shakespeare edition and registered a complaint. Johnson acknowledged his mistake and apologised:

Dear Sir:
I am revising my Edition of Shakespeare and remember that I formerly misrepresented your opinion of Lear. Be pleased to write the paragraph as you would have it, and send it. If you have any remarks of your own upon that or any other play I shall gladly receive them.[46]

The rewriting seems not to have materialised: the next edition (Johnson-Steevens 1773) preserved the paragraph in question as it stood in the 1765 publication.

This *King Lear* stricture was notable for yet another failure. Johnson ignored the actor who had inspired both Warton and Murphy and overlooked the part of the controversy that was most strongly influenced by his acting: the close reading of Lear's turbulent lines. We should not expect Johnson to acknowledge all those concerned in such a brief essay and to live up to our hopes, especially when he himself admitted that '[n]othing is minutely and particularly examined' in it (104). However, when we detect an almost identical case of neglect in the celebrated Preface, where again the editor took it upon himself to defend Shakespeare's 'defective' dramaturgy, Johnson's failure assumes a further significance.

Reality and delusion

Johnson told Joshua Reynolds two things he knew he was good at: 'one is an introduction to any literary work, stating what it is to contain, and how it should be executed in the most perfect manner; the other is a conclusion, shewing from various causes why the execution has not been equal to what the authour promised himself and to the publick'. Johnson's Preface to his edition of Shakespeare, written last and printed just two weeks before the publication, combined the two tasks where he excelled, and proved a 'magnificent piece of Johnsonian prose'.[47]

The editor showed first his appreciation of the naturalness and accuracy of Shakespeare's dramatic portrayal, or as Johnson himself put it:

> that his drama is the mirrour of life; that he who has mazed his imagination, in following the phantoms which other writers raise up before him, may here be cured of his delirious extasies, by reading human sentiments in human language; by scenes from which a hermit may estimate the transactions of the world, and a confessor predict the progress of the passions. (*On Shakespeare*, 65)

He then followed the well-trodden way to examine the playwright's shortcomings, namely: that he 'sacrifices virtue to convenience'; that the 'plots are often so loosely formed, that a very slight consideration may improve them'; that 'in many of his plays the latter part is evidently neglected'; that he had 'no regard to distinction of time or place, but gives one age or nation, without scruple, the customs, institutions, and opinions of another'; that he was 'seldom very successful' in either comic or tragic scenes; that his diction, declamation and sentiment were unwieldy; and, of course, that a 'quibble was to him the fatal Cleopatra' (71–4).

As for Shakespeare's violation of the three unities, however, Johnson decided to defy critical convention and 'adventure to try how I can defend him' (75). Ironically, not unlike his vindication of Lear's probability, Johnson's defence detracted from, rather than added to, Shakespeare's credentials as dramatist. Setting aside the historical plays (where the rule does not apply) and the unity of action (of which Shakespeare was fairly observant), the doctor exploded the fallacy of the unities of time and place. The whole discussion of the unities presupposed that plays could be, and should be, credible, but it is 'false, that any representation is mistaken for reality; that any dramatick fable in its materiality was ever credible, or, for a single moment, was ever credited' (76). Johnson expounded on his rather devastating theory of theatrical verisimilitude as follows:

> The objection arising from the impossibility of passing the first hour at Alexandria, and the next at Rome, supposes, that when the play opens the spectator really imagines himself at Alexandria, and believes that his walk to the theatre has been a voyage to Egypt, and that he lives in the days of Antony and Cleopatra. Surely he that imagines this may imagine more. He that can take the stage at one time for the palace of the Ptolemies, may take it in half an hour for the promontory of Actium. Delusion, if delusion be admitted, has no certain limitation; if the spectator can be once persuaded, that his old acquaintance are Alexander and Caesar, that a room illuminated with candles is the plain of Pharsalia, or the bank of Granicus, he is in a state of elevation above the reach of reason, or of truth, and from the heights of empyrean poetry, may despise the circumscriptions of terrestrial nature. (76–7)

Sherbo hears 'echoes of earlier arguments' in Johnson's contentions and cites Lord Kames's *Elements of Criticism* (1762) as his most important precursor:

> Where the representation is suspended, we can with the greatest facility suppose any length of time or any change of place: the spectator, it is true, may be conscious, that the real time and place are not the same with what are employed in the representation: but this is a work of reflection; and by the same reflection he may also be conscious, that Garrick is not King Lear, that the playhouse is not Dover cliffs, nor the noise he hears thunder and lightning. In a word, after an interruption of the representation, it is no more difficult for a spectator to imagine a new place, or a different time, than at the commencement of the play, to imagine himself at Rome, or in a period of time two thousand years back. And indeed, it is abundantly ridiculous, that a critic, who is willing to hold candle-light for sunshine, and some painted canvasses for a palace or a prison, should be so scrupulous about admitting any latitude of place or of time in the fable, beyond what is necessary in the representation.[48]

The formulations of the two critics look so similar that Sherbo suspects 'conscious or unconscious borrowing' on the part of Johnson. Apart from the omission of 'Garrick' and 'King Lear' from Johnson's version ('his old acquaintance' playing 'Alexander and Caesar' being the editor's anonymous substitute), verbal and figurative echoes are conspicuous enough to justify Sherbo's assertion. However, parallelism here is significant rather for the different conceptions of dramatic credibility that the two critics finally formed. According to Kames, we stop confusing the stage with real life only by 'a work of reflection'. This means that the distinction between reality and illusion is blurred in the heat of performance and that, if it were not for 'the same reflection', we would be scarcely conscious that 'Garrick is not King Lear, that the playhouse is not Dover cliffs, nor the noise he hears thunder and lightning'. Johnson's argument runs emphatically otherwise, which is made clearer in the next paragraph (which Sherbo chooses not to discuss):

> The truth is, that the spectators are always in their senses, and know, from the first act to the last, that the stage is only a stage, and that the players are only players. They come to hear a certain number of lines recited with just gesture and elegant modulation. The lines relate to some action, and an action must be in some place; but the different actions that compleat a story may be in places very remote from each other; and where is the absurdity of allowing that space to represent first Athens, and then Sicily, which was always known to be neither Sicily nor Athens, but a modern theatre. (77)

The unities of time and place are dispensable because the irregularity would not compromise any theatrical verisimilitude, which is nonexistent to begin with.

Johnson did not deny the emotional relevance of theatrical experience because, in his opinion, one can be moved by a performance even when one is not immersed in it. In fact, the drama moves precisely by reminding the spectator of what happens, or can happen, in real life:

> It will be asked, how the drama moves, if it is not credited. It is credited with all the credit due to a drama. It is credited, whenever it moves, as a just picture of a real original; as representing to the auditor what he would himself feel, if he were to do or suffer what is there feigned to be suffered or to be done. (78)

In his view, the audience is moved not by the performance as such but by the possibility of distress in real life of which the stage is a reminder:

> The reflection that strikes the heart is not, that the evils before us are real evils, but that they are evils to which we ourselves may be exposed. If there be any fallacy, it is not that we fancy the players, but that we fancy ourselves unhappy for a moment; but we rather lament the possibility than suppose the presence of misery, as a mother weeps over her babe, when she remembers that death may take it from her. (78)

Here was a curious exchange between Garrick's *King Lear* and Johnson's explanation of tragic distress. As noted above, Garrick portrayed Lear's anguish by imitating the neighbour who had lost his daughter, though Cordelia did not actually die in his stage version. Johnson, on the other hand, regarded stage death as a presentiment of a potential loss of a child in real life. 'Imitations produce pain or pleasure', Johnson continued, 'not because they are mistaken for realities, but because they bring realities to mind.' Johnson established the power of drama precisely by dispelling theatrical delusion.

It is difficult to say how serious Johnson was in pronouncing this idiosyncratic apology for Shakespeare's dramaturgy. The discussion on the unities started as a display of a critical and dialectical *tour de force* in the face of the neoclassical critics ('I shall, with due reverence to that learning which I must oppose, adventure to try how I can defend him', 75) and ended with the same half-joking tone ('I am almost frighted at my own temerity; and when I estimate the fame and the strength of those that maintain the contrary opinion, am ready to sink down in reverential silence', 80–1). To understand Johnson's apparent mistrust of theatrical experience, as well as of Garrick, who was clearly its champion, we can now return to the question Boswell posed.

Punch's feelings

At his memorable first encounter with Samuel Johnson at Thomas Davies's bookshop in 1763, Boswell inadvertently commented on the behaviour of the doctor's old acquaintance and pupil. Although it was Johnson who initiated the animadversion on Garrick, he immediately checked the newcomer: '"Sir, (said he, with a stern look,) I have known David Garrick longer than you have done: and I know no right you have to talk to me on the subject."'[49] Boswell had already been given a fair warning about the complexity of their relationship, or as it was later formulated: 'I [Boswell] once mentioned to him, "It is observed, Sir, that you attack Garrick yourself, but will suffer nobody else to do it." JOHNSON, (smiling) "Why, Sir, that is true."'[50] Even so, when Johnson's edition of Shakespeare was published, Boswell could not help mentioning the glaring omission of the actor's name:

I complained that he had not mentioned Garrick in his Preface to Shakspeare; and asked him if he did not admire him. JOHNSON. 'Yes, as "a poor player, who frets and struts his hour upon the stage"; – as a shadow.' BOSWELL. 'But has he not brought Shakspeare into notice?' JOHNSON. 'Sir, to allow that, would be to lampoon the age. Many of Shakspeare's plays are the worse for being acted: Macbeth, for instance.' BOSWELL. 'What, Sir, is nothing gained by decoration and action? Indeed, I do wish that you had mentioned Garrick.' JOHNSON. 'My dear Sir, had I mentioned him, I must have mentioned many more: Mrs. Pritchard, Mrs. Cibber, – nay, and Mr. Cibber, too; he too altered Shakspeare.'[51]

Joan E. Klingel sees this repartee as an indication of Johnson's antipathy to theatrical alterations of Shakespeare rather than to acting as such. Boswell's 'habitual gadfly query' might also have induced his ironical response.[52] But even the doctor's favourite adaptation, the happy-ending *King Lear*, failed to keep him interested in the performance. Johnson's close friend Hester Lynch Piozzi (Thrale) recorded:

> Garrick was one night coming on the Stage in Lear as I remember, when Johnson laughing or arguing behind the Scenes made such a Noise that the little Man was teized by it – and said at last – do have done with all this Rattle. – it spoyls my Thoughts, it destroys my *Feelings* – No No Sir returns the other – (loud enough for all the players to hear him) – I know better things – *Punch* has no *feelings*.[53]

It may be that Johnson was endearingly teasing his old pupil who self-importantly referred to 'my Thoughts' and 'my Feelings'. It is still not a little surprising that Johnson was laughing and arguing behind the scenes, rather than watching in the auditorium, when the masterpiece tragedy was being performed. This seems a perfect recapitulation of the *King Lear* stricture and the theory of dramatic (non)delusion in the Preface: Johnson came very close to addressing, and paying due respect to, Garrick's Lear but, jokingly or insultingly, avoided doing so in all three cases.

Garrick was miffed to find his name omitted from his friend's edition, of which Johnson was informed: 'Mr Johnson being told that Garrick took umbrage at not being mentioned in His edition of Shakespear: why what is it to me says he as Editor of Shakespear, that Mr Garrick can mouthe a Tragedy, – or skip a Comedy?'[54] Courageously enough, Boswell once again asked 'why he did not mention him in the Preface to Shakspeare' during their tour to the Hebrides (23 September 1773). Johnson answered:

> I would not disgrace my page with a player. Garrick has been liberally paid for mouthing Shakespeare. If I should praise him, I should much more praise the nation who paid him. He has not made Shakespeare better known. He cannot illustrate Shakespeare. He does not understand him. Besides, Garrick got me no subscriptions. He did not furnish me with his old plays. I asked to have them, and I think he sent me one. It was not worthwhile to ask again. So I have reasons enough against mentioning him, were reasons necessary. There should be reasons *for* it.[55]

Johnson's accusation against Garrick regarding the subscription and the antique playbooks was totally unfounded. Garrick did get subscriptions for the Shakespeare edition. It was Johnson who lost the list of subscribers over the many years of editing and, as their correspondence attests, he was aware of his own blunder.[56] And as Boswell recorded, 'Johnson was made welcome to the full use' of Garrick's collection of the antique playbooks and the actor always 'left the key of it with a servant, with orders to have a fire and every convenience for him'. Garrick was not particularly pleased when the doctor took the books out of the library but 'considering the slovenly and careless manner in which books were treated by Johnson, it could not be expected that scarce and valuable editions should have been lent to him'.[57] Making two factually unsound accusations, Johnson seems to have been determined to deny Garrick at all cost the respect that the whole generation of theatregoers and men of letters were more than willing to pay: to Johnson, Garrick was never 'the best commentator of Shakespeare'.

Still undaunted, Boswell then referred to a recent publication in the preface of which Garrick's achievement was acknowledged and applauded: 'I mentioned Mrs. Montagu's high praises of Garrick. JOHNSON. "It is fit she should say so much, and I should say nothing." He said Reynolds was fond of her book, and he wondered at it; for neither he nor Mrs. Thrale nor Beauclerk could get through it.'[58] To examine this further derogation by Johnson, we need to turn to Elizabeth Montagu's 1769 publication.

4 CONFRONTATION AND EVASION: ELIZABETH MONTAGU'S BLUESTOCKING VIEWPOINT

Voltaire and Johnson

In May 1769 Elizabeth Montagu, who was widely regarded as the leader of a group of literary ladies known as 'the Bluestockings' (from the legwear of one of the members), anonymously published her *Essay on the Writings and Genius of Shakespear*, whose table of contents read:

INTRODUCTION.	Page. 1.
On Dramatic Poetry.	P. 25.
On the Historical Drama.	P. 55.
The First Part of Henry IV.	P. 89.
The Second Part of Henry IV.	P. 111.
On the Praeternatural Beings.	P. 133.
The Tragedy of Macbeth.	P. 173.
Upon the Cinna *of* Corneille.	P. 207.
Upon the Death of Julius Caesar.	P. 245.[59]

This looks like a whimsical arrangement of chapters, consisting of three theoretical examinations ('On Dramatic Poetry', 'On the Historical Drama' and 'On the Praeternatural Beings'), interspersed with studies of four Shakespearean plays (the two parts of *Henry IV*, *Macbeth* and *Julius Caesar*) and of *Cinna* by Corneille. However, the depth of Montagu's deliberation becomes abundantly clear when two authoritative literary figures are taken into account: her discussion was carefully organised to challenge the one and avoid the other.

As the subtitle indicates ('Compared with the Greek and French Dramatic Poets, with Some Remarks upon the Misrepresentations of Mons. de Voltaire'), Montagu's publication was not simply 'another study of Shakespeare' but a book of polemic to rebut the French classicist Voltaire's charges against the Bard. Montagu expressed antipathy to the *philosophe* as early as 1755, when she read his *L'Orphelin de la Chine* 'without any concern'. She wrote to her sister:

> When I compare this indifference with the interest, the admiration, the surprise with which I read what the saucy Frenchman calls les farces monstreuses of Shakespear, I could burn him and his tragedy. Foolish coxcomb! rules can no more make a poet, than receipts a cook. There must be taste, there must be skill. Oh! that we were as sure our fleets and armies could drive the French out of America, as that our poets and tragedians can drive them out of Parnassus. I hate to see these tame creatures taught to pace by art, attack fancy's sweetest child.[60]

Throughout the 1760s, Montagu discussed various aspects of drama, from Euripides and Sophocles through Shakespeare to the eighteenth-century dramatists, with her literary friends, and gradually formulated her theses to quash the French writer. By 1769, her opinions were perfectly ready for publication.

Montagu's *Essay* challenged Voltaire by both praising Shakespeare and faulting the Greek and French drama that the *philosophe* championed. After apologising for Shakespeare's neglect of the three unities in the Introduction, Montagu distinguished between truly dramatic expression and mere narration in the first chapter ('On Dramatic Poetry'), criticising French tragedy as no better than 'a tissue of declamations, and some laboured recitals of the catastrophe'.[61] Her next chapter was on historical drama, which was unknown in the age of Aristotle and therefore 'cannot come within any rules which are prior to their existence' (20). With no rules to disfavour the irregular genius, Montagu established Shakespeare's superiority to Voltaire's favourite Corneille by comparing their renditions of historical topics in the next two chapters on *Henry IV*.

Shakespeare's excellent use of supernaturalism was contrasted with the inferior attempts of Greek dramatists in the chapter 'On the Praeternatural Beings' and was subsequently illustrated by the example of *Macbeth*. Montagu discussed two political plays (Shakespeare's *Julius Caesar*, and Corneille's *Cinna*, first staged in 1640, which was Voltaire's favourite) in her final chapters and, while sneering at Voltaire's botched French translation of *Julius Caesar* and criticising his judgment, firmly placed the English conspiracy tragedy over the French counterpart.[62]

While Voltaire was Montagu's direct target, another powerful literary figure influenced her criticism in a less visible, but no less important, way. Samuel Johnson published his Shakespeare edition complete with the brilliant Preface in 1765, putting Montagu's enterprise in a terrible double bind of redundancy and impertinence. She wrote to Elizabeth Carter, another illustrious Bluestocking:

I have sent only one sheet of scrawl, for Mr. Johnson having just published his Shakespear I must see that I do not servilely seem to imitate, or presumptuously contradict him. You will think me perhaps conceited to go on with the work when he has just published a preface on Shakespear, and perhaps it may make me suppress the work, but having begun, I will finish it.[63]

For all her reservations about Johnson's literary judgements, Montagu was intimidated by his 'talent' and 'weight of authority', not to mention 'that prevailing charm of writing which he can throw into his'. Luckily for Montagu, Johnson discussed Shakespeare only in general terms in the Preface, with little reference to particular lines of his plays. Ample room was left for her to explore: 'The method I have persued is quite different from his; I thought there were enough already of vague panegyricks and general criticisms upon Shakespear[']s works, so have taken a larger view of the dramatick art, and a more particular consideration of his merits and faults, excellencies and defects.'[64] Montagu's *Essay* followed the agenda outlined here closely, with the Introduction presenting 'a larger view' on 'dramatic poetry' in general and the ensuing chapters giving 'a more particular consideration' to historical drama, supernatural apparitions and the two conspiracy plays.

Norma Clarke analyses the correspondence between Montagu and Carter and concludes that 'Voltaire and Johnson both served as targets' for the Queen of the Blues, who attacked the English critic 'scornfully' in her letters.[65] Equally significant, however, is that, despite the ample animadversion on Johnson in her private correspondence, Montagu did not make a single negative comment on him in her publication, her only reference to him being in praise of his refutation of the unities of time and place (6). Montagu's strategy was not to attack but to avoid Johnson at all cost and pursue the topics that he had neglected. For instance, the two chapters on *Henry IV* were written not only because Montagu wanted to disclose 'Mr. Voltaire[']s injustice' but because 'Mr. Johnson[']s remarks at the end of Henry the 4th are very short' and 'by no means such as one should expect from a critick'.[66]

Montagu became acquainted with Johnson in 1759 through Carter, who was their mutual friend. They acknowledged each other's intelligence (it was Johnson who famously dubbed her 'the Queen of the Blues') but they were 'never intimates'. According to Clarke, Montagu's consciousness of rank, her dictatorial manner and her love of holding the floor in talk was 'in every way a match for Johnson', and this social and temperamental antagonism prevented them from being truly close.[67] Reflecting their tricky relationship, the doctor's publication helped Montagu's project in a negative way. Through examining Johnson's edition, Montagu clarified what was not to be discussed, rather than what was to be discussed, in her own book.

Voltaire was a good topic for Montagu in this regard for, despite Boswell's encouragement, Johnson did not adequately refute the *philosophe*'s charges against Shakespeare, contenting himself with commenting sardonically, 'These are the petty cavils of petty minds' (*On Shakespeare*, 66). Montagu was more than willing to take up the issue that Johnson had dropped: 'I am sorry Mr. Johnson has pass'd him over with supercilious contempt, it is true that he deserves to be used so, but as he stands high in the opinion of many, I wish Mr. Johnson had exposed him.'[68] Montagu was a firm believer in theatre's intellectual and emotional relevance and here was yet another province for her to explore: 'I think the Theatrical entertainments capable of conveying so much instruction, & exciting such sentiments in the people, that if I am glad he left the task to my unable hand, I dare hardly own it to myself' (173; To Elizabeth Carter, 21 October 1766). Writing once again to Carter, Montagu clarified her project in the interlocking terms of Voltaire, Johnson, theatre and Shakespeare:

I was provoked to this undertaking by the flippancy of Voltaire in a great measure, and also by thinking we had erred widely from the true dramatick art. I have so far proceeded, and am so warm'd by the subject, that I hardly care to drop it, and yet I don[']t know whether after Mr. Johnson people will desire any more criticisms on Shakespear. I understood he was only to write notes upon him, and those merely to rectify the errors of the copies, but alas! his Preface is so ingenious it terrif[ie]s me.[69]

Montagu found both Voltaire and Johnson particularly neglectful, or even ignorant, of the theatricality of Shakespeare's works, to the exploration of which her ambitious first chapter ('On Dramatic Poetry') was devoted.

Description and expression

> BOSWELL. 'But, Sir, we have Lord Kames.' JOHNSON. 'You *have* Lord Kames. Keep him; ha, ha, ha! We don't envy you him.'[70]

Boswell's fellow Scotsman Lord Kames, whose theory of the unities influenced Johnson, published his *Elements of Criticism* in 1762 to explore the psychological rationale of various art forms and to establish the superiority of lifelike expression over formal description. Contrary to Johnson's assertion that the theatre moves by recalling reality, Kames firmly believed in theatrical verisimilitude and the 'real' sympathy evoked in the audience. He downplayed the three unities because dramatic illusion consists not in the continuity in time and place but in the lifelikeness of speeches. For Kames, King Lear's exclamations in front of the hovel (3.4.14–36) and Othello's lamentation over the body of Desdemona (5.2.259–81) epitomised the truly dramatic language, for the 'sentiments here display'd flow so naturally from the passions represented, and are such genuine expressions of these passions, that it is not possible to conceive any imitation more perfect' (2:163). Kames's faith in dramatic verisimilitude also prescribed his preferred acting style. Formalised declamation, which the ornate description of the French school premised, prevents the actor from representing human sentiments:

> Unhappy is the player of genius who acts a capital part in what may be termed a *descriptive tragedy*: after he has assumed the very passion that is to be represented, how must he be cramped in his action, when he is forc'd to utter, not the sentiments of the passion he feels, but a cold description in the language of a by-stander. (2:159)

Kames became acquainted with Montagu in 1766 and, finding her ideas congenial with his own, even invited her to contribute a chapter to *Elements of Criticism*. She did not write a chapter for him but she did send her observations in private correspondence, which the Scotsman cited in a revised edition of his publication.[71] Kames's criticism was not only misused (in his Preface) and abused (see the remark cited at the beginning of this section) by Johnson but also bitterly ridiculed upon its publication by Voltaire.[72] Confronted with these venomous adversaries, Kames found a trustworthy ally in the Queen of the Blues, who developed his insights into theatrical art to wage her battle against the more imposing predecessors.

Like Kames and unlike Johnson, Montagu believed in theatrical verisimilitude (or the 'justness of imitation') and criticised French tragedy on this count. Theatrical sentiments should evoke 'the same passions and affections' in the audience 'as if what was exhibited was real', but French tragedy was no better than 'a tissue of declamations' and 'laboured recitals of the catastrophe', and was too 'faint and feeble' to excite sympathy. Indeed, Montagu saw a truly tragic expression not in the artificial French drama but in real life:

> Experience informs us, that even the inarticulate groans, and involuntary convulsions, of a creature in agonies, affect us much more, than the most eloquent and elaborate description of its situation, delivered in the properest words, and most significant gestures. Our pity is attendant on the passion of the unhappy person, and on his own sense of his misfortunes. (12)

Tragic characters should simulate this natural outburst and express, not narrate, their agony and distress, for '[f]rom description, from the report of a spectator, we may make some conjecture of his internal state of mind, and so far we shall be moved: but the direct and immediate way to the heart is by the sufferer's expression of his passion' (12).

To illustrate the artificial and the lifelike modes of tragic expression, Montagu contrasted Sophocles's *Oedipus Coloneus* on the one hand and passages from Shakespeare's *King Lear*, *King John* and *Macbeth* on the other. In the Greek tragedy Oedipus expostulates with his undutiful son and sets forth the enormity of filial disobedience, but the father's anger and sorrow is conveyed to the audience 'only by the vehemence with which he speaks of them, and the imprecations he utters against the delinquent son'. The audience certainly feels indignation at the conduct of Polynices but it does not empathise with the distressed father, because Oedipus 'has explained to us merely the external duties and relations of parent and child' (12–13). When Shakespeare's father-king expresses his agony in a similar case of ingratitude in *King Lear*, the audience's emotion is stirred in a different way:

> The pangs of paternal tenderness, thus wounded, [are] more pathetically expressed by King Lear, who leaves out whatever of this enormity is equally sensible to the spectator, and immediately exposes to us his own internal feelings, when, in the bitterness of his soul, cursing his daughter's offspring, he adds,
>
> > That she may feel,
> > How sharper than a serpent's tooth it is,
> > To have a thankless child.
>
> By this we perceive how deeply paternal affection is wounded by filial ingratitude. (13)

Reinforcing Kames's explanation of the mechanism of playwriting ('That a passion be adjusted to the character, the sentiments to the passion, and the language to the sentiments'), Montagu speculated on the process through which Shakespeare created such impassioned expressions as Constance's lamentation over the loss of Arthur ('He speaks to me that never had a son') in *King John* and Macbeth's hesitation in saying 'Amen':

> These expressions open to us the internal state of the persons interested, and never fail to command our sympathy. Shakespear seems to have had the art of the Dervise [i.e. Dervish], in the Arabian tales, who could throw his soul into the body of another man, and be at once possessed of his sentiments, adopt his passions, and rise to all the functions and feelings of his situation. (13)

According to this explanation, Shakespeare identified with his characters to express their feelings truthfully. Montagu regarded this power of empathy as essential not only to dramatists but also to actors. (And this sends us back to Montagu's laudation of Garrick of which Boswell reminded the negligent Johnson.) Drawing an analogy between playwriting and acting, Montagu commended Garrick for his empathetic identification with both the dramatist and his dramatic characters: '[Shakespeare's] very spirit seems to come forth and to animate his characters, as often as Mr. Garrick, who acts with the same inspiration with which he wrote, assumes them on the stage' (6).

The publication of Montagu's *Essay* in 1769 coincided with another conspicuous Shakespearean undertaking: Garrick's Stratford Jubilee. These two events were to be associated in people's imagination (and by Garrick and Montagu themselves) as a joint tribute to the great Elizabethan and therefore need to be examined alongside each other. But before turning to Garrick's extraordinary festival and listening to what the actor had to say about Shakespeare and contemporary Shakespeareans, let us take a glance at a curious epilogue that the confrontation of this Bluestocking lady and the French philosopher entailed.

The French Garrick

Some seven years after the publication of her only critical work, Montagu, now widowed, ventured her first (and last) trip to Paris. Her book had not yet been translated into French but it was well known in Parisian literary circles and 'even her coiffeuse was to flatter her on her authorship while she curled her hair'.[73] Coincidentally, a new French translation of three of Shakespeare's plays (*Julius Caesar, Othello* and *The Tempest*) was published at this time under royal patronage and once again infuriated the old champion of classical drama. Voltaire immediately sent an impassioned anti-Shakespearean letter to the Academy to be delivered on 25 August, the feast of St Louis.[74] Montagu obtained a ticket to the public session and joined the audience. The long-term antagonism between the two strong personalities was thus provided with a suitably dramatic finale.

The Academicians were seated around a table and the audience sat or stood 'rows upon rows' behind them. After the transaction of some formal business, D'Alembert delivered the letter from Voltaire. Montagu reported to Elizabeth Vesey (7 September 1776):

> Then rose Monsieur D'Alembert to read a most blackguard abusive invective of Monsr de Voltaire's against Shakespear the translation of whose works he apprehended wd spoil ye taste of ye French Nation. He attributed to Shakespear many things he never said, he gathered together many things the rudeness of the age allowed him to say, & with a few mauvaises plaisanteries season'd ye discourse with as much mauvaise foy. He gave an account of ye Tragedy of Gorboduc, & represented it as ye taste of ye Nation in Drama tho not ten people have for these hundred years read Gorboduc. (196–7)

According to Montagu, the majority of the Academicians disapproved of this invective against the English dramatist, and one of them asked her 'if I wd answer this piece of Voltaires'. Montagu stood up:

> I said Mr l'Abbé Arnauld had done it much better than I could, in ye praises he had given to Original genius, & ye benefits arising from the study of them, that I remembered 60 years [ago] in the same Academy, Old Homer had met with ye same treatment with Shakespear, that they now did justice to Homer, I did not doubt but they wd do so to Shakespear, for that great Genius's survived those who set up to be their Criticks, or more absurdly to be their Rivals. (197)

Apparently Montagu regarded this as the moment of her victory. When one of the Academicians expressed his concern that the reading of Voltaire's violent censure might have distressed her, '*Moi, Monsieur!*' she replied, '*point du tout. Je ne suis pas amie de Monsieur Voltaire.*'[75]

Triumphant and full of herself, she returned home and sent a series of letters to her friends to report on her French adventure. Among them, two letters addressed to Garrick take on an additional resonance when we learn that, while in Paris, Montagu attended a performance of a French actor, one Lekain (Henri-Louis Caïn), who was nicknamed 'the French Garrick' by his compatriots. Lekain met Voltaire when he was still an amateur actor and became his trusted ally. Montagu saw him act in Voltaire's *Mahomet* (1741): 'I was ye other night at ye Theatre to see his Mahomet acted by ye famous actor le Kain. I am so fatigued with the business of ye day that

I have not vivacity enough to describe ye monstrosity of ye entertainment.'[76] Now let Montagu's two letters to Garrick summarise her experience in Paris. In the first letter (20 October 1776), she maliciously described the mock-Aristotelian catharsis that the French performance, with 'the French Garrick' in the title role, brought about on stage:

> Mrs. M[ontagu] cannot help intimating that she never felt such pity and terror, which it is the business of tragedy to excite, as at the French theatre, where Mr. Le Kain roars like a mad bull, and Molé rolls his eyes, and has all the appearance of a man in a phrensy. Every one at Paris talks as they ought to do of Mr. Garrick, and the persons of real taste seem convinced of the false taste prevalent in their tragedies.[77]

In scoffing at Lekain's unavailing efforts at tragic sublimity, Montagu employed the Johnsonian figure of actor as puppet with very different connotations when she added, 'Certainly, Punch in a puppet-show is more like a grave magistrat, than their dramatic characters are like heroes.' By stating that French actors were even less dignified than a puppet, Montagu tactfully complimented the English actor on his lifelike impersonation. To her, Garrick was not a mindless Punch. Montagu's first letter concluded by referring to 'Voltaire's paper, which was read at the Academy', a copy of which she had just forwarded to the Garricks.

After receiving a reply from the actor (26 October 1776), which was full of praise of her admirable performance at the Academy, Montagu sent her second letter (3 November 1776):

> I am rejoiced that you tell me Shakspeare shall be revenged on the base attack made on him at the Academy. I felt the same indignation and scorn at the reading of Voltaire's paper as I should have done if I had seen Harlequin cutting capers, and striking his wooden sword on the monument of a Caesar or an Alexander the Great.[78]

She had shown off her sharp intelligence and wit not only to the French Academicians but also to her correspondents back home, flavouring the accounts of the public session with clever '*variations*':

> to the Greek scholar I complained at the same time of the indignities offered to Homer; to the wit, of the absurdities and inconsistencies so apparent as that, while the study and imitation of great and original genius was recommended, our bard, the greatest and most original of geniuses, was abused and ridiculed for errors to which the most sublime writers are most liable.

In the end, Montagu decided to put off the report to Garrick 'as in you are united all the tastes and all the excellencies of the scholar, the wit, the critic, &c., to provoke the full and utmost of your indignation and contempt, I must repeat to you every offence which genius, wit, and sense received'. Montagu's reference to Garrick as 'the scholar, the wit, the critic, &c.', and not as the best Shakespearean actor, reflected his retirement on 10 June of that year. To Montagu, Garrick's departure from the stage merged with the death of Shakespeare himself ('I must say I felt for Shakspeare the anxiety one does for a dead friend, who can no longer speak for himself. When Mr. Garrick was on the stage, I should have defied the utmost malice, as he was then alive, and consequently invincible'). A nationalistic encomium on Garrick concluded the correspondence:

> Indeed, my dear Sir, you must, from filial piety and paternal duty (for I reckon you both the son and the father of Shakspeare in many respects), defend him against this pert Frenchman. There are many of the French who greatly admire Shakspeare; but, except those who have had the good fortune to see his spirit walk the stage, few I fear that have felt him.[79]

Now let us go back to the year 1769, when Garrick exerted his 'filial piety and paternal duty' to the utmost in hosting the Stratford Jubilee and established himself as the only actor to make Shakespeare's spirit 'walk the stage'.

5 THE USE OF (HYPER)CRITICISM: GARRICK'S POSTSCRIPTS

The Stratford Jubilee of September 1769 was the first festival consecrated to the memory of the famous dramatist born in the small town on the River Avon. It started with a fairly modest request from the Stratford burgesses to David Garrick for a donation of a statue of Shakespeare to adorn the niche of a new town hall. But what was initially envisaged as merely a presentation of a statue proved to be a three-day festival conspicuous enough to engage the attention of the whole nation.[80] Garrick planned, organised and financed the event and was nominated 'the Steward' of the Jubilee. At the end of the theatrical season of the same year, he addressed the audience of Londoners from the Drury Lane stage and invited them to the festivity:

> My eyes, till then [i.e. the next theatrical season], no sights like this will see,
> Unless we meet at *Shakespeare's Jubilee*!
> On Avon's Banks, where flowers eternal blow!
> Like its full stream our Gratitude shall flow!
> There let us revel, show our fond regard,
> On that lov'd Spot, first breath'd our matchless Bard;
> To him all Honour, Gratitude is due,
> To him we owe our all – to Him and You.[81]

The Jubilee scheduled processions, pageants, music of all sorts, dinners and balls, horse racing and fireworks (but not one performance of Shakespeare's plays) among many other attractions, and was to culminate on the second day in a solemn recitation of an ode of Garrick's own making: 'An Ode upon Dedicating a Building and Erecting a Statue to Shakespeare, at Stratford upon Avon'.

This conspicuous undertaking excited much criticism from various sectors both before and after the actual event. Samuel Foote inserted sneering allusions to the Jubilee now and then in his plays, while George Steevens, the up-and-coming Shakespearean and the actor's reasonably close acquaintance, launched malicious attacks on the project anonymously in, among other periodicals, the *Public Advertiser*. Steevens was backed by a team of writers, including Foote, Francis Gentleman, the Rev. Richard Jago, William Kenrick, Charles Macklin, Arthur Murphy and Thomas Sheridan.[82] These journal writers derided the Stratford locals as avaricious and ignorant and pointed to the ironical fact that the intermediary between the town authorities and Garrick had been one George Keate, who was a professed admirer of Shakespeare's archenemy Voltaire. What the critics resented most was that Garrick the actor and manager, and none of their scholastic tribe, stood in charge of the deification of Shakespeare and even composed an ode to his honour:

If this Jubilee is meant to be a serious Meeting in Honour of the greatest Poet ever born in any Nation, or in any Age, why were not literary Men placed at the Head of it? If an Ode was to be written, why not Mr. Gray, Dr. Ak[e]nside, Mr. Warton, or Mr. Mason, requested to furnish out that Part of the Entertainment? Are the Universities supposed to be uninterested on the Occasion? Are Men of Learning the most insufficient Preservers of the Reputation of a Poet? Shakespeare, 'tis true, wrote chiefly for the Stage, but does it follow from thence that he is entitled only to histrionic Honours?[83]

This loud chorus of opponents certainly annoyed Garrick but it did not baffle his enterprise. On the contrary, the Steward of the Jubilee cleverly utilised the adverse publicity to promote his own cause, first rather crudely in the Stratford Rotunda, then more subtly in a Jubilee-related publication, and finally in sheer triumph back on the Drury Lane stage. In concluding this chapter on the interface between Garrick's stage and contemporary theatrical and literary criticism, the actor's own response to, and judicious use of, his critics merits a mention.

Garrick the 'Sick Monkey'

As Drury Lane's star actor and prosperous manager, Garrick was daily exposed to intense publicity, both favourable and hostile, and was highly strategic in dealing with the media.[84] While tirelessly conciliating malicious critics (he is known to have reserved a 'good bed' for Foote at a Stratford inn for the Jubilee), he even anticipated their attacks by writing his own criticism. Indeed, as Mrs Garrick was to confide to Edmund Kean many years later, 'My husband always wrote his own criticisms.'[85] For example, the actor published *An Essay on Acting* anonymously in 1744 to coincide with his first appearance in *Macbeth*. His self-mockery is visible both in the subtitle ('in which will be consider'd the mimical behaviour of a certain fashionable faulty actor, and the laudableness of such unmannerly, as well as inhumane, proceedings') and in the two mottoes cited on the title page:

– *So have I seen a Pygmie strut, mouth, and rant, in a Giant's robe. Tom Thumb.*
– *Oh! Macbeth has murder'd G – k. Shakespear.*

By publishing this pamphlet the diminutive actor forestalled the critics and advertised his new *Macbeth* precisely by derogating it.

Garrick used self-caricature for self-promotion once again in 1765 by publishing *The Sick Monkey: A Fable* anonymously. The actor was returning to London after a self-imposed exile on the Continent ('for health, or quiet / Harras'd with rule, or sick with riot') and wanted to probe the public's reaction to his comeback. In this fable a mimicking monkey falls seriously ill and suffers 'mental fevers', due to press attacks ('*This heap of papers, verse and prose, / Is the joint malice of my foes; / There's not a day but something's sent me, / To fret me, and torment me*'). A doctor gives the monkey a very sensible prescription and cures his disease:

> Never again to cast your eyes
> On what is wrote, or may be writ,
> Whether it is, or is not wit;
> For *there* the magic lies.[86]

In conclusion, Garrick the anonymous pamphleteer advises Garrick the actor and manager to follow the monkey's example and to 'Shut your ears, and close your eyes'.[87] However, Garrick in real life read all the adverse publications carefully and used them to his own advantage. There was even an unconfirmed rumour that some of the most malicious periodical articles on the Stratford Jubilee were actually penned by Garrick.[88] The performance of the Jubilee Ode at Stratford was itself a fair sample of Garrick's media manoeuvring at work.

The Jubilee Ode and a Macaroni

The delivery of 'An Ode upon Dedicating a Building and Erecting a Statue to Shakespeare, at Stratford upon Avon' was the Jubilee's culminating ceremony through which the Elizabethan playwright would metamorphose into a demigod in his Bethlehem. Garrick carefully composed the lyrics, employed the best composer, Thomas Arne, for the music and built an amphitheatre (the Rotunda) by the River Avon for the performance. Departing from his natural style, Garrick also created a brand-new type of declamatory elocution, a sensational 'spoken recitative', for the delivery of the Ode. After repeated rehearsals in London, every detail was brought to perfection.

In spite of the torrential rain, the riverside Rotunda was absolutely packed on 7 September. The orchestra played a brief overture and Garrick began his first recitative:

> TO what blest genius of the isle
>   Shall gratitude her tribute pay,
>   Decree the festive day,
> Erect the statue, and devote the pile?[89]

Although the answer was fairly predictable, the audience was electrified nonetheless: ' 'Tis he! 'tis he! – that demi-god! . . . The god of our idolatry!' With the help of the orchestra and the chorus (pealing '*Shakespeare! Shakespeare! Shakespeare!*'), and with the magic of Garrick's spoken recitative, the performance of this trite poetical composition proved a triumph. As James Boswell reported:

The whole Audience were fixed in the most earnest Attention, and I do believe that if any one had attempted to disturb the Performance, he would have been in Danger of his Life. Garrick in the Front of the Orchestra, filled with the first Musicians of the Nation, with Dr. Arne at their Head, and inspired with an aweful Elevation of Soul, while he looked from Time to Time at the venerable Statue of Shakespeare, appeared more than himself. While he repeated the Ode, and saw the various Passions and Feelings which it contains fully transfused into all around him, he seemed in Extacy, and gave us the Idea of a Mortal transformed into a Demi-god as we read in the Pagan Mythology.[90]

All the audience, even the cynical Charles Dibdin, actor and songwriter, attested to the sheer ecstasy of the recital. To say that 'it was magic; that it was fairy land' or that 'the effect was irresistible, electrical' fell far short of the real impression.[91]

After this ethereal recitation, Garrick addressed the audience and delivered a prose oration on Shakespeare, greatly regretting that 'none of the eminent Poets of our Universities had undertaken the Subject, who were infinitely more capable than himself, to execute that arduous Task'.[92] The actor apologised for his foolhardy poetic venture and judiciously cited a better poetic tribute to Shakespeare (Milton's 'On Shakespeare'). Then, abruptly, he asked the spectators to take an active part in the ceremony: 'Your *Attendance here* upon this Occasion, is a Proof that you felt – powerfully felt his Genius! and that you love and revere him and his Memory: – the only remaining Honour to him now (and it is the greatest Honour you can do him) is to SPEAK for him.'[93] A pause ensued and the audience's embarrassed giggles followed. After offering a piece of music to give the audience time to think, Garrick repeated his proposal: 'Now, Ladies and Gentlemen, will you be pleased to say any Thing *for*, or *against* SHAKESPEARE?'[94] Upon this, a man in a greatcoat stood up and expressed his intention of attacking Shakespeare. He advanced to the orchestra, took off his coat and displayed his fashionable blue satin suit with silver frogs. It was Drury Lane's comic actor Thomas King, who had played the Macaroni, or Frenchified fop, of Garrick and George Coleman's *The Clandestine Marriage* (1766) in the same blue suit.[95] King carped at Shakespeare and the festival by assimilating the styles of both Voltaire and the anti-Jubilee pamphleteers:

[King] complained of his being a vulgar Author, only capable of exciting those vulgar Emotions of laughing and crying. – That it was the Criterion of a Gentleman to be moved at nothing – to feel nothing – to admire nothing. – He owned that he did not much love his Country – yet he could wish that it would submit to be civilized – and as the first Step to it, never to suffer so execrable a fellow as *Shakespeare*, with his *Things*, which are called *Tragedies* and *Comedies*, to debauch their Minds, and Understandings, and produce *Snivelings* and *Horse-laughs* – when the chief Excellence of Man, and the most refined Sensation, was to be devoured by *Ennui*, and only live in a State of insensible Vegetation. – Then he threw out his Sarcasms against the *Jubilee*, the *Steward*, the *Corporation*, and all the *Company*.[96]

Needless to say, King's intrusion was not spontaneous. It was part of the ritual carefully drafted by Garrick himself.[97] Sprinkled with many French words, King's mock invective deliberately confused the two sorts of critical discourse that had hitherto remained fairly separate: the French and neo-classical criticism on Shakespeare and the journalistic attacks on the Stratford Jubilee. As Martha Winburn England correctly points out, the actor's message was clear: 'any attack on the Jubilee was tantamount to an attack on Shakespeare, and both were equally un-English, un-Shakespearean, and unmanly'.[98] In the person of the Macaroni, the malicious critics of Garrick's Jubilee were firmly identified with the French enemies of the national Bard.

Garrick characteristically avoided answering the fop's farcical charge directly: it was his habit to keep away from confrontation of any sort. Instead, he appealed to the ladies in the audience to lend him power:

Garrick, King Lear *and contemporary criticism* 51

O Ladies! it is you, and you alone can put a Stop to this terrible Progress and Irruption of these *Anti-Goths* (as they are pleased to call themselves). *It was you, Ladies,* that restored SHAKESPEARE to the Stage! You formed yourselves into a Society to protect his Fame! and erected a MONUMENT to HIS and YOUR OWN HONOUR in WESTMINSTER ABBEY![99]

The audience's reaction to this curious epilogue was mixed. Most of the visitors from London saw through the thin disguise of their favourite King and appreciated the joke. (According to the theatre manager and writer Benjamin Victor, his performance 'occasioned Mirth, and gave a great Variety to the Entertainment'.) The dignitaries of Stratford were genuinely shocked by the slander poured on their adored dramatist. Boswell immediately understood the situation but regretted that such an unseemly joke was inserted in the sacred rite:

[King's interlude] might have done very well on some other Occasion; but, in my Opinion, it had better have been omitted at this noble Festival: It detracted from it's [*sic*] Dignity; nor was there any Occasion for it. We were all enthusiastic Admirers of Shakespeare. We had not Time to think of his caviling Critics. We were wrapped into Wonder and Admiration of our immortal Bard; and the Levity of the fine Gentleman disturbed the Tone of our Minds. I must be forgiven too for observing that this Exhibition looked so like a Trap laid on Purpose, that it displeased me.[100]

Garrick certainly dissimulated his outright antipathy to the malicious journalists by wrapping the whole procedure in good humour and high spirits. He even excised a direct reference to the '*Advertiser*' and 'scribbling Fools' from the draft of his address to the ladies.[101] Still, his self-vindictive gesture was crude enough to destroy part of the festive atmosphere. His handling of the noisome critics would undergo further sophistication when the Ode was transferred from the stage to the page.

Making everyone testify: the Ode on the page

On 7 September 1769 Mr Montagu congratulated his wife once again on the good reception that her *Essay* had met with, 'though no other than he expected'. He added that her book could not have been published at a more fortunate time than before the Jubilee, as public attention to Shakespeare aroused by the festival no doubt contributed to the sales of her book.[102] Mrs Montagu was also grateful that Garrick mentioned her work favourably in the preface to the printed version of the Ode. She was rather perplexed, though, not only because his kindness was unexpected (there seems to have been some minor squabble between Montagu and Garrick at some point) but also because her name was more strongly associated with the Jubilee than was appropriate:

> I was told the other day I had assisted Mr. Garrick in his Ode. He has made the Author of the Essay a very handsome compliment in his preface to his Ode . . . As Mr. Garrick must probably suspect who is the Author of this Essay, it was very handsome in him, as we have not been always the best friends.[103]

In fact, Garrick's publication not only helped Montagu to sell her book but also made clever use of the *Essay*, along with other literary authorities, to pursue its own end. Garrick's ingenuity as a literary editor, which has been overlooked by researchers, indeed deserves much attention and admiration.

Garrick published the Ode either during or immediately after the Stratford festivity. In the prefatory 'Advertisement' the enemies of Shakespeare and those of his own Jubilee were once again interlaced.[104] After complaining that the 'gentlemen of approved ability' had not supplied a better poem than the Ode, Garrick shifted the target from the anti-Jubilee pamphleteers to the literary critics who 'have illiberally endeavoured to shake the poetic character of our immortal bard'. Direct confrontation with the malignant critics was, however, once again avoided. As in the Macaroni episode at the Rotunda where the support of the ladies was enlisted, Garrick referred the readers to 'a work lately published, called, *An Essay on the Writings and Genius of* SHAKESPEARE, by which they will with much satisfaction be convinced, that *England* may justly boast the honour of producing the greatest dramatic poet in the world'. Garrick again reverted from Shakespeare to the Jubilee in the final paragraph, and offered the Ode 'to his enemies, as a lucky opportunity of venting their wit, humour, criticism, spleen, or whatever else they please, should they think it worthy of their notice'.

After the full text of the Ode, Garrick printed the 'undeniable testimonies . . . of his unequalled original talents' as a way to 'strengthen and justify the general admiration of this Genius'. This impressive appendix, entitled 'Testimonies', consisted of thirty-four excerpts in verse and prose from the First Folio down to the eighteenth-century Shakespeare editions and journals. The authors discussed in the foregoing sections were fairly represented, including both Murphy (from the *Gray's-Inn Journal*) and Joseph Warton (from his poem 'The Enthusiast; or, The Lover of Nature'). Garrick gallantly let even Steevens 'the anti-Jubilite' enter this group of authorities.

The actor exerted a great deal of editorial sagacity in compiling the collection. Ben Jonson's tribute 'To the memory of my beloved, the author Mr. William Shakespeare' was silently purged of the embarrassing reference to his 'small Latin and less Greek' and the quotation from John Dryden's *Of Dramatick Poesie* (1668) missed one crucial sentence from the middle of the (otherwise complete) paragraph: 'He is many times flat, insipid; his Comick wit degenerating into clenches, his serious swelling into Bombast' ('Testimonies', 19–21).

In this congregation of involuntary testifiers, the most unexpected were Voltaire, who was Shakespeare's sworn enemy, and Samuel Johnson, who thoroughly neglected the Stratford Jubilee. Garrick represented these French and English literary giants with utmost ingenuity. As self-nominated defender of Shakespeare and 'like a good Englishman', Garrick abhorred Voltaire's attack on the dramatist but was nonetheless unwilling to upset this imposing Frenchman with his own Bardolatry.[105] In the appendix Garrick quoted diplomatically from Voltaire's earliest essay on Shakespeare (*Lettres philosophiques*, 1733), where the critic is not altogether derogatory:

SHAKESPEARE created, as it were, the *English* theatre: that he boasted a strong, fruitful genius: that he was nature and sublime: that his scenes are beautiful and noble, though sometimes dreadful: that his passages are strong and forcible, and atone for all his faults: and that his dramatic pieces dart such resplendent flashes as amaze and astonish! ('Testimonies', 29)

Johnson required even more delicate treatment. Once again to the greatest regret of his biographer, the doctor not only missed the Stratford festival but sullenly ignored the whole Jubilee enterprise:

Upon this occasion I particularly lamented that he [Johnson] had not that warmth of friendship for his brilliant pupil, which we may suppose would have had a benignant effect on both. When almost every man of eminence in the literary world was happy to partake in this festival of genius, the absence of Johnson could not but be wondered at and regretted.[106]

In fact, this 'brilliant pupil' knew better, and made the unwilling master participate in his festival. In this appendix Johnson was made to testify twice for Shakespeare and for Garrick; first in verse (from the 'Prologue Spoken at the Opening of the Theatre in Drury-Lane'), and then in prose (from the Preface to the Shakespeare edition).[107] The latter especially was an editorial feat. The extract consisted of two distant paragraphs stitched together backwardly: the first came from after the discussion of the three unities in the original Preface (*On Shakespeare*, 79–80) while the second was part of the eulogy on Shakespeare's natural genius discussed much earlier (65). The first quoted paragraph reads:

> If such another poet could arise, should I very vehemently reproach him, that his first act passed at *Venice*, and his next at *Cyprus*. Such violations of rules merely passive, become the comprehensive Genius of SHAKESPEARE, and such censures are suitable to the minute and slender criticism of Voltaire:
>
> > *Non usque adeo permiscuit imis*
> > *Longus summa dies, ut non, si voce Metelli*
> > *Serventur leges, malint a Caesare tolli.* ('Testimonies', 31)[108]

Garrick omitted a 'Nor' from the first sentence (the original reads: 'Nor, if such another poet could arise ...') and substituted the original epithet 'positive' with 'passive' in the second. Shakespeare's uniqueness was thereby made to stand out and his fault to look smaller. Even more importantly, this was one of the rare passages in the Preface where Johnson referred to Voltaire at all. In this way the negligent doctor was made to wage surrogate warfare for his former pupil against the blasphemous French critic.

The last two quotations in the collection made the anti-Gallic message even clearer. One was from Horace Walpole ('*Voltaire* is a genius, but not of SHAKESPEARE's magnitude') and the other was a long paragraph from, of course, Montagu's *Essay*, where she refuted Voltaire's argument that Shakespeare is 'barbarous':

> Such is SHAKESPEARE's merit, that the more just and refined the taste of the nation has become, the more he has increased in reputation ... His merit is disputed by little wits, and his errors are the jests of little critics; but there has not been a great poet, or great critic, since his time, who has not spoken of him with the highest veneration, Mr. *Voltaire* excepted. ('Testimonies', 34)

Just as he had appealed to the ladies for help at the Stratford Rotunda, Garrick countered Voltaire by resorting to the Bluestocking queen in both the Advertisement and the testimonies of the publication. In a later poem entitled 'The Dream' (1771), Garrick would style Montagu as a 'Pallas' protecting 'the Bard' against the 'Gallic God of literary War'.[109] Indeed, Garrick should have acknowledged not only Shakespeare's but also his own indebtedness to her bravery.

While making the critics undermine Voltaire's authority, Garrick himself remained disengaged from the controversy. He even sent a copy of his Ode to the French sage with a courteous covering note, citing the *philosophe*'s own view of Shakespeare as the founder of the English stage:

Sir,
I have taken the liberty of offering my small poetical tribute to the first Genius in the World – As nobody has written so well & so forcibly against the principles of intoleration, as MonSr de Voltaire, I hope he will excuse the excess of Zeal with which I have Endeavor'd to paint in this Ode the Powers of our great dramatic Poet, Shakespeare, who is both the founder and chief Supporter of the English Stage.
I am Sir Your most Obedient humble Servant & sincere Admirer

D. Garrick.[110]

The Frenchman was not displeased with this foremost Shakespearean actor. Voltaire criticised the Jubilee bitterly but 'never spoke of Garrick as being in any way responsible for the affair, and from first and last there was no derogation of him'.[111]

Serving a glass of 'Jubilee Punch': back in London

Garrick's theatrical career hit its all-time low in the latter half of September 1769. Apart from the triumphant recitation of the Ode, most of the Jubilee entertainments had to be cancelled owing to torrential rain. The costly costumes transported all the way from Drury Lane were destroyed and the riverside Rotunda was brought to near collapse. Despite months of assiduous preparation, logistical problems were never solved and the Jubilee guests kept complaining about poor accommodation and transport or, more exactly, about lack of them. It is estimated that Garrick suffered a personal loss of more than £2,000, which would have been enough to build two town halls.[112]

The '*Avarice*, and shameful *Extortions*' of 'the very *low* People' of Stratford and 'their absurd Notions relating to the *Jubilee*' disappointed its Steward, Garrick. Victor recorded that

They [the townspeople] were, in general, much dissatisfied, and greatly afraid of Mischief – they had not the least Comprehension of *what*, or about *whom*, such Preparations were making. – They looked upon Mr. *Garrick* as a *Magician*, who could, and would raise the Devil! And, instead of being delighted with the approaching *Festival*, many of them kept at home, and were afraid to stir abroad. – They were confirmed in their Absurdities by the black Looks and secret Operations of those who were employed in making the *Fireworks* – and looked on the heavy Rains that fell during the *Jubilee*, as a mark of Heaven's Anger.[113]

Victor concluded his detailed account of the Jubilee by commenting ironically, 'It seems as if *Providence* had created *Shakespeare* to shew what Wonders the intellectual Powers of Man might perform! and by having bestowed so much upon one of that *Town*, was resolved to take away all Ideas from three-fourths of the rest of the Inhabitants.'

This theatrical, financial and organisational debacle attracted much harsh criticism, and the euphoric songs that Garrick had prepared for the festival were repeatedly parodied with a malicious sneer. To make the situation even worse, the rival Covent Garden theatre announced a production of George Colman's *Man and Wife; or, The Shakespeare Jubilee* to cash in on the public attention provoked by Garrick's disastrous venture. Something had to be done to recoup the losses.

Garrick promptly decided to produce a retributive *Jubilee* on the London stage. In this afterpiece he carefully resurrected the pageants and songs that had failed to ornament the Stratford theatre and streets and good-humouredly retaliated on the anti-Jubilites. *The Jubilee* was plotted around an Irishman who 'come[s] from Dublin to See ye Pageant – he is oblig'd to lye in a post Chaise all Night – undergoes all kind of fatigue & inconvenience to see ye Pageant, but unluckily goes to Sleep as ye Pageant passes by; & returns to Ireland without knowing any thing of ye Matter'.[114] In the prologue, spoken by King, the rivalry of two pubs, the old Magpie (Drury Lane) and the new Magpie (Covent Garden), serving differently flavoured 'Jubilee Punch', provided a further frame of reference.

Set in this metadramatic structure, the hyperoptimistic Jubilee songs and pageants, together with the hurly-burly of the visitors and townspeople, gained fresh self-reflexivity and depth. For example, to the lighthearted 'Warwickshire' ballad with the well-known refrain 'the lad of all lads was a Warwickshire lad', the sleepless Irishman adds an irritable coda:

> The devil burn me, but I believe you are T[h]ieves.
> Jubilee thief,
> 'Tis my belief,
> The thief of all thieves is a Jubilee thief. (1.2.122–5)

The ecstatic hymn to 'Shakespeare's Mulberry-Tree' sung by Garrick 'with a Cup in his Hand made of the Tree' at Stratford is also fully recuperated in this afterpiece:

> Behold this fair goblet, 'twas carved from the tree
> Which, O my sweet Shakespear, was planted by thee.
> As a relic I kiss it and bow at the shrine,
> What comes from thy hand must be ever divine!
>   All shall yield to the Mulberry Tree,
>   Bend to thee,
>   Blest Mulberry,
>   Matchless was he
>   Who planted thee,
>   And thou like him immortal be! (1.3.126–35)

Unlike at Stratford, however, the performance is preceded by two ridiculous mulberry episodes this time. In the first the Steward of the Jubilee is reported to be practising 'his fine Ode to music' in a hotel room appropriately named '*Much Ado About Nothing*', preciously cuddling a mulberry box given by the town authorities upon his breast (1.2.77–81). In the second the Irishman narrowly escapes two peddlers who try to dupe him into buying fake mulberry souvenirs (1.3.69–89).

The corny hymn to 'sweet Willy O' ('The pride of all nature was sweet Willy O, / The first of all swains, / He gladdened the plains, / None ever was like to the sweet Willy O') is also given an appropriately nonsensical dramatic context and sung by one of the 'sweet Jubilee wenches' who 'dote upon Shakespur'. These cheerful Stratford girls keep confusing the 'Jubilee' with 'Jewbill' or 'Jubillo', and 'Pageant' with 'Pagan', but have enough sensitivity to cry 'a whole night together' after seeing 'Romy and July' in the polite city of Birmingham (2.1.1–38).

Most characteristic of all, Garrick even parodied the parodist Foote, who had offered 'the Devil's Definition' of the Stratford disaster:

A Jubilee, as it hath lately appeared, is a public invitation circulated and arranged by puffing, to go posting without horses to an obscure borough without representatives, governed by a Mayor and Aldermen who are no magistrates, to celebrate a great poet whose works have made him immortal by an ode without poetry, music without melody, dinners without victuals and lodgings without beds; a masquerade where half the people appear barefaced, a horse race up to the knees in water, fireworks extinguished as soon as they were lighted, and a gingerbread amphitheatre, which like a house of cards tumbled to pieces as it was finished.[115]

In *The Jubilee* a musician sings a five-stanza song version of this definition, which begins:

> This is, Sir, a Jubilee
> Crowded without company.
> Riot without jollity,
> That's a Jubilee.
> Thus 'tis night and day, Sir,
> I hope that you will stay, Sir,
>   To see our Jubilee. (1.2.37–43)

Garrick's Irishman shrewdly points to the old rhyme from which Foote had stolen:

IRISHMAN 'Tis a comical kind of a song to be sure, and you did not stale it from what they say of little Kilkenny. There we have –

> Fire without smoke
> Wit without joke
> Air without fog
> Land without bog
> Men without heads
> Lodging without beds.
> O no! that's your Jubilee Rig. (1.2.60–8)

Here, as in all the other parts of *The Jubilee*, Garrick succeeded not only in parodying the parodists, the hypercritics and his own bardolatry, but also in creating a thoroughly enjoyable metatheatrical entertainment. *The Jubilee* proved a blockbuster, too. It achieved an unprecedented eighty-eight performances in the 1769–70 season and was revived from time to time for many years after. The success of the first season alone allowed Garrick to make up for the original loss of £2,000 four times over. This was the sweetest use that the Sick Monkey ever made of his own adversities.

Among the various portrayals of the Stratford festival and townspeople, the centrepiece of *The Jubilee* was the pageant procession of Shakespearean characters (which the unfortunate Irishman naturally misses). Garrick skilfully mounted pantomimes of characteristic scenes from nineteen plays, scattering muses and goddesses, music and dance here and there. When the afterpiece was revived yet again in Garrick's final season (1775–6), a young actress made her debut as Venus on the Drury Lane stage. Jealous of her youth and beauty, senior actresses blocked this debutante from the sight of the audience in the final scene, but Garrick, who was also in the pageant as Benedick of *Much Ado About Nothing*, walked up to her, took her hand and led her to the front of the stage. The young woman was Sarah Siddons, who will be the heroine of our next chapter.

2

'Who dares do more': Kemble, Siddons and the question of sublimity in Macbeth

1 ENCOUNTERING A STAGE GHOST: SIR ROGER, MR PARTRIDGE AND SIR JOSHUA

Suppose that Dr Johnson was in the right. Suppose that the spectator is level-headed enough to know 'from the first act to the last' that the stage is only a stage, the players only players. Suppose that the tragedy moves not by deluding him into believing the heartrending spectacle to be real, but by reminding him of a possibility of misery and danger in real life. Does this spectator's emotion have relevance to the Aristotelian catharsis? Would he feel the mixture of pity and fear, or pity and 'terror' as eighteenth-century critics preferred to style it, as he attends the tragic performance? And if the onstage misery is to do with witches, ghosts and visions, which have no counterparts in real life, how would he be moved?

By way of introduction to the late eighteenth- and early nineteenth-century representations of *Macbeth*, with John Philip Kemble and his sister Sarah Siddons as the regicide couple, let me cite three interlocking episodes on theatrical verisimilitude and its reception. In the first two you will encounter an extremely naïve spectator who is thrilled about, and as a result strongly conscious of, being in the theatre throughout the performance. (Will they manage to be moved?) The third episode is about someone who teaches you the way to forget that you are in the theatre. (Is his argument convincing?) The stories are as follows.

'Natural Criticism'

In March 1712 the *Spectator*'s fictional narrator, Mr Spectator, accompanied his old friend Sir Roger de Coverly to Drury Lane to see the performance of *The Distrest Mother*, an English rendition of Racine's *Andromaque* (1667) by Ambrose Philips. In the theatre Mr Spectator was just as intent on listening to Sir Roger's remarks on the show as on enjoying the show itself:

3 Thomas Beach, *Kemble and Siddons in* Macbeth.

this goodly knight 'had not been at a Play these twenty Years' and his comments were 'a piece of Natural Criticism'.[1] In December 1745 Henry Fielding, no doubt inspired by the example of the *Spectator*, sent his eponymous hero Tom Jones and his alleged father, Mr Partridge, to Drury Lane to attend the performance of David Garrick's *Hamlet*. Tom, who was himself not the most sophisticated of the theatre audience, expected from Partridge 'the simple Dictates of Nature, unimproved indeed, but likewise unadulterated by Art'.[2] Despite the parallelism between the two theatrical experiences, tragedy as seen by these spectators afforded entirely different outlooks: for Sir Roger, it was predominantly the plot that mattered, while Mr Partridge was preoccupied with something more immaterial.

As soon as the play began, Sir Roger was innocently impressed by the stylish posture of the actors and, upon the entrance of Pyrrhus, pronounced rather irrelevantly that 'he did not believe the King of *France* himself had a better Strut'. But this spectator's attention was emphatically on what would happen next. He confessed to his companion that 'he could not imagine how the Play would end'. He was deeply concerned about the destiny awaiting Andromache and Hermione, and was 'extremely puzzled to think what would become of *Pyrrhus*'. He also posed several knowledgeable questions to Mr Spectator regarding the neoclassical rules: 'But pray, says he, you that are a Critick, is this Play according to your Dramatick Rules, as you call them? Should your People in Tragedy always talk to be understood? Why, there is not a single Sentence in this Play, that I do not know the Meaning of' (3:241). The knight showed certain interest in the strong tragic emotions that Orestes evinced while reporting the death of Pyrrhus and subsequently in his madness ('Seeing afterwards *Orestes* in his raving Fit, he [Sir Roger] grew more than ordinarily serious, and took Occasion to moralize (in his way) upon an Evil Conscious'). But this was as far as it got: Sir Roger was satisfied by simply observing that '*Orestes, in his Madness, looked as if he saw something*' (3:242).

In Book 16 chapter 5 of *Tom Jones*, Partridge experienced Garrick's *Hamlet* in a very different way. Certainly he made naïve observations on the theatre and its ambience in the wake of his predecessor, wondering 'how so many Fidlers could play at one Time, without putting one another out' and, upon seeing a man lighting the candles in the auditorium, drawing an awkward analogy between reality and art ('Look, look, Madam [i.e. Mrs Jones, who was also present], the very Picture of the Man in the End of the Common-Prayer Book, before the Gunpowder-Treason Service', 2:852). When the show began, again like Sir Roger, Partridge failed to accept theatrical premises and to enter into the dramatic illusion. Upon the entrance of King Hamlet, even after Tom's explanation, he declared with unassailable confidence that what he saw on stage could never be a ghost: '"Perswade me to that, Sir, if you can. Though I can't say I ever actually saw a Ghost in my Life, yet I am certain I should know one, if I saw him, better than that comes to. No, no, Sir, Ghosts don't appear in such Dresses as that, neither"' (2:853).

The situation changed when Garrick's young Hamlet encountered the apparition. All of a sudden, Partridge began to tremble, his knees knocking against each other. Tom asked him what the matter was, wondering if, again by some gross misunderstanding of the dramatic situation, he was afraid of the warlike costume of King Hamlet. Partridge's explanation deserves close scrutiny:

'O, la! Sir,' said he, 'I perceive now it is what you told me. I am not afraid of any Thing; for I know it is but a Play: And if it was really a Ghost, it could do one no Harm at such a Distance, and in so much Company; and yet if I was frightened, I am not the only Person.' (2:853–4)

'"Why, who"', cried Tom, '"dost thou take to be such a Coward here besides thyself?"' Partridge exclaimed, '"Nay, you may call me Coward if you will; but if that little Man there upon the Stage is not frightned, I never saw any Man frightned in my Life."' Partridge was not afraid of the apparition, whose supernatural status he was unable to register ('"Not that it was the Ghost that surprized me neither; for I should have known that to have been only a Man in a strange Dress"'). What frightened him was the sense of terror that the diminutive actor expressed in the person of Hamlet upon encountering the late king. Tom then asked if he believed that Garrick was 'really' frightened. Partridge's answer was slightly irrelevant to the enquiry but showed the depth of his sympathetic understanding of the tragedy: '"Nay, Sir," said *Partridge*, "did not you yourself observe afterwards, when he found it was his own Father's Spirit, and how he was murdered in the Garden, how his Fear forsook him by Degrees, and he was struck dumb with Sorrow, as it were, just as I should have been, had it been my own Case"' (2:854–5). It was through sympathy for, and identification with, the fear and horror the tragic actor displayed that this innocent viewer shuddered. He explained that '"when I saw the little Man so frightned himself, it was that which took Hold of me"' and claimed that '"it is *natural* to be surprized at such Things"' (2:854; emphasis added). Partridge's identification with Garrick's Hamlet was such that, during the speech of the ghost, he fixed his eyes 'partly on the Ghost, and partly on *Hamlet*, and with his Mouth open; the same Passions which succeeded each other in *Hamlet*, succeeding likewise in him' (2:854).

Fielding put three more scenes from *Hamlet* to the test of this natural critic: another ghost scene in Gertrude's closet, the play-within-the-play and the grave-digging in the final act.[3] While continually dropping naïve comments on the performance, Partridge was interested less in the plot than in the ways in which Garrick and other players reacted to the situation. His response to *The Mousetrap* was exemplary. Partridge at first failed to understand the metatheatrical situation but, after Tom's explanation, 'he no sooner entered into the Spirit of it, than he began to bless himself that he had never committed Murder' (2:856). Partridge, with Hamlet, devouringly observed Claudius's reaction to the performance rather than the play-within-the-play itself, while Tom amused himself more by looking at Partridge react to the play than by watching *Hamlet*.[4] In the end, while still confusing the dexterity of the actor playing Claudius and the cunning of Claudius himself, Partridge nonetheless reached the same conclusion as Hamlet and asked Mrs Miller "'[i]f she did not imagine the King looked as if he was touched; though he is ... a good Actor, and doth all he can to hide it'" (2:856).

After the performance, Tom asked "'which of the Players he had liked best'". Partridge answered, "'The King, without Doubt.'" Being informed that Hamlet was acted by the best player who ever was on stage:

'He the best Player!' cries *Partridge* with a contemptuous Sneer, 'why I could act as well as he myself. I am sure if I had seen a Ghost, I should have looked in the very same Manner, and done just as he did. And then, to be sure, in that Scene, as you called it, between him and his Mother, where you told me he acted so fine, why, Lord help me, any Man, that is, any good Man, that had such a Mother, would have done exactly the same. I know you are only joking with me; but, indeed, Madam, though I was never at a Play in *London*, yet I have seen acting before in the Country; and the King for my Money; he speaks all his Words distinctly, half as loud again as the other. – Any Body may see he is an Actor.' (2:856–7)

Critics often cite this passage as Fielding's tribute to Garrick's natural acting, as opposed to the conventionalised theatrical expression. Just as noteworthy is that Partridge's 'natural' theatrical criticism was based on Garrick's reaction to the dramatic action rather than to the action itself and that he thoroughly empathised with the tragic feeling that the Hamlet actor represented. Indeed, Partridge's identification with the tragic character went so deep that he 'durst not go to Bed all that Night, for Fear of the Ghost, and for many Nights after, sweated two or three Hours before he went to sleep, with the same Apprehensions, and waked several Times in great Horrors, crying out, "Lord have Mercy upon us! there it is"' (2:857). The theatrical ghost, which Partridge had dismissed as a nonentity, materialised and haunted the poor man off stage.

Apparently following the *Spectator* article, Fielding drastically revised the way in which theatrical illusion was received, interpreted and recreated in a spectator's mind, shifting the focus from the tragic action to the actor's reaction to it. The question, and explanation, of theatrical illusion would undergo a further transformation when Sir Joshua Reynolds reread (and in many ways misread) Fielding's discussion and denounced the 'Natural Criticism'.

Discourses on Art

Joshua Reynolds's fifteen *Discourses* constitute a deeply ambivalent work of art criticism. They were originally delivered as annual presidential lectures at the Royal Academy from its establishment in 1769 to Reynolds's retirement in 1790. With their emphasis on rules and imitation of old masters, these treatises were seen as exemplarily neoclassical and quite understandably infuriated the pre-Romantic poet and engraver William Blake, who wrote in the margin of his copy, 'This Man was Hired to Depress Art.' Reynolds, however, sounded a noticeably 'unneoclassical' note when he discussed his favourite painters: Raphael and Michelangelo. Curiously anticipating Samuel Taylor Coleridge's discussion of artistic creativity, Reynolds defined Raphael as a painter of 'Taste' and 'Fancy', and Michelangelo of 'Genius' and 'Imagination', and consistently preferred the more 'Romantic' painter of the two. In *Discourse* 5 (10 December 1772), he still passed his judgement in a reticent way:

> To the question therefore, which ought to hold the first rank, Raffaelle or Michael Angelo, it must be answered, that if it is to be given to him who possessed a greater combination of the higher qualities of the art than any other man, there is no doubt but Raffaelle is the first. But if, as Longinus thinks, the sublime, being the highest excellence that human composition can attain to, abundantly compensates the absence of every other beauty, and atones for all other deficiencies, then Michael Angelo demands the preference.[5]

In the final *Discourse* 15 (10 December 1790), however, the painter professed his unconditional love and adoration of the sublime maestro. Unlike Michelangelo, Reynolds excelled in the low-category art of portraiture and failed to achieve the divinity and grandeur of 'history' (meaning religious and mythological as well as historical) painting. 'Yet however unequal I feel myself to that attempt, were I now to begin the world again, I would tread in the steps of that great master: to kiss the hem of his garment, to catch the slightest of his perfections, would be glory and distinction enough for an ambitious man' (282). This infirm painter, with his eyes nearly blind, finished his swansong lecture by ecstatically pronouncing the name of the god of his idolatry:

> I FEEL a self-congratulation in knowing myself capable of such sensations as he intended to excite. I reflect not without vanity, that these Discourses bear testimony of my admiration of that truly divine man, and I should desire that the last words which I should pronounce in this Academy, and from this place, might be the name of – MICHAEL ANGELO. (282)

Torn between the placidity of neoclassical discipline and the unrestrained sublimity of Michelangelo, Reynolds's *Discourses* challenges the reader with many paradoxes and incongruities hidden in its impeccable eloquence.

In *Discourse* 13 (11 December 1786), Reynolds compared the art of painting with the principles of other arts, theatrical representation among them. Once again anticipating the nineteenth-century theorisers of Romanticism, he related the arts to imagination and sensibility and decried 'the false system of reasoning, grounded on a partial view of things' (231–2). Reynolds counted Plato's theory of mimesis as an example of such 'poor, partial, and so far, false' reasoning. Imitative art is simply lacking in imagination and only 'naturally' pleasing to an uneducated spectator, when painting 'ought to be as far removed from the vulgar idea of imitation, as the refined civilized state in which we live, is removed from a gross state of nature' (232–3). Reynolds then applied the distinction between the imitative and nonimitative representations to theatrical art. Citing Hamlet's famous formulation (which has negative implications in this context), he argued:

> THE Theatre, which is said *to hold the mirrour up to nature*, comprehends both those ideas. The lower kind of Comedy, or Farce, like the inferior style of Painting, the more naturally it is represented, the better; but the higher appears to me to aim no more at imitation, so far as it belongs to any thing like deception, or to expect that the spectators should think that the events there represented are really passing before them, than Raffaelle in his Cartoons, or Poussin in his Sacraments, expected it to be believed, even for a moment, that what they exhibited were real figures. (238)

The 'lower' and 'higher' levels of theatrical representation often get confused and 'the world is filled with false criticism' as a result. Reynolds singled out Fielding's rendition in *Tom Jones* of Garrick's performance to exemplify this fallacy. Just as Raphael was often mistakenly 'praised for naturalness and deception',

> our late great actor, Garrick, has been as ignorantly praised by his friend Fielding; who doubtless imagined he had hit upon an ingenious device, by introducing in one of his novels, (otherwise a work of the highest merit,) an ignorant man, mistaking Garrick's representation of a scene in Hamlet, for reality. A very little reflection will convince us, that there is not one circumstance in the whole scene that is of the nature of deception. The merit and excellence of Shakspeare, and of Garrick, when they were engaged in such scenes, is of a different and much higher kind. (238–9)

Unlike most of his contemporaries, Reynolds saw artifice, rather than naturalness, in Garrick's acting requiring artistic literacy on the part of the audience. To do justice to Fielding, however, Partridge actually did not once mistake the physicality of the stage or the plot of the play for reality. On the contrary, he failed to accept theatrical conventions and was even unable to follow the basic storyline. Reynolds laid an unjustifiable charge against the novelist on this latter count as well: 'But what adds to the falsity of this intended compliment, is, that the best stage-representation appears even more unnatural to a person of such a character, who is supposed never to have seen a play before, than it does to those who have had a habit of allowing for those necessary deviations from nature which the Art requires' (239). In fact, Reynolds's contention was the very import of Partridge's theatrical adventure. The painter denounced Fielding's enchanting parable of naïvety to propose his own doctrine of discipline and refinement. To appreciate theatre:

great allowances must always be made for the place in which the exhibition is represented; for the surrounding company, the lighted candles, the scenes visibly shifted in your sight, and the language of the blank verse, so different from common English; which merely as English must appear surprising in the mouths of Hamlet, and all the court and natives of Denmark.

There was no room for natural theatrical criticism, for 'the more low, illiterate, and vulgar any person is, the less he will be disposed to make these allowances, and of course to be deceived by any imitation' (239).

Concluding his overview of theatrical verisimilitude, Reynolds went on problematically to deny the 'naturalness' of tragic emotion. In this he certainly parted company with Fielding, who saw Garrick's onstage horror as natural and made the unsophisticated spectator appreciate and sympathise with the feeling. Reynolds's final paragraph on theatre deserves full quotation:

THOUGH I have no intention of entering into all the circumstances of unnaturalness in theatrical representations, I must observe, that even the expression of violent passion, is not always the most excellent in proportion as it is the most natural: so great terror and such disagreeable sensations may be communicated to the audience, that the balance may be destroyed by which pleasure is preserved, and holds its predominancy in the mind: violent distortion of action, harsh screamings of the voice, however great the occasion, or however natural on such occasion, are therefore not admissible in the theatrick art. Many of these allowed deviations from nature arise from the necessity which there is, that every thing should be raised and enlarged beyond its natural state; that the full effect may come home to the spectator, which otherwise would be lost in the comparatively extensive space of the Theatre. Hence the deliberate and stately step, the studied grace of action, which seems to enlarge the dimensions of the Actor, and alone to fill the stage. All this unnaturalness, though right and proper in its place, would appear affected and ridiculous in a private room; *quid enim deformius, quam scenam in vitam transferre*? (239–40)[6]

My three fables on naturalness in tragic expression and its reception conclude here. I shall now turn to John Philip Kemble and Sarah Siddons playing in, and writing about, *Macbeth* by briefly noting that a contemporary biographer of Kemble (James Boaden) used the last quoted paragraph from Reynolds as the best illustration of the actor's histrionics, and that the painter in his turn regarded Kemble's sister as the ultimate tragedienne and painted his celebrated *Sarah Siddons as the Tragic Muse* in 1782, significantly echoing a masterpiece of Michelangelo which he adored when he visited the Sistine Chapel as a young man.

2 KEMBLE, SIDDONS AND *MACBETH*

The tragedy of *Macbeth* marked the milestones in the theatrical careers of John Philip Kemble (1757–1823) and Sarah Siddons (1755–1831), the two eldest of the twelve children (eight if whom eventually went on the stage) of strolling actor and manager Roger Kemble and actress Sarah Ward, whose parents, John and Sarah Ward, had also managed a respected troupe of itinerant players. The two siblings acted in their father's company when they were small and went on to perform at various provincial theatres in the 1770s. Acting was in their blood. After a disappointing first season under David Garrick's management in 1775–6 and a long stint in provincial theatres, Siddons made a triumphant comeback to Drury Lane in 1782. She played Lady Macbeth for the first time on 2 February 1785 and, although her mediocre partner (William 'Gentleman' Smith) delivered only a 'very passable tyrant', already departed from the stereotype established by Hannah Pritchard, who had been Garrick's Lady Macbeth. After a chance appearance in the title role in a supplementary 'benefit' performance in March 1785, Kemble began to play opposite his sister in the tragedy regularly from the season of 1788–9.

On 21 April 1794 Kemble, then manager and principal actor, opened a new Drury Lane theatre with *Macbeth*, which was 'now attended with much novelty' of lavish scenery, costume and stage effects.[7] The siblings moved to the rival Covent Garden in 1803 but the tragedy remained the mainstay of their repertory. After an atrocious fire, the theatre reopened on 18 September 1809 with *Macbeth*, amid the disturbances of the notorious O[ld] P[rice] riots. The mob demanding reduction of the ticket prices and removal of the additional boxes caused so much noise that the show 'proceeded in pantomime; not a word was heard, save now and then the deeply modulated tones of the bewitching Siddons'.[8] On 29 June 1812 the great actress bade her official farewell to the theatre as Lady Macbeth. This performance was left incomplete for, after her celebrated sleepwalking, 'the applause of the spectators became ungovernable: they stood on the benches, and demanded that the performance of the piece should not go further than the last scene in which she appeared'.[9] Even after this grand ceremony, Siddons would make odd appearances as Lady Macbeth until her brother's retirement in 1817 and would give public readings of the tragedy at the Argyll Rooms.[10]

At the time of Kemble's staging, *Macbeth* was often labelled a second-rate tragedy in comparison with *Hamlet* and *King Lear*, with its impressive array of intrigues, murders and supernatural apparitions overwhelming genuinely tragic characterisation. (According to Samuel Johnson, 'it has no nice discriminations of character, the events are too great to admit the influence of particular dispositions, and the course of the action necessarily determines the conduct of the agents', *On Shakespeare*, 795). Theatrical managers subordinated characterisation further to showy spectacles by importing some witch scenes (3.5 and 4.1 most probably) from Thomas Middleton's *Witch* (*c.* 1610) 'after Shakespeare had ceased to be active with the King's Men',[11] and, in William Davenant's adaptation, by making the witches fly, sing and dance. Indeed, Macbeth had not been deemed 'a character of the first rate; all the pith of it was exhausted, they said, in the first and second acts of the play', until Garrick restored Shakespeare's text and deepened tragic characterisation.[12] The actor, however, largely retained the undignified Restoration business and let 'the low comedians' play the witches, rendering 'those sentiments ridiculous which were designed by him [Shakespeare] to be spoken with gravity and solemnity' as a result.[13]

The siblings' innovation was to study their respective characters critically and interlace the dark, bloody, terrifying episodes of the tragedy with the tortured psychology of the usurper and his wife, thereby combining effective staging with compelling characterisation. The relationship between the siblings' critical and theatrical interpretations of their roles was nevertheless a precarious one. In clear contrast with the studied wavering and infirmity of his onstage persona, the only important contention of Kemble's character criticism (*Macbeth Reconsidered*, 1786) was that 'Macbeth has a just right to the reputation of intrepidity; that he feels no personal dread of Banquo and Macduff; and that he meets equal, not to say superior, trials, as boldly as Richard [III]'.[14] Siddons's 'Remarks on the Character of Lady Macbeth' (first published by the actress's biographer Thomas Campbell in 1834 but according to her written much earlier) also baffles our expectation by portraying the ferocious Scottish queen as a 'fair, feminine, nay, perhaps, even fragile' woman complete with 'starry' dark blue eyes, when the actress herself was dark and statuesque. Joseph Donohue believes that their sympathetic character criticism naturally led to a portrayal of 'two essentially virtuous persons, victimised by exterior forces and interior passions' on stage,[15] but what actually struck the audience was their awe-inspiring portrayal of the 'present fears' and 'horrible imaginings' of the criminal couple. As the following discussion will show, character study was a way for Kemble and Siddons to explore the dark psychology of guilt, terror and anguish empathetically.

Fighting apprehensions

As the subtitle makes clear, Kemble's *Macbeth Reconsidered* was 'an answer' to Thomas Whately's *Remarks on Some of the Characters of Shakespeare* published posthumously in 1785, which singled out apprehension as a distinguishing feature of Macbeth's character. Dismissing the mechanical 'Rules of Drama' on the one hand and the intangible 'poet's imagination' on the other, Whately defined 'the distinction and preservation of *Character*' as the true province of literary criticism and compared the characterisations of Shakespeare's two usurper-kings, Macbeth and Richard III, to illustrate his point: 'Ambition is common to both; but in Macbeth, it proceeds only from vanity, which is flattered and falsified by the splendour of a throne: in Richard, it is founded upon pride; his ruling passion is the lust of power.'[16] In accordance with their different characters, 'a distinction still stronger is made in the article of courage': 'in Richard it is intrepidity, and in Macbeth no more than resolution: in him it proceeds from exertion, not from nature; in enterprise he betrays a degree of fear, though he is able, when occasion requires, to stifle and subdue it' (29). Whately underlined Macbeth's apprehensiveness by attending to 'the circumstances of horror' on which his imagination dwells before the regicide, and to his 'agony and despair' after it (31–2). 'Anxiety' arising from 'apprehension' motivates his murders of Banquo and the Macduffs, while the witches and Banquo's ghost 'ruffle' and 'terrify' him, and reveal his 'natural timidity' (39–43, 47–9).

Courage had been a central issue in *Macbeth* criticism ever since the time of Johnson, who admired Macbeth's answer to his wife's indictment of his timidity ('I dare do all that may become a man; / Who dares do more, is none', 1.7.46–7):

> The arguments by which Lady Macbeth persuades her husband to commit the murder, afford a proof of Shakespeare's knowledge of human nature. She urges the excellence and dignity of courage, a glittering idea which has dazzled mankind

from age to age, and animated sometimes the housebreaker, and sometimes the conqueror; but this sophism Macbeth has for ever destroyed by distinguishing true from false fortitude, in a line and a half; of which it may almost be said, that they ought to bestow immortality on the author, though all his other productions had been lost. (*On Shakespeare*, 767)[17]

Johnson's appreciation notwithstanding, we should rightly question the quality of Macbeth's courageousness and doubt whether his wife's sophism is 'for ever destroyed', as the usurper contradicts his own definition of fortitude in no time and 'dares do more' to become a king. However, fresh from a successful benefit performance in the title role, Kemble apparently took Whately's insistence on Macbeth's apprehensiveness as an affront to him and his hero. He published an essay that 'concerns itself only with the sentiments of the hero' of the tragedy, in the belief that 'they will more effectually serve ethicks, if, in analysing his character, it shews that there is no distinction between him and king Richard, in the quality of personal courage' (*Macbeth Reconsidered*, 4). While Whately judged people's character with reference to their predominant temperament, Kemble turned to 'the simple character of Macbeth, as it stands before any change is effected in it by the supernatural soliciting of the weird sisters' (5). This 'simple character' seems a very tricky supposition, as Macbeth is mesmerised by the witches the moment he enters in Act 1 scene 3. Kemble regarded the dialogue between Duncan and his subordinates in the preceding scene 2, Ross's greeting to Macbeth (1.3.89–100) and the king's gratitude to him in scene 4 as definitive of Macbeth's 'simple character' and 'the tribunal of Shakspeare himself' on his intrepidity (5–10). The actor posed several rhetorical questions regarding the Captain's 'brave Macbeth (well he deserves that name)' (1.2.16):

Could Shakspeare call a man brave, and insist upon his well deserving that appellation; could he grace a man with the title of valour's minion, and deem him, as he does in a subsequent passage, worthy to be matched even with the goddess of war; – could he do this, and not design to impress a full idea of the dignity of his courage? (7)

T. S. Eliot has taught us to distinguish between the artist and his artistic persona and to answer in the affirmative to all these questions, but this advocate of Macbeth's valour was convinced: 'Such is the character Shakspeare attributes to Macbeth' (10).

Kemble went on to refute Whately's contention that 'Macbeth is personally afraid of Banquo' and that 'his fear is founded on the superior courage of the other', first by pointing out that Banquo is just as agitated as

Macbeth on seeing the witches (10–16), and then by rereading the usurper's crucial confessions: 'Our fears in Banquo / Stick deep, and in his royalty of nature / Reigns that which would be fear'd' (3.1.48–50), and 'There is none but he / Whose being I do fear' (3.1.53–4). The actor paraphrased the sequence beginning 'To be thus, is nothing, / But to be safely thus' (3.1.47–54) as follows:

> I have possess'd myself of the sovereignty; but to what avail, when, in a moment, it may be wrested from me? Banquo's eye is fix'd upon it; and there reigns in his very nature a royalty, that seems to realize his expectations: he is not only a soldier of uncommon bravery, but so consummate a politician, that, should he revolt against my government, he would infallibly carry his designs successfully into execution. He is the only man alive, whose attempts I dread. (17–18)

Kemble politicised the usurper's fear of Banquo (and later similarly of Macduff), to say that Macbeth is afraid only of losing kingship and is therefore fully ambitious and 'courageous'.

Donohue holds that Kemble's argument 'followed the tendency of almost all eighteenth-century *Macbeth* criticism in making the central character a virtuous man seduced by false prophets, a scheming wife, and his own ambition into a crime revolting to his nature', and that his emphasis on the protagonist's courage 'is connected with the concern of the sentimental movement, from Shaftesbury on, to demonstrate the innate goodness of man'.[18] Kemble's professed critical objective was certainly ethical and 'virtuous' ('If Macbeth be what Mr. Wheatley describes him, we must forego our virtuous satisfaction in his repugnance to guilt, for it arises from mere cowardice; and can gain no instruction from his remorse, for it is only the effect of imbecility', 4). However, the actor clearly overstated his case in refuting Whately and almost glorified his hero's grandeur in iniquity. When Buckingham hesitates to conspire in murdering the young princes, the impervious Richard immediately looks for another partner in crime. Whately argued that '[h]ad Macbeth been thus disappointed in the person to whom he had opened himself, it would have disconcerted any design he had formed' (37). Kemble rejoined:

> It appears, however, that the persons Macbeth open'd himself to [i.e. the two murderers of Banquo], were not wrought to his purpose on their first interview; yet it does not disconcert his designs; he sends for them again, repeats his former conversation, and prevails with them by strong arguments, and large promises, to undertake a murder, the execution whereof he steadily persists in. (25)

This is more a picture of a scheming Machiavellian than a 'virtuous' man seduced by evil forces. Similarly, while Whately believed that 'all the crimes

Richard commits are for his advancement, not for his security' (43), Kemble argued otherwise: 'Richard removes Clarence and Hastings, as Macbeth does Duncan, for his advancement; but he murders his nephews and his wife, as Macbeth does Banquo, to secure himself in that advancement' (25). It is difficult to see how these comparisons 'more effectually serve ethicks'. On the contrary, the implication is that Macbeth is no less wicked than Shakespeare's archvillain.

James Boaden observed that his friend Kemble's critical excess was judiciously corrected in his performances and that Macbeth's alleged 'courage' remained only a sentimental undertone upon which the actor's onstage character was built ('if, in combating Mr. Whateley, our great actor had seemed to carry his respect for Macbeth's courage rather higher than, without controversy, he would have done in his performance of the character, his feelings were correctly true; and from this, his first exhibition of Macbeth in town, to his last, it maintained the same features of discrimination').[19] Kemble certainly maintained 'a *stately* posture' and 'studied dignity' in encountering the witches (1.3), and stayed '*easy* and *serene*' in Duncan's court (1.4). This early composure, by way of contrast, only highlighted the anxiety of the dagger scene and the overwhelming horror that ensued from the regicide:

That scene particularly, 'I have done the deed', was beyond all possibility of description, fine, beautiful, sublime, and indeed it paid us with double usury, for one patience throughout the evening. – The face, the looks, the *every thing* of that moment in MACBETH, appalled us with hellish terror, and brought before us the corse of DUNCAN.[20]

Nevertheless, in one way at least, this 1786 publication directly affected Kemble's staging. For the opening performance of the new Drury Lane theatre in 1794, Kemble subtly revised the Garrick version ('As Shakespeare wrote it') that had replaced Davenant's adaptation from 1744.[21] While retaining Garrick's major excisions and additions, Kemble cut some thirteen lines out of the total sixty-eight of Act 1 scene 2, but the twenty-five lines he had cited in the pamphlet as indicative of Macbeth's courage remained intact. Macbeth's reference to Banquo's 'royalty of nature' (3.1.49–56), on the other hand, was edited out.[22] The third murderer of Banquo, whom Whately had cited as 'a further proof of the same imbecility' of Macbeth (62), was also omitted. Most conspicuously, the lines and stage business associated with Macbeth's premature request for his armour before the final battle, which Whately believed demonstrated his nervousness (70–1), were dropped entirely:

MACBETH	Give me my armour.
SEYTON	'Tis not needed yet.
MACBETH	I'll put it on ... Give me mine armour ... Come, put mine armour on ... Come, sir, despatch ... Pull't off, I say. (5.3.33–54)[23]

In this way Kemble quietly helped his hero to vindicate himself from the charges of timidity on stage.

There are two more issues of interest in Kemble's publication. First, the actor referred to Macbeth's awesome wife only once in the entire essay, quoting a mere four lines. Second, the word 'coward', which so annoyed Kemble, was not actually used at all in Whately's *Remarks*.[24] In fact, this crucially insulting word exists only in those very four lines cited, and refuted, by Kemble (and this is the Lady's 'sophism' to incite Macbeth's 'I dare do all that may become a man; / Who dares do more is none' that impressed Johnson):

> Would'st thou have that
> Which thou esteem'st the ornament of life,
> And live a *coward* in thine own esteem,
> Letting 'I dare not' wait upon 'I would'. . .? (1.7.41–4; emphasis added)

Kemble's essay obviously needs to be complemented by what his prodigious sister had to say about the other half of the regicide couple.

The fragile woman within

Here is another ghost story which is not unlike Mr Partridge's. Sarah Siddons, then twenty years of age, was having a late night preparing for her first performance as Lady Macbeth at a provincial theatre the following evening. She thought that she would finish it easily as 'the character is very short' and 'the necessity of discrimination, and the development of character, at that time of my life, had scarcely entered into my imagination'. In the silence of the night, she went on with tolerable composure until she came to the regicide scene:

> when the horrors of the scene rose to a degree that made it impossible for me to get farther. I snatched up my candle, and hurried out of the room, in a paroxysm of terror. My dress was of silk, and the rustling of it, as I ascended the stairs to go to bed, seemed to my panic-struck fancy like the movement of a spectre pursuing me. At last I reached my chamber, where I found my husband fast asleep. I clapt my candlestick down upon the table, without the power of putting the candle out; and I threw myself on my bed, without daring to stay even to take off my clothes.[25]

This episode, indicative as it was of a burgeoning of her impassioned character portrayal, concluded with a rather didactic note. Her first appearance as Lady Macbeth turned out to be a failure ('so little did I know of my part when I appeared in it'), and 'my shame and confusion cured me of procrastinating my business for the remainder of my life'.[26] Siddons certainly took this lesson to heart and subsequently honed her acting tirelessly by visiting asylums, observing somnambulists and studying Egyptian statues. Tragedy in her own family also helped to improve her impersonation. When consumption claimed two of her teenage daughters, Mrs Piozzi recalled to Mrs Pennington, "'Do you not remember dear Siddons saying she never acted so well as once when her heart was heavy concerning the loss of a child?'"[27]

Unlike her predecessor Hannah Pritchard, whom Johnson once disparaged as 'a vulgar idiot' who 'never read any part of the Play, except her own part',[28] Siddons studied the promptbook of *Macbeth* in great detail and even tried Lady Macbeth's mere two words ('We fail', 1.7.60) in three different ways, by at first saying 'We fail?' as a contemptuous interrogation to her husband, modifying it later to 'We fail!' with a note of indignant astonishment, and finally fixing on the simple 'We fail', modulating her voice to a deep, low, resolute tone and thereby creating a 'sublime, almost awful' effect.[29] She also wrote an essay on the character of Lady Macbeth and let her biographer Thomas Campbell publish it as part of his volume. Campbell, however, found her critical interpretation of Lady Macbeth as 'fair, feminine, nay, perhaps, even fragile' woman considerably less convincing than her onstage rendition:

[Lady Macbeth] is a splendid picture of evil ... a sort of sister of Milton's *Lucifer*; and, like him, we surely imagine her externally majestic and beautiful. Mrs. Siddons's idea of her having been a delicate and blonde beauty, seems to me to be a pure caprice. The public would have ill exchanged such a representative of *Lady Macbeth*, for the dark locks and the eagle eyes of Mrs. Siddons.[30]

Donohue explains the departure of Siddons's criticism from her own acting in terms of Lady Macbeth's 'original' character, or the 'character as it might exist *before the play begins*', against which the actress 'can play from the moment she steps on stage'.[31] This original character, which is equivalent to Kemble's 'simple character', is true as far as it goes: Siddons even envisioned the girlhood of Lady Macbeth in her essay. However, the theatrical relevance of her criticism lay less in her conception of the early Lady Macbeth than in the insights it gave her into the gaps and inconsistencies in the part and into the ways for her to piece them together.

While Kemble based his analyses on the second Johnson-Steevens edition published in 1778, Siddons studied the current theatrical version that excised Lady Macbeth from both Act 2 scene 3 and Act 3 scene 1. To ensure an emotional consistency between the regicide (2.2) and the interview with Macbeth (3.2), Siddons postulated Lady Macbeth's repentance directly after the regicide: 'The golden round of royalty now crowns her brow, and royal robes enfold her form; but the peace that passeth all understanding is lost to her for ever, and the worm that never dies already gnaws her heart.'[32] Siddons's promptbook did not specifically point to Lady Macbeth's tortured conscience yet, but it did not contradict her interpretation either. While the critical editors since Nicholas Rowe had added a stage direction ('*Seeming to faint*') at Lady Macbeth's 'Help me hence, ho!' (2.3.116) to emphasise her unregenerate deceitfulness even at the revelation of the regicide, stage versions customarily cut the swooning sequence to prevent her '[c]oarse hypocrisy' from exciting 'derision' in the audience.[33] Siddons was therefore entitled to assume 'the dejection of countenance and manners' as soon as she entered in Act 3, for (as the actress herself put it) 'though the author of this sublime composition has not, it must be acknowledged, given any direction whatever to authorize this assumption, yet I venture to hope that he would not have disapproved of it'. The audience, however, might not have perceived the agony of Siddons's Lady Macbeth quite as clearly yet, for 'so far from adding to the weight of his [i.e. Macbeth's] affliction the burthen of her own, she endeavours to conceal it from him with the most delicate and unremitting attention'. It must have been extremely difficult for Siddons to convey to the audience the agony that the wife hides from her husband. The actress continued, 'Yes; smothering her sufferings in the deepest recesses of her own wretched bosom, we cannot but perceive that she devotes herself entirely to the effort of supporting him.'[34]

Another gap for Siddons to fill in was between the banquet scene, where the wife strong-mindedly chides her husband into keeping composure (3.4), and the deranged sleepwalking (5.1). According to Siddons, Lady Macbeth's hidden vulnerability already surfaces in the banquet scene and prepares the way for her final collapse. Seeing Macbeth's consternation at the sight of Banquo's ghost, she reproves:

> O proper stuff!
> This is the very painting of your fear:
> This is the air-drawn dagger, which, you said,
> Led you to Duncan. O! these flaws and starts
> (Impostors to true fear), would well become

> A woman's story at a winter's fire,
> Authoris'd by her grandam. Shame itself!
> Why do you make such faces? When all's done,
> You look but on a stool. (3.4.59–67)

In fact, Lady Macbeth is already '[d]ying with fear, yet assuming the utmost composure' and is 'writhing ... under her internal agonies'. The agitated glances she darts at Macbeth throw the guests into amazement 'in spite of all her efforts to suppress them'.[35] Macbeth's broken references to the ghastly vision begin to reveal his heinous crime to the guests, and when Ross enquires, 'What sights, my Lord?' (3.4.115):

> What imitation, in such circumstances as these, would ever satisfy the demands of expectation? The terror, the remorse, the hypocrisy of this astonishing being, flitting in frightful succession over her countenance, and actuating her agitated gestures with her varying emotions, present, perhaps, one of the greatest difficulties of the scenic art, and cause her representative no less to tremble for the suffrage of her private study, than for its public effect.[36]

About 1807 the Scottish solicitor G. J. Bell took down Siddons's marvellous delivery of Lady Macbeth's inner anxiety in a series of notes. While Kemble's Macbeth spoke to the murderer at the beginning of the banquet, the actress was already performing an excellent byplay: 'During all this a growing uneasiness in her; at last she rises and speaks.' And upon Macbeth's 'The table's full' (3.4.45), 'Her secret uneasiness very fine. Suppressed, but agitating her whole frame.'[37] Siddons walked up to Macbeth, caught his hand and whispered with suppressed voice, 'Are you a man?' (3.4.57). She sounded 'peevish and scornful' upon 'O proper stuff!' (3.4.59), but when she interrogated him, 'Why do you make such faces? ... You look but on a stool' (3.4.66–7), 'Her anxiety makes you creep with apprehension: uncertain how to act. Her emotion keeps you breathless.'[38] Returning to her throne, Siddons whispered low, 'Fie! for shame!' (3.4.73). But when Macbeth again cried out, 'Avaunt! and quit my sight!' (3.4.92), her 'secret agony again agitates her'. Siddons's Lady Macbeth kept speaking 'sweetly to the company', but upon Ross's 'What sights, my Lord?': '[She d]escends in great eagerness; voice almost choked with anxiety to prevent their questioning; alarm, hurry, rapid and convulsive as if afraid he should tell of the murder of Duncan.'[39]

When the guests withdrew, Siddons stepped yet further forward and prepared for Lady Macbeth's somnambulism and subsequent death. The nervewracking night was nearly over: 'Almost at odds with morning, which is which' (3.4.126). Now Lady Macbeth was 'Very sorrowful. Quite exhausted.'⁴⁰ She told her husband to sleep and have a rest ('You lack the season of all natures, sleep', 3.4.140), though it was this former 'sister of Milton's *Lucifer*' that was badly in need of the 'balm of hurt minds'. She was feeble, 'as if preparing for her last sickness and final doom'.⁴¹ Simultaneously reading into and supplementing the promptbook, Siddons invented the process of Lady Macbeth's decline into the frenzied sleepwalking. The actress gave excellent theatrical expression to Lady Macbeth's inmost vulnerability, though some of her interpretations probably remained 'hidden' not only from Macbeth and other dramatic characters but also from her audience.

There was another important rereading of the play, again not quite backed by the text, that might have found its way to the stage. Siddons believed that Lady Macbeth correctly guesses at her husband's intention to kill Banquo (and Fleance) in Act 3 scene 2, and even insinuates the idea of the murder into him when she says, 'But in them [i.e. Banquo and Fleance] Nature's copy's not eterne' (3.2.38). In her interpretation Lady Macbeth is as guilty of Banquo's death as her husband, and therefore:

Having ... now filled the measure of her crimes, I have imagined that the last appearance of *Banquo*'s ghost became no less visible to her eyes than it became to those of her husband. Yes, the spirit of the noble *Banquo* has smilingly filled up, even to overflowing, and now commends to her own lips the ingredients of her poisoned chalice.⁴²

Anna Brownell Jameson's observation strongly suggests that Siddons actually tested the theory on stage:

Mrs. Siddons, I believe, had an idea that Lady Macbeth beheld the spectre of Banquo in the supper scene, and that her self controul and presence of mind enabled her to surmount her consciousness of the ghastly presence. This would be superhuman, and I do not see that either the character or the text bear out this supposition.⁴³

Siddons's 'superhuman' impersonation merits careful scrutiny in conjunction with her brother's partnership in acting and stage direction of the play's supernaturalism.

3 MATERIALISING THE IMMATERIAL: THE 1794 PERFORMANCE

Besides scaring theatrical audiences, the ghosts and witches in *Macbeth* have sorely perplexed literary critics and eluded their scrutiny with great success. Their supernatural status disturbed Samuel Johnson's commonsensical thinking and faith in plausible plotting to such an extent that he set about seeking 'probability' in them in *Miscellaneous Observations on the Tragedy of Macbeth* (1745):

> A poet who should now make the whole action of his tragedy depend upon enchantment, and produce the chief events by the assistance of supernatural agents, would be censured as transgressing the bounds of probability, he would be banished from the theatre to the nursery, and condemned to write fairy tales instead of tragedies; but a survey of the notions that prevailed at the time when this play was written, will prove that Shakespeare was in no danger of such censures, since he only turned the system that was then universally admitted to his advantage, and was far from overburthening the credulity of his audience. (*On Shakespeare*, 3)

Johnson sharply contrasted the cultural milieu of Shakespeare's days with that of his own, to say that the playwright had only followed the current belief 'with great exactness', and that the scenes of enchantment, 'however they may now be ridiculed', would have been believable and affecting to his original audience (6).[44]

Johnson even tried to see practical utility in the Weird Sisters in the 'stricture' of his Shakespeare edition, where he argued with uncharacteristic reticence: ' I know not whether it may not be said in defence of some parts which now seem improbable, that, in Shakespeare's time, it was necessary to warn credulity against vain and illusive predictions' (795). According to this explanation, the witches were not only probable but also useful: they were there not to frighten but to teach. However, this historical apology for the witchcraft, firmly based as it was on such Johnsonian values as 'judgement', 'knowledge' and 'exactness', did not secure the tragedy's relevance to eighteenth-century readers and, more specifically, to theatregoers, for whom the very presence of the apparitions was at issue. If the witches had ceased to be probable and useful, does it follow that *Macbeth* should now be 'banished from the theatre to the nursery' and labelled as a 'fairy tale' rather than a tragedy?

Elizabeth Montagu's *Essay* vindicated the tragedy to a greater extent than Johnson had done by regarding the preternatural creatures as a means for transcendence:

> The agency of witches and spirits excites a species of terror, that cannot be effected by the operation of human agency, or by any form or disposition of human things. For the known limits of their powers and capacities set certain bounds to our apprehensions; mysterious horrors, undefined terrors, are raised by the intervention of beings whose nature we do not understand, whose actions we cannot control, and whose influence we know not how to escape. (65)

This formulation, however, poses a new difficulty when examined specifically in theatrical terms. On the stage the 'witches and spirits' have to be 'effected by the operation of human agency' and are necessarily influenced by the 'form' and 'disposition' of the actors involved. Montagu did not clarify whether the physicality of actors and of stage could produce such superhuman sensation.

Opening the new Drury Lane theatre in 1794, John Philip Kemble enhanced visual effects at various levels and, in an effort to excite such 'a species of terror' as Montagu suggested, handled the problematic apparitions with meticulous care. To take advantage of the expanded theatre space, Kemble not only kept all the spectacles available in the Garrick version but also introduced a big chorus of fifty to sixty singing witches and groups of children.[45] He ordered new scenery and stage property and reformed the costumes, especially of the witches, who were still played by men but 'no longer wore mittens, plaited caps, laced aprons, red stomachers, ruffs, &c . . . or any human garb, but appeared as preternatural beings, distinguishable only by the fellness of their purposes, and the fatality of their delusions'. Kemble was determined 'to strike the eye with a picture of supernatural power, by such appropriate vestures, as marked neither mortal grandeur nor earthly insignificance' as well as 'to avoid all buffoonery in those parts, that Macbeth might no longer be deemed a Tragi-Comedy'.[46]

Kemble also materialised some of Shakespeare's poetic imageries. His Hecate descended and rose again on a 'cloud machine', which embodied the lines: 'Hark! I am call'd: my little spirit, see, / Sits in a foggy cloud, and stays for me' (3.5.34–5). Likewise, he personified the spirits from the song that traditionally accompanied Hecate's exit from the cave ('*Black Spiritts, and white: Red Spiritts, and Gray, / Mingle, Mingle, Mingle, you that mingle may*', 4.1.43).[47] Kemble's friend Walter Scott witnessed the 'four bands of children' respectively representing the colours mentioned in the song, but was not particularly pleased, as there was 'perhaps little taste in rendering these aerial beings visible to the bodily eye'.[48] This personification proved unpopular with the generality of the audience, too, and was subsequently omitted.

In Act 4 scene 1 the resourceful director heightened the supernatural atmosphere of the witches' den by teaming a solemn scene ('The Cave – Moonlight and Eclipse') with a screen of black gauze set before the stage.[49] As Scott accurately observed, by 'causing the descendants of the murdered thane to pass behind a screen of black crape', Kemble successfully 'diminished their corporeal appearance' and achieved the solemnity only possible

4 Henry Fuseli, *Lady Macbeth Seizing the Daggers*.

in the audience's imagination.[50] Kemble explored this metaphysical representation of terror further in the important banquet and sleepwalking scenes, with a great deal of help from his prodigious sister.

Visible and invisible terror

Shakespeare's *Macbeth* is haunted by hallucinatory noises and visions that are even more elusive than the witches and ghosts: they are not even cited in the *Dramatis Personae* or stage directions. The protagonist is led into Duncan's bedchamber by an illusory dagger:

> Art thou not, fatal vision, sensible
> To feeling, as to sight? or art thou but
> A dagger of the mind, a false creation,
> Proceeding from the heat-oppressed brain? (2.1.36–9)

And when the atrocity transpires, he is tortured by a voice crying, 'Sleep no more! ... Macbeth shall sleep no more!' (2.2.34–42). Shakespeare portrayed these illusions as embodiments of Macbeth's ambition and guilt rather than as external evil spirits, and the audience registers them only as they are described by the usurper.

Some sounds and visions are even more transient. While Macbeth is carrying through the regicide, strange noises frighten his wife: 'Hark! – Peace! / It was the owl that shriek'd' (2.2.2–3), and again, 'Hark!' (2.2.11). She rationalises them as 'the owl' and 'the crickets' but, as no stage direction for a sound effect is supplied, the audience is left uncertain about the nature of the scary noises.[51] When Macbeth returns, the guilty couple exchange anxious interrogations:

LADY MACBETH	*Did not you speak*?
MACBETH	When?
LADY MACBETH	Now.
MACBETH	As I descended?
LADY MACBETH	Ay.
MACBETH	*Hark*!
	Who lies i'th' second chamber?
LADY MACBETH	Donalbain.
MACBETH	*This is a sorry sight*. (2.2.16–20; emphases added)

Characteristically, the three italicised lines are not accorded any audible or visual referents in the text. The conversation fails to clarify whether Macbeth actually spoke as he descended, or whether Donalbain in the second chamber made any noise to trigger Macbeth's 'Hark!'. At 'This is a sorry sight', actors customarily lift their bloody hands near their faces according to the stage direction supplied by editors from Alexander Pope onwards. The ultimate 'sorry sight', however, lies offstage in the blood-besmeared carcass of Duncan, Macbeth's crimson hands being its weak metonymy.

Banquo's ghost itself entails much ambivalence. According to the stage direction in F1, the apparition manifests itself selectively to Macbeth and the audience but not to other dramatic characters, and therefore could be seen either as 'existent' in a similar manner to the late King Hamlet, or (in the words of Lady Macbeth) as 'the very painting' (3.4.60) of the usurper's anxiety and guilt.

In the 1794 production Kemble in effect corroborated the second interpretation by eliminating the stage ghost and by miming the usurper's terrified reaction to the (really) vacant stool.[52] This new theatrical situation is comparable to Henry Fielding's rendition of the second ghost scene of *Hamlet* discussed above: while Partridge was interested in David Garrick's reaction (as Hamlet) to the apparition rather than to the apparition itself, Kemble cut the ghost altogether and invited the audience to attend exclusively to his masterly performance. It is not known whether Sarah Siddons played her 'superhuman' interpretation of the banquet scene in this production. If she did, her reaction to the nonexistent ghost must have been even subtler than Kemble's, as she needed to signify to the audience that she was witnessing the invisible *and* disguising it from both her husband and the guests.

The audience's response to the omission of the ghost was mixed. Thomas Campbell was infuriated and condemned it as 'a mere crotchet' and 'a pernicious departure from the ancient custom'. According to him, spectators were Shakespeare's guests, as distinguished from the guests at Macbeth's table, and were entitled to see 'what he [Macbeth] sees, and to feel what he feels'. The elimination of the ghost was, therefore, 'a violation of the spiritual peerage of the drama, an outrage on the rights of ghosts, – and a worthier spectre than *Banquo*'s never trode the stage'.[53] Those who supported Kemble's staging felt that the stage gained emotional intensity precisely by excluding the corporeal stage ghost. 'Nothing real', noted a *Monthly Mirror* critic, 'can approach in horror what the imagination can conceive – to attempt, indeed, to realize what is horribly conceived by the mind, is to deprive it of half its horror.'[54] As a matter of fact, Kemble would restore the ghost later in his career, only to invite just as much approbation and criticism all over again.

Kemble and Siddons represented invisible terror in a more sophisticated, and unanimously successful, way in the sleepwalking scene, where all the atrocities of the tragedy are revived in Lady Macbeth's perturbed mind. Kemble had replaced the conventional stage direction of '*A bell rings*' (2.1.61) to cue Macbeth to regicide with '*A clock strikes two*', and thereby underpinned the parallelism between the tragic action and Lady Macbeth's nightmare. Now the memory of the horrid moment tortures her guilty conscience. (Bell's comments on Siddons's somnambulism are supplied in brackets.)

One; [Listening eagerly] two: why, then 'tis time to do't. [A strange unnatural whisper] – Hell is murky. – Fie, my Lord, fie! a soldier, and afeard? – What need we fear who knows it, when none can call our power to accompt? – Yet who would have thought the old man to have had so much blood in him? (5.1.36–41)[55]

Being projected in Lady Macbeth's mind, the 'sorry sight' of the blood-besmeared Duncan, which was kept offstage in Act 2, was visualised to the audience at long last.

After the regicide, Lady Macbeth, with her hands still red with Duncan's blood, famously declares, 'A little water clears us of this deed' (2.2.66).

Presumably she then washes her hands somewhere offstage. While sleepwalking, she is terrified at the sight of her hands, which are clean in reality. Hannah Pritchard, who was Garrick's Lady Macbeth, held the taper throughout the scene and only emblematically signified the 'damned spot' by looking at her palm. Siddons set down the candle as soon as she entered and mimed a handwashing.[56] The audience thereby not only registered Lady Macbeth's hallucination (as in Pritchard's rendition) but also witnessed (with Siddons) the blood once again staining her hands. The effect was striking. To an enquiry from the American tragedian Edwin Forrest about Siddons's sleepwalking, Sheridan Knowles answered 'with a sort of shudder', 'Well, sir, I smelt blood! I swear that I smelt blood!'[57]

Interestingly, Lady Macbeth remembers the murders of Banquo and the Macduffs in her frenzy although, as far as can be seen from the theatrical and reading texts, she has not been even informed of them: 'I tell you yet again, Banquo's buried: he cannot come out on's grave' (5.1.64–5), and 'The Thane of Fife had a wife [Very melancholy tone]: where is she now?' (5.1.43–4). As Siddons's Lady Macbeth was implicated in the intrigue against Banquo, the parallelism between his murder and the nightmare was maintained in her rendition. (Following a similar reasoning, we could suppose her Lady Macbeth's involvement in the massacre of the Macduffs, though she is entirely absent from the crucial Act 4.) Whatever the case, Siddons's sleepwalking gave the play's carnage a powerful metaphysical expression. Her Lady Macbeth had admirably endured the actual atrocities but in the end succumbed to their images, or as the actress herself put it, 'During this appalling scene, which, to my sense, is the most so of them all, the wretched creature, in imagination, acts over again the accumulated horrors of her whole conduct.'[58] Siddons's Lady Macbeth had been '[d]ying with fear, yet assuming the utmost composure' and 'writhing thus under her internal agonies' ever since the regicide. In the sleepwalking the 'feminine, nay, perhaps, even fragile' woman with all her suppressed vulnerabilities finally revealed her true self. By both portraying and suppressing the terror of the tragedy, Kemble and Siddons gave a compelling theatrical expression to the 'present fears' and 'horrible imaginings' of the regicide couple.

Some five years before this successful opening performance at Drury Lane, a respected artist was struggling to paint Shakespeare's Cardinal Beaufort (*Henry VI Part 2*). Anticipating Kemble's four-colour spirits, the painter superimposed a physical shape of a fiend behind the pillow of the dying Cardinal and depicted his 'gnawing demon of despair'. This little pictorial demon would share the destiny of Kemble's short-lived spirits, too, and would be obliterated from the canvas under tremendous objections from the reviewers. Let us turn now to Joshua Reynolds's problematic Shakespearean pictures and see how the supernatural could be expressed on the pictorial plane.

4 'ASK REYNOLDS': THE WAY TO PAINT TRAGEDY

Ugolino's distress

When Joshua Reynolds collected the quintessentially Johnsonian comments on David Garrick into two imaginary dialogues between the doctor and two of his friends (the painter himself and Edward Gibbon), the notorious 'Punch has no feelings' was accorded an interesting discursive context. Against Gibbon's assertion that Garrick was a man of acute sensibility and that his fine feelings made him the great actor he was, Johnson replied tersely, 'This is all cant, fit only for kitchen wenches and chambermaids: Garrick's trade was to represent passion, not to feel it. Ask Reynolds whether he felt the distress of Count Hugolino when he drew it.'[59]

When Gibbon retorted that 'surely he feels the passion at the moment he is representing it', Johnson elaborated on the distinction between artistic expression and feeling, beginning, 'About as much as Punch feels.'

Tantalisingly, the painter left the question of 'whether he felt the distress of Count Hugolino when he drew it' unanswered in this fictional conversation, but a contemporary testimony suggests that he actually *did not*. According to Reynolds's disciple and biographer, James Northcote, the picture (*Count Ugolino and His Children*, 1773; figure 5) started simply as a head of an old man painted on a half-length canvas sometime before 1771. The theme of Ugolino and his family was introduced as an afterthought at the suggestion of 'either ... Mr. Edmund Burke, or Dr. Goldsmith', who recognised in the initial portrayal 'the precise person, countenance, and expression of the Count Ugolino, as described by Dante in his "Inferno"'.[60]

Dante's *Inferno* (Canto 33) tells the affective story of Count Ugolino and his family in a barricaded dungeon, its keys having been thrown into the River Arno. The children and grandchildren die of starvation one by one, offering their flesh to Ugolino to feed on. In order to fit in the story, Reynolds enlarged the canvas, painted the Count's four offspring and transformed the background into a dark prison. Also added were a grated window and a dawn light entering through it, just as described by Dante.

5 Joshua Reynolds, *Count Ugolino and His Children*.

Reynolds captured Ugolino's hidden anguish over the bolted door in the picture, and underscored the reference by printing the relevant passage from *Inferno* in the exhibition catalogue:

> Turned to stone I could not cry,
> but heard *them* cry and my Anselmo say,
> 'Father, how you do stare! But why?'
> I could not weep – all through that day,
> and through the night – and I did not reply. (Canto 33, 49–53)[61]

Throughout this drastic transformation, the face of the old man remained untouched: it was 'in point of expression, exactly as it now stands' from when it was first painted.[62] The countenance is ambivalent in itself. It signifies Ugolino's agony only in the additional narrative and pictorial context of the heartrending family tragedy. What was originally a study of an obscure beggar (one George White) expanded into a history painting as it was situated in the strife between the Guelphs and the Ghibellines.

Unfortunately, Northcote's account is not entirely trustworthy. The canvas was certainly extended, but he was wrong at least as regards the date of composition. Nicholas Penny points out that already in 1770,

Reynolds's pocketbook included references to 'Beggar Hugolino' and 'Hugolino Boy'. Penny argues that probably 'Reynolds's decision to extend the canvas was not related to a change in the subject, but simply reflected his decision to include more figures'.[63] Moreover, the painter's initial conception can be traced further back in Jonathan Richardson's *Two Discourses* (1719), of which he was an avid reader from when he was eight years old.[64] Examining the various renditions of Ugolino in history (by Villani), poetry (by Dante), and sculpture (by 'Michelangelo', or Pierino da Vinci), Richardson regretted that Michelangelo had not also painted the story and urged future painters to take on the challenge.[65] As Northcote implied, Richardson's suggestion was probably at the back of the painter's mind as he worked on the tragic motif.[66] It is not clear, however, at which stage of composition Reynolds remembered Richardson and decided to emulate his great predecessors.

White was Reynolds's favourite model and sat for him on many occasions.[67] In the end, we are left uncertain as to when exactly 'another study' of a haggard man metamorphosed into a rendition of Count Ugolino and his sorrow, and whether Reynolds (or White for that matter) intended, and felt, Ugolino's agony during the composition. Johnson's analogy between Garrick and Reynolds cannot be carried too far, either: while an actor assimilates his character's emotion through the medium of his own body, a painter represents it on an objective canvas. Henry Fuseli dismissed any such emotional involvement on the side of the painter and pointed out drily: 'From whatever cause this face became that of Ugolino – whether its original were that of a noble or a pauper, it is a standard of grief.'[68] Ugolino's countenance was indeed modelled on the representation of '*horreur*' in Charles Le Brun's *Expression des passions*.[69] Incidentally, eighteenth-century actors are known to have used Le Brun's treatise as a standard textbook on facial expression.[70]

The comparison between an actor's and a painter's expressive skills was given a further twist when Walter Scott compared his friend John Philip Kemble's acting of Macbeth once again to Reynolds's masterpiece. The actor was at best only equal to Garrick in such roles as Lear and Hamlet but 'in Macbeth, Kemble has been as yet unapproachable'. The novelist was particularly impressed with his acting subsequent to the initial murder, where Macbeth's terror and anxiety was both expressed and suppressed:

We can never forget the rueful horror of his look, which by strong exertion he endeavours to conceal, when on the morning succeeding the murder he receives Lennox and Macduff in the ante-chamber of Duncan. His efforts to appear composed, his endeavours to assume the attitude and appearance of one listening to Lennox's account of the external terrors of the night, while in fact he is expecting the alarm to arise within the royal apartment, formed a most astonishing piece of playing.[71]

Interestingly, Kemble's acting in this nervewracking scene reminded Scott of Reynolds's Ugolino, especially on account of the emotional turmoil hidden under the actor's composed appearance: 'Kemble's countenance seemed altered by the sense of internal horror, and had a cast of that of Count Ugolino in the dungeon, as painted by Reynolds.'[72] Unlike Johnson, Scott believed that the actor's feeling defined the countenance that he assumed on stage and, against Northcote's account of the origin of the painting, he also believed in the internal agony behind the painted face of the unfortunate Count. This interface between theatrical and pictorial expressions of tragedy needs to be illustrated further by Reynolds's three Shakespearean paintings with their assorted ghosts and fairies, as well as by his masterly portrayal of Siddons as the embodiment of tragedy itself.

Painting the supernatural: the three Boydell pictures

In 1786, when John Boydell projected a permanent gallery of Shakespearean paintings to be financed by the sale of prints made from them, he thought it of absolute necessity to procure some pictures from the President of the prestigious Royal Academy. Reynolds was unwilling to participate in this Shakespeare Gallery venture at first, 'as if he thought it degrading himself to paint for a print-seller', but after Boydell's repeated solicitations and 'a bank bill of five hundred pounds' delivered by his ally, the editor George Steevens, the painter finally complied.[73]

Boydell's commission extended to thirty-five painters, and their handlings of the Shakespearean topics were varied: some pictures were primarily theatrical, reproducing specific stage performances or portraying identifiable players in stage costume, while others defied stage conventions and depicted offstage events.[74] For his three Boydell pictures (*Puck*, *The Death of Cardinal Beaufort* and *Macbeth and the Witches*), Reynolds opted out of the portraiture for which he was widely acclaimed and squarely tackled Shakespeare's poetic reality. Unfortunately, his performance in this particular department left something to be desired. His younger colleague Henry Fuseli, who was committed to history painting throughout his life and whose domain was 'in air and hell, the clouds and the grave',[75] would have some hard words on the fashionable portraitist's Shakespearean endeavours, especially regarding his handling of the supernatural.

The last to be undertaken, but finished in no time, was the lighthearted *Puck* (figure 6). The history of its composition, as recorded by the antiquarian William Cotton, is reminiscent of Northcote's *Ugolino* episode in many ways. Cotton's grandfather accompanied Boydell to Reynolds's studio one day to inspect the progress of *The Death of Cardinal Beaufort*. In the studio Boydell was 'much taken with the portrait of a naked child, and wished it could be brought into the Shakespeare'. It was a picture of a little child whom Reynolds had found sitting on his doorstep. Cotton's grandfather then said, 'Well, Mr Alderman, it can very easily come into the Shakespeare, if Sir Joshua will kindly place him on a mushroom, give him faun's ears, and make a Puck of him.' Reynolds retouched the picture according to the suggestion, adding pointed ears, a giant mushroom and the figures of Titania and Bottom in the background.[76]

At the Royal Academy exhibition in 1789 and subsequently at the Shakespeare Gallery, critical response to the picture was unfavourable. To the *Morning Post* reviewer (1 May), the piece had 'no claim to praise' apart from fine colouring and was indeed 'rather disgusting', as it looked like 'a portrait of a *foetus* taken from some anatomical preparation'. The reviewer continued, 'It is really offensive, and we wonder the taste and feeling of this admirable artist should ever have been employed on such a subject. The *toad-stool* on which this praeternatural infant is sitting, is one of such disproportionate magnitude, that it seems to have been brought from *Brobdingna[g]* for the occasion, particularly as the trees are very small.'[77] This reviewer was probably not informed of the origin of the picture but he instinctively reacted against the dissonance between the overtly fantastic setting of the giant mushroom and the corporeality of the infant boy. Fuseli noticed the same incongruity and criticised Reynolds's infirm grasp of the poetic subject: 'This is a fairy whom fancy may endow with the creation of a midnight mushroom, a snow drop, or a violet; but he surely cannot be mistaken for the Robin of Shakespeare or Milton.'[78] Fuseli's own Boydell piece (figure 7) certainly captured Puck's supernatural quality without recourse to such props as a toadstool, though the overriding uncanniness of the scene seems to have partaken more of a haunting nightmare than an elusive midsummer night's dream.

Reynolds's second Boydell painting, *The Death of Cardinal Beaufort* (figure 8), interpreted the following passage from *Henry VI Part 2*:

KING   (*Kneels.*)
          O Thou eternal mover of the heavens,
          Look with a gentle eye upon this wretch.

6 Joshua Reynolds, *Puck (Robin Goodfellow)*. Engraved by Luigi Schiavonetti.

7 Henry Fuseli, *Robin Goodfellow-Puck*.

8 Joshua Reynolds, *The Death of Cardinal Beaufort*. Engraved by S. W. Reynolds.

	O beat away the busy meddling fiend
	That lays strong siege unto this wretch's soul,
	And from his bosom purge this black despair.
WARWICK	See how the pangs of death do make him grin.
SALISBURY	Disturb him not; let him pass peaceably.
KING	Peace to his soul, if God's good pleasure be.
	Lord Cardinal, if thou thinkst on heaven's bliss,
	Hold up thy hand, make signal of thy hope.
	(*Cardinal dies.*)
	He dies and makes no sign. O God, forgive him! (3.3.19–29)

This picture was noted for the literal representation of the 'grin' of the Cardinal and for the materialisation of the 'busy meddling fiend' on the canvas. William Mason witnessed the process through which Reynolds created the peculiar facial expression of the dying villain. The painter 'scumbled in' the positions of the subordinate figures and then began to work on the main character. The model for the Cardinal was 'a porter, or coal heaver, between fifty and sixty years of age, whose black and bushy beard he had paid for letting grow'. The model was stripped naked to the waist and, with his profile turned to the painter, sat 'with a fixed grin, showing his teeth':

I could not help laughing at the strange figure, and recollecting why he had ordered the poor fellow so to grin, on account of Shakespeare's line:
Mark [*sic*] how the pangs of death do make him grin.
I told him, that in my opinion Shakespeare would never have used the word 'grin' in that place, if he could have readily found a better ... He did not agree with me on this point, so the fellow sat grinning on for upwards of one hour, during which he sometimes gave a touch to the face, sometimes scumbled on the bedclothes with white much diluted with spirits of turpentine.[79]

According to Mason, Reynolds 'could not catch the expression he wanted' and 'rubbed the face entirely out; for the face and attitude in the present finished picture, which I did not see till above a year after this first fruitless attempt, is certainly different, and on an idea much superior'. However, even in the finished painting, the Cardinal does sport quite a grin.

Closely related to the Cardinal's facial expression was the fiend painted behind his pillow. Critics censured the daring invention and Edmund Burke even tried to persuade Reynolds to eliminate the demon, as he found it 'an absurd and ridiculous incident, and a disgrace to the artist'.[80] Northcote, however, supported his master's artistic intention, if not the final product. Reynolds needed to indicate unequivocally in the picture that 'the dying man's agonies do not proceed from bodily pain, so much as from the horrors of a guilty conscience'. The distinction was 'of so nice a kind in respect to its being pourtrayed, that perhaps Raffaelle himself would have found it difficult to execute it', but 'this important article of information must of necessity be decidedly and distinctly pronounced, or the subject is not explained'.[81] When Garrick faced a similar challenge in acting the fatally wounded Macbeth, he added to the Davenant ending the following eight lines (an abbreviated form of which Kemble inherited), and emphasised the moral nature of the usurper's agony by not once referring to his bodily pain:

> 'Tis done! the scene of life will quickly close.
> Ambition's vain, delusive dreams are fled,
> And now I wake to darkness, guilt and horror.
> I cannot bear it! Let me shake it off. –
> 'T wa' not be; my soul is clogged with blood.
> I cannot rise! I dare not ask for mercy.
> It is too late, hell drags me down. I sink,
> I sink – Oh! – my soul is lost forever!
> Oh! (*Dies.*) ('Garrick', 5.4.73–81)

Unfortunately, a history painter is not allowed a lengthy narrative and, as Reynolds himself pointed out in one of his *Discourses*, '[w]hat is done by Painting, must be done at one blow' (*Discourse* 8, 146). The demon behind the pillow was a pictorial counterpart to Macbeth's dying speech and a device to prevent 'the possibility, even for a moment, of mistaking it for the representation of a man dying in a mere painful bodily disease'.[82]

According to Northcote, the problem with the fiend was elsewhere: while Reynolds's artistic intention was fully vindicable, his execution fell short of perfection. He painted the fiend too distinctly to signify immaterial agony:

had he given this fiend a visionary, mysterious, and awful appearance, no one would or could have questioned its usefulness in the composition: but, on the contrary, he has made the figure too palpable and material, and much too vulgar and mean in the idea of its form. Nay, its distinctness is such, that, had it not been rendered unfit and improbable, from its hideousness, it might have passed or been mistaken for an attendant page or dwarf, instead of a terrible and supernatural agent.[83]

In fact, Reynolds's invention was quite similar to the incubus of Fuseli's *The Nightmare* (figure 9), which was a runaway success at the Royal Academy exhibition of 1782. Fuseli's incubus did not simply signal the theme of nightmare but formed an organic part of the haunting terror of

9 Henry Fuseli, *The Nightmare* (1781).

the picture, reverberating with both the vulnerable sensuality of the girl and the male aggression symbolised by the horse. Reynolds's demon only looked bizarre and out of place in the company of the demure nobles. Fuseli himself sneered at Reynolds's 'infernal monkey', whose 'ludicrous meanness destroys that terror which is the soul of the scene'.[84]

To achieve 'visionary, mysterious, and awful' effects using paints and canvas must be a challenge. Before Reynolds, quite a few painters had illustrated the death of Beaufort but they avoided painting the supernatural in one way or another. In Nicholas Rowe's Shakespeare edition (1709), the Cardinal was painted as dead already (figure 10). Both H. François Gravelot (for Thomas Hanmer's Shakespeare edition, figure 11) and Fuseli himself (figure 12) illustrated Beaufort's encounter with the ghost of Gloucester ('He hath no eyes ... look, look, it stands upright / Like lime twigs set to catch my winged soul!', 3.3.14–16)[85] but did not paint the apparition itself: their Cardinals only stared into vacancy. By painting in the little demon, Reynolds gave a tangible expression to an emotional reality, at the (very real) risk of looking ludicrous.

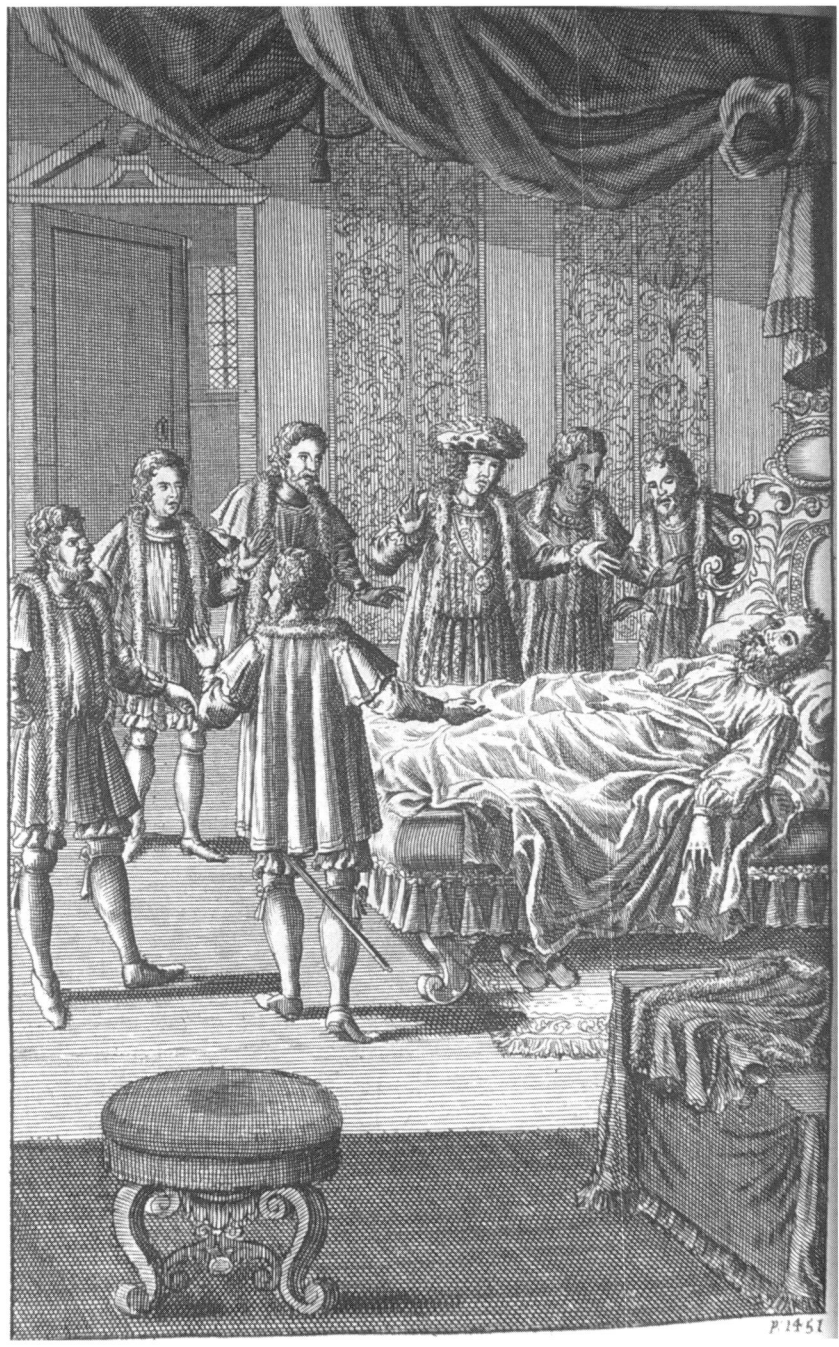
10 [François Boitard], *Henry VI Part 2* (Nicholas Rowe's 1709 edition of Shakespeare).

11 H. François Gravelot, *Henry VI Part 2* (Thomas Hanmer's 1744 edition of Shakespeare).

12 Henry Fuseli, *The Death of Cardinal Beaufort*. Engraved by Moses Haughton.

Reynolds's fiend lived a curious afterlife. It was included in the first stage of Caroline Watson's 1790 engraving of the piece but was partially erased from the second stage (1792; figure 13) onwards, apparently at Boydell's discretion. Probably after the death of the President himself, the noisome presence either faded or was obliterated to near invisibility in the original painting, too.[86]

Macbeth and the Witches (figure 14) was the first piece commissioned by Boydell but was left unfinished at Reynolds's death in 1792. The painter illustrated the play's most supernatural scene, Act 4 scene 1, set in the witches' den, and included not only the hags and other apparitions but also the grotesque objects itemised by the Weird Sisters ('Fillet of fenny snake' and so on) in the canvas.[87] For all his literal-mindedness, Reynolds did not follow the script slavishly but, on the contrary, captured a moment that did not exist in any reading or theatrical versions of the tragedy. Hecate was painted at the pictorial centre, sitting on a bizarre bone throne and frightening Macbeth with an awesome gesture. Unlike in some modern editions that give an exit cue to Hecate (4.1.43) before the entrance of Macbeth

13 Joshua Reynolds, *The Death of Cardinal Beaufort*. Engraved by Caroline Watson.

14 Joshua Reynolds, *Macbeth and the Witches*. Engraved by Robert Thew.

(4.1.47), eighteenth-century reading texts certainly kept her mute on stage until the exit of the witches (4.1.132), and some stage versions also let her speak with the protagonist. However, even in the theatre, the audience had not been treated to as striking a spectacle as this. Probably owing to technical staging difficulties, William Davenant omitted 'an armed Head', 'a bloody Child' and 'a Child crowned with a tree' from his adaptation. Even after Garrick's restoration, the three apparitions entered one by one, while they appear side by side in Reynolds's painting. On stage the witches danced around the cauldron at the beginning of the scene, and the procession of the eight kings and Banquo began only after the cauldron descended. Reynolds painted them all together. Painters do often take liberties with their source materials and Rowe's illustration already included both the cauldron and the procession (figure 15). Reynolds's remarkable composition nonetheless outdid all others in the thoroughgoing exploitation of the supernatural ingredients.

Northcote's response to Reynolds's *Macbeth* curiously contrasted with his reaction to *The Death of Cardinal Beaufort*. Scathing reviews

15 [François Boitard], *Macbeth* (Nicholas Rowe's 1709 edition of Shakespeare). Engraved by Elijah Kirkall (?).

notwithstanding, 'my opinion of this piece is, that the visionary and awful effect produced, both in the conception and execution of the back ground of this picture, is certainly without a parallel in the world – its novelty and its excellence bid defiance to all future attempts at rivalry'. His only reservation concerned the portrayal of Macbeth: 'Had the figure of Macbeth been but equal in its requisite to this appalling scene, the picture would have stood without a companion on earth.'[88] While the fiend behind the pillow looked out of place in the realistic picture of the Cardinal and other nobles, the corporeal Macbeth was incongruous in the predominantly supernatural setting of the witches and apparitions, despite Reynolds's apparent effort to avoid the conflict by shadowing the protagonist heavily and turning his countenance more than half away from the spectator.

Fuseli did not comment on Reynolds's *Macbeth* directly but was by principle against such apposition of terrifying items: 'It is not by the accumulation of infernal or magic machinery, distinctly seen, by the introduction of Hecate and a chorus of female demons and witches, by surrounding him with successive apparitions at once, and a range of shadows moving above or before him, that Macbeth can be made an object of terror.'[89] Fuseli certainly interpreted the terror of the tragedy very differently in *Macbeth Consulting the Vision of an Armed Head* (1793) painted for James Woodmason's *Illustrations of Shakespeare* (figure 16).[90] The painter explained his own invention thus:

I have endeavoured to shew a colossal head rising out of the abyss, and that head Macbeth's likeness. What, I would ask, would be a greater object of terror to you, if, some night on going home, you were to find yourself sitting at your own table, either writing, reading, or otherwise employed? would not this make a powerful impression on your mind?[91]

Lacking Fuseli's tact and inspiration in dealing with the supernatural, Reynolds's Boydell pictures failed to convince the critics. In the 1783 masterpiece, *Sarah Siddons as the Tragic Muse*, however, he had captured an ethereal subject in a very different, and much more forceful, way.

'Bestow upon me some grand Idea': Sarah Siddons as the Tragic Muse

> Sir Joshua often honoured me by his presence at The Theatre ... He always sat in the Orchestra, and in that place were to be seen (O glorious constellation!) Burke, Gibbon, Sheridan, Windham, and 'though last not least', the illustrious Fox of whom it was frequently observed that 'Iron tears were drawn down Plutos cheek'; and these

16 Henry Fuseli, *Macbeth Consulting the Vision of an Armed Head*.

great men would often visit my Dressing Room after the Play, to make their bows and honour me with their applauses.[92]

As she recalled in the last year of her life (1831, aged seventy-five), Sarah Siddons kept a friendly intercourse with Reynolds, among other theatre-going luminaries, from her meteoric London launch in 1782 until his death ten years later, seeking his suggestions on her costume, hairstyle and makeup. He is believed to have proposed the shroudlike white dress that

Siddons wore for Lady Macbeth's sleepwalking.[93] However, in the celebrated *Sarah Siddons as the Tragic Muse* (figure 17), Reynolds did not paint the actress in any of her famous tragic roles, firmly convinced that if 'a Painter should endeavour to copy the theatrical pomp and parade of dress and attitude ... we should condemn such Pictures as painted in the meanest style' (*Discourse* 13, 240). He also avoided painting an intimate portrait of the beautiful woman. His was a representation of Siddons 'as' the Tragic Muse, and the image hovered somewhere between the very personal (Sarah Siddons without theatrical trappings) and the very generic and transcendent (the muse of tragedy).[94] As an indication of the uniqueness of this portraiture, Reynolds even retouched the Muse's countenance to make it look *less* like Siddons. Amid an almost unanimous chorus of admiration, some critics faulted the picture specifically for its excessive idealisation and lack of personal likeness. The *St James Chronicle* reviewed the 1784 Royal Academy exhibition thus:

> This picture last year, for we then had the pleasure of seeing it, gave some intimation and hopes of sublimity. Sir Joshua, it seems, was not satisfied with his first thoughts; and by endeavouring to correct them we think he has lost considerably of their spirit and energy. It is not a strong likeness of the original, it is rather an ideal representation of despair than a copy of Mrs. Siddons' countenance when affected by that passion.[95]

As is well known, Reynolds regarded the predominance of the general over the particular as essential in a grand-style painting: a painter should elevate his picture by eliminating the accidental blemishes and irregularities that abound in the natural world.[96] This principle of generalisation was also applied to portraiture: 'if a portrait-painter is desirous to raise and improve his subject, he has no other means than by approaching it to a general idea', even at the expense of personal likeness (*Discourse* 4, 72). Reynolds apparently followed this rule in *Sarah Siddons as the Tragic Muse*, which critics consider to be in the painter's most elevated style, and achieved the awe-inspiring solemnity requisite in a goddess by retouching the actress's features.

The posture of the actress also delicately balanced the accidental and the transcendental. There are three legends about how the pose was decided. Samuel Rogers claimed that he was in Reynolds's studio 'when Mrs Siddons came in, having walked rapidly to be in time for her appointment': 'She threw herself, out of breath, into an armchair; having taken off her bonnet and dropped her head upon her left hand – the other hand drooping over the arm of the chair. Suddenly lifting her head she said, "How shall I sit?" "Just as you are," said Sir Joshua, and so she is painted.'[97] Another account, by the painter Thomas Phillips, has it that she sat as posed by the artist when she

17 Joshua Reynolds, *Sarah Siddons as the Tragic Muse*.

turned her head to look at a picture on the studio wall. Reynolds liked this new accidental posture and painted it.[98] Siddons's own explanation is the most dramatic and self-congratulatory:

> When I attended him for the first sitting, after many more gratifying encomiums than I dare repeat, he took me by the hand, saying, 'Ascend your undisputed throne, and graciously bestow upon me some grand Idea of The Tragick Muse.' I walked up the steps & seated myself instantly in the attitude in which She now appears. This idea satisfyd him so well that he, without one moment[']s hesitation, determined not to alter it.[99]

All these versions claim that, whether by accident or by inspiration, the posture was determined instantaneously without any preconceived idea on the painter's side. However, at the 1784 Royal Academy exhibition, critics noted Reynolds's borrowing from the prophets and sybils of Michelangelo's Sistine Chapel. As James Boaden recorded:

> Among the triumphs of Mrs. Siddons this year is to be noticed the completion and exhibition of her portrait as the Tragic Muse, by Sir Joshua Reynolds. There were persons, at one time, who affected to doubt the sincerity of that great artist, in his praises of Michael Angelo. But this picture alone proves the intimate feeling by Sir Joshua of his sublime conceptions. Whoever looks at Volpato's engraving of the prophet Joel, one of the sublime series of sybils and prophets in the Sistine Chapel at Rome, will see what he has used, and admire his use of it, in the fine composition of the Tragic Muse. The sway and balance of the figures are the same. The magnificent effect of the drapery, suggested by the Italian, is rivalled by the encreased facility afforded to the English artist by the female habiliments.[100]

By combining the accidents in his studio with the divine example of the sublime maestro, Reynolds surpassed the mere physicality of the actress and ephemeral stage performances. With his usual modesty tinged with uncontainable exultation, the painter reportedly exclaimed upon the work's completion, 'See, gentlemen, behold *my* obligations to MICHAEL ANGELO.'[101]

Ironically, this lofty portrayal of Siddons as muse of tragedy was to make a curious stage appearance at Drury Lane in 1785, when Garrick's *Jubilee* was revived yet again. As a special attraction, Siddons appeared in the Shakespearean procession not in her debut role of Venus but in the same costume and posture as in *Sarah Siddons as the Tragic Muse*:

> The Jubilee was now revived, with what they at that time called splendour, and one grace it had, which no time will ever surpass – Mrs. Siddons drawn in state, as the muse of tragedy; and as well as mere mechanism and motion could compensate the want of back-ground, resembling Sir Joshua Reynolds's sublime portrait of her.[102]

18 Michelangelo, *Isaiah*.

Reynolds's grand-style Tragic Muse, who supposedly surpassed any particular actress, or any single tragedy or performance, was incorporated into the comedy that was occasional and trifling *par excellence*.

Recent X-ray analyses of the canvas show that, while the posture of the Muse remained unchanged, the iconography of the painting went through a considerable modification.¹⁰³ While removing a kneeling putto presenting a scroll from the Muse's feet, Reynolds retouched the facial expression and iconography of one of her attendants in the background. Originally, the figures of Pity (to the left) and Melancholy (to the right) accompanied the Muse, but the right-hand figure was modified into 'Terror' with reference to the facial expression of Reynolds's *Self Portrait as a Figure of Horror* (*c.* 1784). In this way the painter not only accommodated the Aristotelian definition of tragedy, but also paid tribute to the new aesthetics of the sublime of which terror formed a vital part.

Being a popular society painter, Reynolds did not fail to add a fine finishing touch to the portraiture, either. After assuring Siddons that the colours would not fade 'as long as the Canvass would hold them together', he added flatteringly, 'And to confirm my opinion, here is my name, for I have resolved to go down to posterity upon the hem of *your* Garment'. Accordingly, his name was signed on the border of the Muse's drapery.¹⁰⁴

This takes us back to the lecture room of the Royal Academy, 10 December 1790, where Reynolds was rounding up his farewell *Discourse* with an encomium on the sublime Italian painter: 'Yet however unequal I feel myself to that attempt, were I now to begin the world again, I would tread in the steps of that great master: to kiss the hem of his garment, to catch the slightest of his perfections, would be glory and distinction enough for an ambitious man.' Yes, indeed. Reynolds signed his name on the hem of the garment in a portrait in which he got as near as possible to the sublimity of his great predecessor through the process of generalisation and iconographical allusion: 'I reflect not without vanity, that these Discourses bear testimony of my admiration of that truly divine man, and I should desire that the last words which I should pronounce in this Academy, and from this place, might be the name of – MICHAEL ANGELO.' 'Unnerved and tremulous from the exertion of his lecture, he bowed again and again to the hearty plaudits of those whose faces he could but dimly see, and then as with slow uncertain step he was about to quit the chair, Edmund Burke on the impulse of the moment hurried forward, and grasping his old friend's hand warmly in his own, repeated aloud the lines from Milton:

> The angel ended, and in Adam's ear
> So charming left his voice, that he awhile
> Thought him still speaking, still stood fix'd to hear.'¹⁰⁵

My next section is about the aesthetics of the sublime and its relation to the sense of terror as explored by this emotional Irishman, whose Miltonian quotation hazarded a grave unintentional irony, as 'the angel' here referred to is Raphael, not Michael.

5 PUNCH AND THE MADMAN: THE THEATRICAL CAREER OF EDMUND BURKE

> I think often of our Dispute about murdering Sleep and as I have since read that excellent play of my favourite Shakespear I am rather more in love with the passage observe with what horror it's attended. Macbeth, immediately after murdering his royal Guest and all his attendants and describing the Stings of conscience that afflicted him during that horrid work he speaks thus to his Wife
>
> > Macb. Methought I heard a Voice cry, Sleep no more!
> > Macbeth doth Murther Sleep.

Thus wrote Edmund Burke, aged sixteen, to his school friend Richard Shackleton.[106] Two years later, this young theatre fan went on to publish a mock supplication to Thomas Sheridan, father of Richard Brinsley and then manager of the Theatre Royal Dublin, for employment as one of his comedians ('PUNCH's Petition to Mr. S – n, to be admitted into the THEATRE ROYAL').[107] His campaign proved unsuccessful. In the event, Burke would forge his career first as the author of an aesthetic treatise and then as a Whig MP and political thinker in London, and theatre would cease to be his foremost concern. Nevertheless, Burke's early speculations about the art of theatre would define his aesthetic stand and help to deepen his insights into political events, most notably the French Revolution. An obscure theatrical essay from his Dublin days therefore merits a mention here.

Burke, Shackleton and some other local friends published the *Reformer*, featuring theatrical and literary topics, weekly from 28 January to 21 April 1748, and set out 'to expose [the] dullness' of Dublin's Theatre Royal.[108] The single theatrical paper (dated 11 February 1748) that we are sure Burke contributed analysed a recent performance of William Davenant's *Macbeth* at Smock Alley and recommended a general reform of the stage.[109] Burke was exasperated by Davenant's alteration of the masterpiece tragedy as well as by the actors' undignified style and the audience's vulgar taste:

> the Scene of the Witches in *Macbeth*, perhaps the most solemn that can be represented, is burlesqued in such a Manner, that it is surprizing how the People bear, much less applaud it; to see the ridiculous Jiggs they dance, the heavy Jest of the Brooms, the smutty Entendre of the *red hair'd Wench*, *Hecates* Spectacles, and the other such choice Buffooneries; all this before an Audience who profess themselves Admirers of *Shakespear*. (1:78)

David Garrick's (partial) restoration of *Macbeth* at Drury Lane (from 7 January 1744) might have prompted Burke's reprimand that, although the players did not themselves alter the text, they are still 'charg[e]able with all its Faults', as they 'have the Election of two Pieces, and chu[s]e the worst' (1:78).[110]

The stage mirrors the times, and he who regards 'the Honour of his Country' should aim for 'the Correction of Stage Abuses'. Sadly, reformation did not seem imminent in Dublin: 'such a Transition from the grossest of Buffooneries to real Action, cannot be soon expected, on People long immersed in Folly, Conviction works but slowly'. The theatrical vice was perpetuated equally by actors, the audience (who 'may be rather called Spectators'), and playwrights and adapters. The actors and the audience owed their bad taste to each other ('We know the Actors will say . . . they comply with the Taste of their Audience; we answer . . . were they [i.e. spectators] used a while to better Plays, and better Customs, they would as much despise these Things as they now approve them'). The poor taste of the audience in its turn impoverished the art of playwriting, 'for the Poet depending as well for his Reputation, as Subsistence on the People, is often oblig'd to please them at the Expence of his Judgment' (1:79–80).

Athenians used to show exquisite taste in drama and even banned Euripides' *Hippolytus* 'because some Things were said in it, to invalidate the Sanction of Oaths, tho' in the Mouth of one who spoke them in Character'. Dubliners, on the other hand, were 'far from being disgusted at seeing any thing immoral represented' and indeed they were 'seldom better pleas'd'. There was scarcely an English tragedy 'in which there is not some Body butchered on the Stage' thanks to 'the Passion the People have for the Actor's Dying', though onstage fighting and killing never really succeeded 'in raising Terror' and even carried 'something ridiculous with it'. The audience's 'Taste for what is vicious, what is unnatural' coupled with the custom of 'impertinent Clapping' and 'hissing' killed tragedy in Dublin (1:80–2).

For all its naïvety and narrowness of scope, this contrast of true and false tragedy, as well as of good and bad theatrical performance and reception, would provide a framework for Burke's aesthetic and political deliberations, to which I turn.

Translating the sublime: Orestes *and* Macbeth

On the evening of 16 October 1769, Dr Johnson and company indulged in their favourite pastime of gossiping about recent literary publications. To Joshua Reynolds's assertion that Elizabeth Montagu's *Essay* 'does her honour', Johnson replied: 'Yes, Sir; it does *her* honour, but it would do nobody else honour. I have, indeed, not read it all. But when I take up the end of a web, and find it packthread, I do not expect, by looking further, to find embroidery. Sir, I will venture to say, there is not one sentence of true criticism in her book.' Fresh from the Stratford Jubilee, David Garrick felt obliged to defend Montagu: 'But, Sir, surely it shews how much Voltaire has mistaken Shakspeare, which nobody else has done.' Johnson, who himself had failed to perform the critical mission in his Shakespeare edition, was unflappable. He argued it was only because 'nobody else has thought it worth while' and that Montagu was like a schoolmaster 'whipping a boy who has construed ill': 'No, Sir, there is no real criticism in it: none shewing the beauty of thought, as formed on the workings of the human heart.'[111]

Then the doctor referred to several publications that had managed to impress him somehow or other, of which Lord Kames's *Elements of Criticism* was one ('I do not mean that he has taught us any thing; but he has told us old things in a new way'). But what still struck Johnson as genuine critical achievement was a publication some twelve years old: 'We have an example of true criticism in Burke's "Essay on the Sublime and Beautiful"; and, if I recollect, there is also Du Bos; and Bouhours, who shews all beauty to depend on truth. There is no great merit in telling how many plays have ghosts in them, and how this ghost is better than that.'[112] Johnson defined the true province of literary criticism against Montagu's flat recounting of preternatural beings in drama: 'You must shew how terrour is impressed on the human heart. – In the description of night in Macbeth, the beetle and the bat detract from the general idea of darkness, – inspissated gloom.'[113] The reference to *Macbeth* might seem somewhat irrelevant in this context, as Burke already preferred actual political drama to theatrical representation and did not even mention the Shakespearean tragedy in the treatise. Johnson's association of *Macbeth* with Burke's sublimity was nonetheless very much along the lines of contemporary discussion on supernaturalism and imagination.

In 1709 Nicholas Rowe introduced his Shakespeare edition with a special remark on the power of 'Imagination' that enabled the playwright to transcend the visible world: 'the greatness of this Author's Genius do's no where so much appear, as where he gives his Imagination an entire Loose, and raises his Fancy to a flight above Mankind and the Limits of the visible World'.[114] Joseph Addison's 'Pleasures of Imagination' (*Spectator*, 3:535–82; nos. 411–21, 21 June–3 July 1712) enlarged on the image-making genius of Shakespeare and applauded his supernatural apparitions in particular. Addison distinguished between the primary pleasures which 'entirely proceed from such Objects as are before our Eyes', and the secondary pleasures which 'flow from the Ideas of visible Objects, when the Objects are not actually before the Eye, but are called up into our Memories, or form'd into agreeable Visions of Things that are either Absent or Fictitious' (3:537). Literary representation of the last-mentioned 'Visions' was discussed in a subsequent instalment ('THERE is a kind or Writing, wherein the Poet quite loses sight of Nature, and entertains his Reader's Imagination with the Characters and Actions of such Persons as have many of them no Existence, but what he bestows on them. Such are Fairies, Witches, Magicians, Demons, and departed Spirits', 3:570). English people generally handle this literary genre well, as they are 'naturally Fanciful, and very often disposed by that Gloominess and Melancholly of Temper ... to many wild Notions and Visions', but Shakespeare 'has incomparably excelled all others':

There is something so wild and yet so solemn in the Speeches of his Ghosts, Fairies, Witches, and the like Imaginary Persons, that we cannot forbear thinking them natural, tho' we have no Rule by which to judge of them, and must confess, if there are such Beings in the World, it looks highly probable they should talk and act as he has represented them. (3:572–3)

Reflecting the contemporary taste for the gothic and the grotesque, Rowe and Addison clearly preferred Shakespeare's unrestrained genius to neo-classical sophistication and decorum.

To the eighteenth-century critics, (pseudo-)Longinus's *On the Sublime* was another epitome of unbridled imagination.[115] Allegedly following the Greek philosopher, John Dennis's *The Grounds of Criticism in Poetry*, for one, analysed the 'Enthusiastick Passion, which is Terror' in relation to 'Gods, Daemons, Hell, Spirits and Souls of Men, Miracles, Prodigies, Enchantments, Witchcrafts, Thunder, Tempests, raging Seas, Inundations, Torrents, Earthquakes, Volcanos, Monsters, Serpents, Lions, Tygers, Fire, War, Pestilence, Famine, &c'.[116] While Longinus's treatise was first and foremost about high rhetorical style, Dennis emphasised violence and transcendental terror disproportionately by subordinating 'all other literary qualities ... to the emotion'.[117]

Shakespearean and Longinian discussions of supernatural imagination merged in a definitive manner in William Smith's influential English translation of the Greek treatise published in 1739.[118] Smith annotated Longinus by quoting from English writers and conjured up not only John Milton but also Shakespeare especially to elucidate the technique of visualisation (*phantasiai*) or, in the translator's wording, 'imagination'.[119] According to Longinus, visualisation 'has now come to be used predominantly of passages where, inspired by strong emotion, you seem to see what you describe and bring it vividly before the eyes of your audience'.[120] He illustrated the device with a passage from Euripides' *Orestes*, where the protagonist in his madness envisions his mother Clytemnestra sending the Furies against him:

> Mother, I beg you, do not drive against me
> These snake-like women with blood-reddened eyes.
> See there! See there! They leap upon me close. (*Orestes* ll. 255–7)

Longinus's other example was from *Iphigenia in Tauris*, where the deranged Orestes is reported as exclaiming, 'Ah, she will slay me, whither shall I flee?' (l. 291). According to him, 'the poet himself saw Furies and compelled the audience almost to see what he had visualized' (217) in these passages. This being a rhetorical treatise, Longinus's interest was in the effective transmission of Euripides' vision to his audience, and the role of the dramatic medium (Orestes) was significantly underplayed.

Smith's annotation deviated significantly from the original discussion in this regard. After quoting from Addison's *Pleasures of Imagination* ('There is not a Sight in Nature so mortifying as that of a Distracted Person, when his Imagination is troubled, and his whole Soul disordered and confused. *Babylon* in Ruins is not so melancholly a Spectacle', 3:579), the translator explained visualisation from the tragic character's point of view:

The consciousness of what he [Orestes] has done is uppermost in his Thoughts, disorders his Fancy, and confounds his Reason. He is strongly apprehensive of divine Vengeance, and the violence of his Fears places the avenging Furies before his Eyes. Whenever the Mind is harrassed [*sic*] by the Stings of Conscience, or the Horrors of Guilt, the Senses are liable to infinite Delusions, and startle at hideous imaginary Monsters.[121]

Smith certainly registered Euripides' excellent portrayal of consternation and was aware that this 'is what *Longinus* commends in *Euripides*'. The emphasis, however, shifted from oratorical technique to dramatic immediacy. Smith amplified his explanation with reference to the visionary dagger in *Macbeth*:

When *Mackbeth* is preparing for the murder of *Duncan*, his Imagination is big with the Attempt, and is quite upon the Rack. Within, his Soul is dismayed with the Horror of so black an Enterprize, and every thing without looks dismal and affrighting. His Eyes rebel against his Reason, and make him start at Images that have no reality;

[Cites 2.1.33–5 ('Is this a dagger ... and yet I see thee still').]
He then endeavours to summon his Reason to his Aid, and convince himself that it is mere Chimera; but in vain, the Terror stamped on his Imagination will not be shook off.
[Cites 2.1.40–1 ('I see thee yet, in form as palpable / As this which now I draw').]
Here he makes a new Attempt to reason himself out of the Delusion, but it is quite too strong.
[Cites 2.1.45–7 ('I see thee still ... There's no such thing').] (146–7 note)

Smith's preoccupation was clearly not Shakespeare's delineation of the 'dagger of the mind' but the murderer's perturbed psychology. Attending likewise to the half-imaginary noises that surprise the guilty couple ('The least Noise, the very sound of their own Voices is shocking and frightful to both', 147 note), Smith went far beyond the Longinian image-making rhetoric and analysed the horror shared by the dramatic characters and the audience: 'Every single Image seems reality, and alarms the Soul. They seize the whole Attention, stiffen and benumb the Sense, the very Blood curdles and runs cold, thro' the strongest abhorrence and detestation of the Crime' (148 note). Annotating Longinus's discussion of the ghost of Achilles from *Polyxena* some pages later, Smith referred once again to Shakespeare:

Ghosts are very frequent in *English* Tragedies; but Ghosts as well as Fairies seem to be the peculiar Province of *Shakespeare*. In such Circles none but he could move with Dignity. That in *Hamlet* is introduced with the utmost Solemnity, awful throughout and majestic. At the appearance of *Banquo* in *Macbeth* ... the Images are set off in the strongest Expression, and strike the Imagination with high degrees of Horror, which is supported with surprising Art through the whole Scene. (151 note)

While Longinus commended Euripides' vivid verbal portrayal of the invisible, Smith discussed Shakespeare's ghosts not only as a piece of rhetoric but also as drama. Judging by such words as 'introduce' and 'appearance' in the quotation above, Smith might even have had theatrical effects in mind.

Longinus's discussion was so transformed in Smith's footnote as to anticipate Burke and to explore 'How terrour is impressed on the human heart'. In fact, this confluence of Longinian sublimity and Shakespearean tragedy in Smith was of special importance to Burke's thinking, as he bought his second copy of the translation on 24 January 1746/7 and gave it to Shackleton, recommending it as 'a very good translation' with 'no bad notes'.[122]

A recipe for terror: the sublime, the beautiful and the tragic

Burke's *Philosophical Enquiry into the Origin of Our Ideas of the Sublime and the Beautiful* is conspicuous for its exclusive attention to terror as the source of the strong emotion he called the sublime. According to his theory, 'Whatever is fitted in any sort to excite the ideas of pain, and danger, that is to say, whatever is in any sort terrible, or is conversant about terrible objects, or operates in a manner analogous to terror, is a source of the *sublime*; that is, it is productive of the strongest emotion which the mind is capable of feeling.'[123] Unlike the counterpart concept of 'the beautiful', which stems from the enjoyment of 'society' and is accompanied by the sense of pleasure, sublimity arises when the principle of 'self-preservation' is threatened. The sublime is a much stronger emotion than the beautiful as 'the torments which we may be made to suffer, are much greater in their effect on the body and mind, than any pleasures which the most learned voluptuary could suggest, or than the liveliest imagination, and the most sound and exquisitely sensible body could enjoy' (1:216–17). Burke illustrated his point by citing a striking example: 'Nay I am in great doubt, whether any man could be found who would earn a life of the most perfect satisfaction, at the price of ending it in the torments, which justice inflicted in a few hours on the late unfortunate regicide in France' (1:217). This being a 1757 publication, the 'late unfortunate regicide' cannot be one of the Jacobin chiefs who guillotined Louis XVI and Marie-Antoinette in 1793. In fact, Burke's reference was to one Robert Francis Damiens, who made an attempt on the life of Louis XV on 5 January 1757 and, after cruel tortures, was put to death by *écartèlement* on 28 March. Nevertheless, this aesthetic treatise not only looked back to Burke's earlier interest in theatrical performances but also looked forward with curious anticipations to the French Revolution and the Reign of Terror with which his name is most strongly associated.

Burke's sublimity departed from the Longinian model at several points. His interest was not primarily verbal, and the evocative power of language was discussed only cursorily in the final section (1:309–20). Second, while Longinus demanded vivid visualisation even of ghosts and hallucinations, Burke extolled obscurity, reminding the reader 'how much the notions of ghosts and goblins, of which none can form clear ideas, affect minds, which give credit to the popular tales concerning such sorts of beings'. It was 'one thing to make an idea clear, and another to make it *affecting* to the imagination', and it was 'our ignorance of things that causes all our admiration, and chiefly excites our passions'. For Burke, a clear idea was 'another name for a little idea' (1:231–5). Third, while the Longinian sublime required highly sophisticated rhetoric, Burke emphasised natural emotion. His sublimity 'anticipates our reasonings, and hurries us on by an irresistible force' (1:230). The popular 'associationism' was repudiated on this count. Defying John Locke's view that darkness is terrible because of the associated ideas of ghosts and goblins, Burke firmly believed that darkness is 'terrible in its own nature' (1:294–6).

In Burke's aesthetic system tragedy occupied a precarious position. While tragic experience was predominantly terrible and sublime, 'the EFFECTS of TRAGEDY' were discussed in terms of 'sympathy', which was among the 'passions belonging to general society' constituting 'the beautiful'. The Aristotelian attributes of tragedy (terror and pity), therefore, were translated into Burke's binary system of the sublime (consisting of terror, pain and delight, and self-interest) and the beautiful (pity, pleasure and grief, and altruism) as follows: 'terror is a passion which always produces delight when it does not press too close, and pity is a passion accompanied with pleasure, because it arises from love and social affection'. Against the critical commonplace that tragedy pleases because it is only an imitation of reality, Burke believed that tragic events in real life are pleasurable in themselves and that 'we shall be much mistaken if we attribute any considerable part of our satisfaction in tragedy to a consideration that tragedy is a deceit, and its representations no realities'.[124] Theatre could be quite interesting and engaging, but 'be its power of what kind it will, it never approaches to what it represents' (1:221–4). He illustrated his point by comparing a theatrical and a political tragedy:

> Chuse a day on which to represent the most sublime and affecting tragedy we have; appoint the most favourite actors; spare no cost upon the scenes and decorations; unite the greatest efforts of poetry, painting and music; and when you have collected your audience, just at the moment when their minds are erect with expectation, let it be reported that a state criminal of high rank is on the point of being executed in the adjoining square; in a moment the emptiness of the theatre would demonstrate the comparative weakness of the imitative arts, and proclaim the triumph of the real sympathy. (1:223)

Once our own safety is guaranteed, the sublimity and beauty of a tragedy only increases if the distress is real: 'We delight in seeing things, which so far from doing, our heartiest wishes would be to see redressed' (1:223).

Some thirty years after the publication of the *Enquiry*, Edmond Malone encouraged his old friend to revise the treatise to incorporate the insights that experience of the world had furnished. Burke declined the entreaty, saying that 'the train of his thoughts had gone another way, and the whole bent of his mind turned from such subjects; that he was much fitter for such speculations at the time he published that work ... than now'.[125] We have every reason to believe that the 'train of his thoughts' had gone a very different way, as Malone's entreaty was made in the critical July of 1789. Nevertheless, Burke's response to the French Revolution strongly echoed both his youthful theatrical theory and his aesthetics of the sublime, which is the topic of my final section.

Burke's regicide show: Reflections on the Revolution in France

> I cannot consider Mr Burke's book in scarcely any other light than a dramatic performance; and he must, I think, have considered it in the same light himself, by the poetical liberties he has taken of omitting some facts, distorting others, and making the whole machinery bend to produce a stage effect.[126]

In *The Rights of Man* (1791), the defender of the French Revolution Thomas Paine accused Burke's *Reflections on the Revolution in France*, published the year before, of factual inaccuracy and arbitrary (and deliberate) sentimentalisation of the 'tragic' French royal family:

> As to the tragic paintings by which Mr Burke has outraged his own imagination, and seeks to work upon that of his readers, they are very well calculated for theatrical representation, where facts are manufactured for the sake of show, and accommodated to produce, through the weakness of sympathy, a weeping effect. But Mr Burke should recollect that he is writing History, and not Plays; and that his readers will expect truth, and not the spouting rant of high-toned exclamation. (71–2)

Paine was certainly right. Burke did regard the Revolution as a piece of theatre. He resented, however, that the performance was not genuinely tragic. Echoing his own *Reformer* essay on *Macbeth*, he looked on the Revolution as a 'monstrous tragic-comic scene' where 'the most opposite passions' alternated and mixed with each other: 'The most wonderful things are brought about in many instances by means the most absurd and ridiculous; in the most ridiculous modes; and, apparently, by the most contemptible instruments.'[127] To Burke, the members of the National Assembly were 'like the comedians of a fair' staging a 'profane burlesque' or 'farce of deliberation with as little decency as liberty' before 'a mixed mob of ferocious men, and of women lost to shame, who, according to their insolent fancies, direct, control, applaud, explode them' (229–30).

The centrepiece of his *Reflections* was the mob's attack on the royal family at Versailles on 6 October 1789. Apparently inspired by the massacre of the Macduffs, this Irish 'playwright' made the most of the drama of the Bourbons' sleepless night:

the king and queen of France, after a day of confusion, alarm, dismay, and slaughter, lay down, under the pledged security of public faith, to indulge nature in a few hours of respite, and troubled melancholy repose. From this sleep the queen was first startled by the voice of the centinel at her door, who cried out to her, to save herself by flight – that this was the last proof of fidelity he could give – that they were upon him, and he was dead. Instantly he was cut down. A band of cruel ruffians and assassins, reeking with his blood, rushed into the chamber of the queen, and pierced with an hundred strokes of bayonets and poniards the bed, from whence this persecuted woman had but just time to fly almost naked, and through ways unknown to the murderers had escaped to seek refuge at the feet of a king and husband, not secure of his own life for a moment. (232)

This best-known passage of *Reflections* is notable for its factual inaccuracies: the sentinel was not murdered (Burke's son was to meet him in Cologne many years after the Revolution and report him well), nor did the queen fly naked.[128] The mob enacted this horrible spectacle only in Burke's mental theatre. Two gentlemen of the king's guard were beheaded: 'Their heads were stuck upon spears, and led the procession; whilst the royal captives who followed in the train were slowly moved along, amidst the horrid yells, and shrilling screams, and frantic dances, and infamous contumelies, and all the unutterable abominations of the furies of hell, in the abused shape of the vilest of women' (233).

Since Hindson and Gray's innovative study, Burke's theatrical metaphors have been explored extensively.[129] But it was not only the burlesqued tragic performance that enraged him: the Revolution was also an issue of playwriting and theatrical criticism. While the Revolutionary legislators used 'the declamations and the buffooneries of satirists' (341) to regulate the society, the leaders of the Enlightenment supplied them with the promptbooks. David Hume informed Burke of the dramaturgy of a representative Enlightenment playwright:

Mr. Hume told me, that he had from Rousseau himself the secret of his principles of composition. That acute, though eccentric, observer had perceived, that to strike and interest the public, the marvellous must be produced; that the marvellous of the heathen mythology had long since lost its effect; that giants, magicians, fairies, and heroes of romance which succeeded, had exhausted the portion of credulity which belonged to their age; that now nothing was left to a writer but that species of the marvellous, which might still be produced, and with as great an effect as ever, though in another way; that is, the marvellous in life, in manners, in characters, and in extraordinary situations, giving rise to new and unlooked-for strokes in politics and morals. (342)

Jean-Jacques Rousseau and other leaders of the Enlightenment composed the new political drama as 'a sport of fancy, to try their talents, to rouze attention, and to excite surprize' (342). To them, the political disturbance was only a substitute for the preternatural beings that once entertained the readers and spectators by titillating their base curiosity. The leaders of the Revolution mistook Rousseau's sardonic work for a high tragedy and put on the incongruous regicide show.

Back in Britain, the Revolution was an issue of true and false drama criticism. Burke contrasted his own genuine appreciation of tragedy with the ignoble delight indulged by the Rev. Richard Price. Once again echoing *Macbeth*, Burke compared Price's pro-Revolutionary preaching at the Old Jewry on 4 November 1789 to a dubious 'cauldron' ('a very extraordinary miscellaneous sermon, in which there are some good moral and religious sentiments, and not ill expressed, mixed up in a sort of porridge of various political opinions and reflections: but the revolution in France is the grand ingredient in the cauldron', 155). Price's exultation over the 'Theban and Thracian Orgies, acted in France' was detestable to Burke, as it was a facile and undignified theatrical response: 'Is this a triumph to be consecrated at alters? to be commemorated with grateful thanksgiving? to be offered to the divine humanity with fervent prayer and enthusiastick ejaculation? . . . At first I was at a loss to account for this fit of unguarded transport' (233–4). Burke's response to this 'revolution in sentiments, manners, and moral opinions' was entirely different: 'Why do I feel so differently from the Reverend Dr. Price, and those of his lay flock, who will choose to adopt the sentiments of his discourse?'

> For this plain reason – because it is *natural* I should; because we are so made as to be affected at such spectacles with melancholy sentiments upon the unstable condition of mortal prosperity, and the tremendous uncertainty of human greatness; because in those natural feelings we learn great lessons; because in events like these our passions instruct our reason; because when kings are hurl'd from their thrones by the Supreme Director of this great drama, and become the objects of insult to the base, and of pity to the good, we behold such disasters in the moral, as we should behold a miracle in the physical order of things. (243)

Burke rejected the crowd-pleasing spectacles and chose to see in them an authentic tragedy. He regarded his own response to the Revolution as 'natural' and believed that instinctive reactions ('our passions') would transcend the post-Enlightenment 'reason'. The burlesque of the French mob was reread and sublimated in Burke's mind as 'this great drama' staged by the 'Supreme Director', so as to create a purely Aristotelian catharsis: 'We are alarmed into reflexion; our minds (as it has long since been observed) are purified by terror and pity; our weak unthinking pride is humbled, under the dispensations of a mysterious wisdom' (243).

Continuing in this conspicuous passive construction, Burke revealed his theatrical perception of the Revolution when he added, 'Some tears might be drawn from me, if such a spectacle were exhibited on the stage.' Echoing his aesthetic discussion of many years ago, but in considerably stronger terms, Burke prioritised the real over the theatrical tragedy, the excellence of his favourite actor and actress notwithstanding:

> I should be truly ashamed of finding in myself that superficial, theatric sense of painted distress, whilst I could exult over it in real life. With such a perverted mind, I could never venture to shew my face at a tragedy. People would think the tears that Garrick formerly, or that Siddons not long since, have extorted from me, were the tears of hypocrisy; I should know them to be the tears of folly. (243)

In fact, compared with churches where such as Price preach, theatres were 'a better school of moral sentiments' where people would follow 'their *natural* impulses' rather than 'the odious maxims of a Machiavelian policy' (224; emphasis added). Burke still entertained the same misgivings over contemporary theatregoers as in the early *Reformer* pamphlet but hoped that they would behave better this time. Once again citing the banishment of Euripides' *Hyppolitus* by Athenians:

> They would reject them [i.e. distorted political ideas] on the modern, as they once did on the antient stage, where they could not bear even the hypothetical proposition of such wickedness in the mouth of a personated tyrant, though suitable to the character he sustained. No theatric audience in Athens would bear what has been borne, in the midst of the real tragedy of this triumphal day. (244)

In the theatre 'the first *intuitive* glance, without any elaborate process of reasoning, would shew, that this method of political computation, would justify every extent of crime' but, because of the dogmatic 'rights of men', people had lost 'all *natural* sense of wrong and right' (244; emphases added). No doubt Burke would have liked the people in France to behave and respond to the tragedy of the Bourbons after the good examples of Sir Roger de Coverly and Mr Partridge.

From a dramaturgical point of view, something was grievously missing from the French performance at this stage. The king and queen of France were imprisoned but were still alive. Burke's reference to 'regicide' was still very premature and revealed not only a strong anxiety but also a hidden expectation of a tragic denouement in this defender of the French monarchy. Burke imputed this anticipation to the bad taste of the French mob (here ironically called 'worthy gentlemen'):

> There was, however (as in all human affairs there is) in the midst of this joy something to exercise the patience of these worthy gentlemen, and to try the long-suffering of their faith. The actual murder of the king and queen, and their child,

was wanting to the other auspicious circumstances of this *'beautiful day'*. The actual murder of the bishops, though called for by so many holy ejaculations, was also wanting. A groupe of regicide and sacrilegious slaughter, was indeed boldly sketched, but it was only sketched. It unhappily was left unfinished, in this great history-piece of the massacre of innocents. What hardy pencil of a great master, from the school of the rights of men, will finish it, is to be seen hereafter. (234–5)

Burke advised, 'If it had been thought justifiable and expedient to make such a revolution by such means, and through such persons, as you have made yours, it would have been more wise to have completed the business of the fifth and sixth of October' (371).

Louis XVI was executed on 21 January 1793. Burke had been enquiring after and worrying over the fate of the French royals and had 'looked for something of that kind as inevitable, from the day that the Rights of man were declared'. The execution overwhelmed him nonetheless. In a letter to Lord Loughborough, he expressed his emotion once again in dramatic terms: 'Since I saw you last, the Catastrophe of the Tragedy of France has been compleated. It was the necessary result of all the preceeding parts of that monstrous Drama.'[130] Burke would spend the rest of his years preaching a holy war against the French 'regicides' and earning the reputation of 'an ingenious madman'.[131] Let me cite a final ghost story from Burke's impassioned anti-France propaganda, *Four Letters on the Proposals for Peace with the Regicide Directory of France* (1796). The erstwhile theoriser of aesthetic terror was now to end his life witnessing the drama of the Terror and its aftermath ('I shall not live to behold the unravelling of the intricate plot, which saddens and perplexes the awful drama of Providence, now acting on the moral theatre of the world').[132] In Burke's mental theatre 'a vast, tremendous, unformed spectre' rose out of the tomb of the Bourbons 'in a far more terrific guise than any which ever yet have overpowered the imagination and subdued the fortitude of man'. This frightful ghost, which Burke called 'the Republick of Regicide', confounded the world with its 'unnatural' principles:

Going straight forward to its end, unappalled by peril, unchecked by remorse, despising all common maxims and all common means, that hideous phantom overpowered those who could not believe it was possible she could at all exist, except on the principles, which habit rather than nature had persuaded them were necessary to their own particular welfare and to their own ordinary modes of action. (7–8)

The French public indulged in ignoble spectacles in the meantime. While courts of justice and churches were thrust out by revolutionary tribunals, 'there were no fewer than nineteen or twenty theatres, great and small, most of them kept open at the public expense, and all of them crowded every night':

> Among the gaunt, haggard forms of famine and nakedness, amidst the yells of murder, the tears of affliction, and the cries of despair, the song, the dance, the mimick scene, the buffoon laughter, went on as regularly as in the gay hour of festive peace. I have it from good authority, that under the scaffold of judicial murder, and the gaping planks that poured down blood on the spectators, the space was hired out for a shew of dancing dogs. (77–8)

3

'Speak the speech, I pray you': Kean, Hamlet and the Romantic 'playwrights'

I SEVERAL MIRRORS UP TO NATURE: REYNOLDS AND JOHNSON, BLAKE AND HAZLITT

Difference of opinion: a pitiful case

> The villain at the gallows tree
> When he is doomed to die,
> To assuage his misery
> In virtue's praise does cry.
>
> So Reynolds, when he came to die
> To assuage his bitter woe,
> Thus aloud did howl and cry
> 'Michael Angelo! Michael Angelo!'[1]

However genuine the anger, William Blake hardly did justice to the critical and artistic integrity of the President of the Royal Academy, either in his series of incredibly malicious verses that included 'A Pitiful Case', cited above, or in his equally ferocious marginal notes in his copy of the first eight *Discourses*.[2] In the latter case Blake condemned Reynolds's inconsistencies by deliberately neglecting the discursive context and confusing the different levels of artistic sophistication that each lecture addressed. He was also in the nasty habit of regarding the President's humility and reverence for other artists as a mere hypocritical gesture.[3] As Blake himself admitted, the acrimony was due in part to the all-too-common resentment felt by a frustrated young artist towards an authoritative figure of the preceding generation ('Having spent the Vigour of my Youth & Genius under the Op[p]ression of Sr Joshua & his Gang of Cunning Hired Knaves Without Employment & as much as could possibly be Without Bread, The Reader must Expect to Read in all my Remarks on these Books Nothing but Indignation & Resentment').[4] Despite (or even because of)

19 Daniel Maclise, *The Play Scene in* Hamlet *exhibited 1842*.

the arbitrariness and the unfairness to the imposing predecessor, the marginalia pointed sharply to the issues of difference by which the pre-Romantic engraver and poet defined his own artistic stand.

Annotating the (for him final) *Discourse* 8, Blake reviewed his own marginalia and noticed a curious coincidence:

Burke's Treatise on the Sublime & Beautiful is founded on the Opinions of Newton & Locke; on this Treatise Reynolds has grounded many of his assertions in all his Discourses. I read Burke's Treatise when very Young; at the same time I read Locke on Human Understanding & Bacon's Advancement of Learning; on Every one of these Books I wrote my Opinions, & on looking them over find that my Notes on Reynolds in this Book are exactly Similar. I felt the Same Contempt & Abhorrence then that I do now. (316)

Unfortunately, Blake's marginalia on these writings do not survive,[5] but they must primarily have been to do with their empiricism and mechanical explanations of human behaviour and psychology. For these philosophers, there was no such thing as born genius or divine inspiration, or as Blake put it in the subsequent passage: 'They mock Inspiration & Vision. Inspiration & Vision was then, and now is, & I hope will always Remain, my Element, my Eternal Dwelling place; how can I then hear it Contemned without returning Scorn for Scorn?' (316).

While preaching mistrust of born genius ('You must have no dependence on your own genius', *Discourse* 2, 35), Reynolds encouraged artistic imitation or 'the following other masters': only by patiently imitating the examples of the past masters can a painter acquire the proficiency and style necessary to achieve grandeur. Artistic servility of this sort was totally unacceptable to Blake:

Bacon's Philosophy has Destroy'd [word cut away] Art & Science. The Man who says that the Genius is not Born, but Taught – Is a Knave.
  O Reader, behold the Philosopher's Grave!
  He was born quite a Fool, but he died quite a Knave. (309)

Reynolds's faith in diligent learning certainly resonated with the empiricism of *The Advancement of Learning* and understandably offended Blake's Romantic belief in man's individuality and unadulterated (or unadulterable) personality: 'How ridiculous it would be to see the Sheep Endeavouring to walk like the Dog, or the Ox striving to trot like the Horse; just as Ridiculous it is to see One Man Striving to Imitate Another. Man varies from Man more than Animal from Animal of different Species' (309). Reynolds's version of the *tabula rasa* theory ('The mind is but a barren soil; a soil which is soon exhausted, and will produce no crop') enraged Blake, who wrote that 'The mind that could have produced this Sentence must have been a Pitiful, a Pitiable Imbecillity. I always thought that the Human Mind was the most Prolific of All Things & Inexhaustible. I certainly do Thank God that I am not like Reynolds' (310). Reynolds's emphasis on imitation and training was an unmistakable part of the empirical tradition that Blake detested.

  Blake's association of Edmund Burke with the *Discourses* must have been strengthened by what Reynolds variously denominated as 'the general character', 'the grand (or great) style', or most explicitly 'the sublime' in painting, as well as their counterpart concepts of 'the elegant', 'the central form' and 'the beauty'. Unlike in Burke's formulation, Reynolds's sublimity was concerned less with danger and horror than with lofty conception and forceful execution and effects. His grand style was also a technical question of imitation, and should be achieved by imitating nature, along with past masters, in a specific way. While dimness and obscurity contributed to Burke's sublimity, Reynolds would leave out accidental details and blemishes when painting natural objects so as to transcend occasionality and achieve grandeur. The very first anecdote of Reynolds's inaugural *Discourse*, which portrayed the moment of epiphany when the young Raphael achieved his grand style, housed all his artistic creeds:

RAFFAELLE, it is true, had not the advantage of studying in an Academy; but all Rome, and the works of MICHAEL ANGELO in particular, were to him an Academy. On the sight of the CAPELLA SISTINA, he immediately from a dry,

Gothick, and even insipid manner, which attends to the minute accidental discriminations of particular and individual objects, assumed that grand style of painting, which improves partial representation by the general and invariable ideas of nature. (15–16)[6]

Blake was outraged by Reynolds's repudiation of Raphael's 'own genius' and preference for the 'general' and 'invariable' over the 'minute' and 'accidental' in nature:

Minute Discrimination is Not Accidental. All Sublimity is founded on Minute Discrimination.
 I do not believe that Rafael taught Mich. Angelo, or that Mich Angelo taught Rafael, any more than I believe that the Rose teaches the Lilly how to grow, or the Apple tree teaches the Pear tree how to bear Fruit. I do not believe the tales of Anecdote writers when they mitigate against Individual Character. (292)

However righteous (or otherwise) the assertion, Blake was rather too cruel and harsh to the President, who was just opening an Academy and was strongly expected to say something uplifting to the new teachers who were to teach young artists of various degrees of mediocrity. How could the President have denounced the possibility of one artist teaching another in his inaugural lecture? This regrettable episode of artistic antagonism between the two excellent painters assumed a further significance when another critic and sometime painter joined the chorus quite independently of Blake and criticised the *Discourses*. This third writer did away with Blake's acrimony but shared all his disagreements with the senior painter. Interestingly to us, he would reuse the tenets of the artistic controversy to contest with another imposing authority in the field of Shakespeare studies, too.

Painter's eye

William Hazlitt's early ambition was to become a portrait painter. He learnt the basic elements of the art from his brother John, who in his turn had studied under Reynolds. Hazlitt then spent four months in Paris in 1802–3 and copied several pictures in the Louvre. After returning to London, he painted quite a few portraits, including that of Hartley Coleridge, William Wordsworth (which was destroyed as unsatisfactory) and the famous one of Charles Lamb as a Venetian Senator.[7] But he gave up on the idea of painting professionally around 1805, realising that his pictures did not meet his own high artistic standards. However, a lifelong love for art was nurtured. He subsequently published insightful essays on paintings and art theories and, I would contend, this painter's viewpoint affords a key to understanding Hazlitt's various writings, Shakespeare criticism among them.[8]

The achievements of Reynolds as painter and art theorist were a topic to which Hazlitt frequently recurred.[9] The most comprehensive survey of the *Discourses* appeared in four instalments in the *Champion* from 27 November 1814 to 8 January 1815. Unlike the furious Blake, Hazlitt appreciated Reynolds's eloquence and taste but still believed that his opinions were 'liable ... to various objections' and that his errors were 'not casual, but systematic'. Reynolds's conclusions were 'either false or only true in part' and led English painters to a fatal error: 'The English school of painting is universally reproached by foreigners with the slovenly and unfinished state in which they send their productions into the world, with their ignorance of academic rules and neglect of the subordinate details; in other words, with aiming at *effect* only in all their works of art' (18:62–3). Concluding the first essay, Hazlitt summarised Reynolds's harmful doctrines under six headings, covering the same issues of imitation of other artists (no. 1) and of nature (nos. 2–6) as in Blake's marginalia:

1. *That genius or invention consists chiefly in borrowing the ideas of others, or in using other men's minds.*
2. *That the great style in painting depends on leaving out the details of particular objects.*
3. *That the essence of portrait consists in giving the general character, rather than the individual likeness.*
4. *That the essence of history consists in abstracting from individuality of character and expression as much as possible.*
5. *That beauty or ideal perfection consists in a central form.*
6. *That to imitate nature is a very inferior object in art.* (18:63)

The second essay ('On Genius and Originality') exploded the fallacies of Reynolds's theory of artistic imitation. Hazlitt criticised as 'vague', 'contradictory' and 'biased' such beliefs as 'by imitation [of past masters] only, variety, and even originality of invention, is produced' (*Discourse* 6, 96). Unlike the furious Blake, Hazlitt understood the pedagogical context of Reynolds's discussion ('[Reynolds] was apprehensive that if genius were allowed to stand for any thing, industry would go for nothing in the minds of "the vain, the ignorant, and the idle"'), but regretted that the President 'from his unwillingness to admit one extreme, has fallen into the other' (18:70). By overemphasising industry, he slighted genius and originality. Hazlitt also suspected that Reynolds was glossing over the process of artistic imitation (or even poaching) 'from which he himself derived such felicitous results' but which 'can only produce mediocrity and imbecility' when employed indiscriminately in educating young artists (18:66).[10]

Hazlitt's main objection was to Reynolds's theory of imitation of nature, and the two remaining instalments respectively examined the possibility and validity of likeness mainly in portraiture ('On the Imitation of Nature') and in history painting ('On the Ideal'). While Reynolds advocated generalisation and idealisation 'from supposing the imitation of particulars to be inconsistent with general truth and effect', Hazlitt believed that artistic excellence depends 'not on the separation, but on the union (as far as possible) of general truth and effect with individual distinctness and accuracy' (18:70). The critic not only challenged Reynolds's artistic use of nature but also reversed his whole conception of it when he added, 'Nature contains both large and small parts, – both masses and details; and the same may be said of the most perfect works of art' (18:71). For Reynolds, any individual component of nature was 'irregular', 'accidental' and full of 'defects', and had to be patched up by an artist's hand. Even such a celebrated beauty as Sarah Siddons was no exception. For Hazlitt, it was nature that achieved the exemplary combination of seemingly incongruous details and the whole.

Hazlitt applied the same reasoning to history painting in the final instalment. While portraiture represents a sitter 'such as he is in himself', history painting delineates a character 'as he is likely to be' and shares its fictionality with poetry, novel and drama. History painters, therefore, should emulate the natural characterisation of Chaucer, Shakespeare and Henry Fielding. Hazlitt epitomised his belief by quoting from *Hamlet*: the optimum combination of the whole and the detail should be achieved in history painting, or indeed any painting, 'whose end and use both at the first, now is, and was, to hold as 'twere the mirror up to nature' (18:80).

At this point the critic regretted that an eminent scholar shared Reynolds's false doctrines and emphasised the overall effect of Shakespeare's characterisation to the detriment of his excellent details: 'Dr. Johnson, proceeding on the same theoretical principles as his friend Sir Joshua, affirms, that the excellence of Shakespeare's characters consists in their generality. We grant in one sense it does; but we will add that it consists in their particularity also' (18:80). This was the claim that Hazlitt set out to demonstrate in *Characters of Shakespear's Plays* (1817).

Characters of Shakespear's Plays

The preface to Hazlitt's 1817 publication included substantial quotations from three distinguished Shakespeareans. First, the critic cited Alexander Pope's tribute to Shakespeare's originality and inspiration ('If ever any author deserved the name of an *original*, it was Shakespear . . . The poetry of Shakespear was inspiration indeed') and his natural characterisation ('His *characters* are so much nature herself') from his Shakespeare edition. Hazlitt's criticism aimed to 'illustrate these remarks [from Pope] in a more particular manner by a reference to each play' (4:171), by following the models supplied by such character critics as Thomas Whately and William Richardson (*A Philosophical Analysis and Illustration of Some of Shakespeare's Remarkable Characters*, 1774).[11]

Second, A. C. Schlegel's eulogy on Shakespeare's genius (in *A Course of Lectures on Dramatic Art and Literature*, 1809–11) was conjured up to refute the third Shakespearean, the formidable Samuel Johnson ('We have the rather availed ourselves of this testimony of a foreign critic in behalf of Shakespear, because our own countryman, Dr. Johnson, has not been so favourable to him', 4:174). Johnson shared Pope's, and Hazlitt's, view in part and stated in his Preface that Shakespeare was 'the poet of nature; that holds up to his readers a faithful mirrour of manners and of life' (*On Shakespeare*, 62). However, Johnson conceived nature in general terms, as can be seen in the additional citation from Reynolds (*Discourse* 4, 73) in the fourth edition of his *Dictionary* published in 1773:

NATURE. 7. The constitution and appearances of things.
The works, whether of poets, painters, moralists, or historians, which are built upon general *nature*, live for ever; while those which depend for their existence on particular customs and habits, a partial view of nature, or the fluctuation of fashion, can only be coeval with that which first raised them from obscurity. *Reynolds*

Johnson's appreciation of Shakespeare's 'natural' portrayal was premised on this general conception: 'Nothing can please many, and please long, but just representations of general nature. Particular manners can be known to few, and therefore few only can judge how nearly they are copied' (*On Shakespeare*, 61). According to Johnson, Shakespeare's characters are not distorted by 'the customs of particular places', 'the peculiarities of studies or professions' or by 'the accidents of transient fashions or temporary opinions'. They are 'the genuine progeny of common humanity, such as the world will always supply, and observation will always find', and they act and speak 'by the influence of those general passions and principles by which all minds are agitated, and the whole system of life is continued in motion'. In short, the Shakespearean character is 'commonly a species' rather than 'an individual' (62).

Hazlitt regarded Johnson's assumptions, or even his critical temper, as unsuitable for understanding Shakespeare. Johnson's thinking was cast 'in a given mould, in a set form', and his understanding 'dealt only in round numbers: the fractions were lost upon him' (4:175). As a result, the unique details of Shakespeare's characterisation were lost sight of. Like Reynolds, who faulted Rubens's landscape for using such accidents as 'a rainbow, storm, or some particular accidental effect of light' (*Discourse* 4, 70), Johnson failed to appreciate the irregular and transient manifestations of beauty that abound in Shakespeare's plays. Hazlitt continued, 'To him an excess of beauty was a fault; for it appeared to him like an excrescence; and his imagination was dazzled by the blaze of light. His writings neither shone with the beams of native genius, nor reflected them. The shifting shapes of fancy, the rainbow hues of things, made no impression on him: he seized only on the permanent and tangible' (4:175). Hazlitt regarded Johnson as not only a faulty Shakespearean but, potentially, a painter of very limited capacity: 'he was to the poet what the painter of still life is to the painter of history' (4:175). The pictorial analogy continued into the following paragraph on Shakespeare's *ekphrates*:

> According to Dr. Johnson, a mountain is sublime, or a rose is beautiful; for that their name and definition imply. But he would no more be able to give the description of Dover cliff in *Lear*, or the description of flowers in *The Winter's Tale*, than to describe the objects of a sixth sense; nor do we think he would have any very profound feeling of the beauty of the passages here referred to. (4:176)

The doctor would have been less than masterly even in the modest genre of landscape and still life.[12]

Johnson's blindness to the particularities of Shakespeare is related to 'the very structure of his style'. In a manner reminiscent of Reynolds's 'central form', Johnson continually balanced out the merits and faults of the dramatist ('He no sooner acknowledges the merits of his author in one line than the periodical revolution of his style carries the weight of his opinion completely over to the side of objection'), and was more concerned with 'maintaining the equilibrium of his style than the consistency or truth of his opinions' (4:177–8). Hazlitt's criticism was diametrically opposed to Johnson's generalised approach ('If Dr. Johnson's opinion was right, the following observations on Shakespear's Plays must be greatly exaggerated, if not ridiculous', 4:178) though it was, in real fact, also a perfect match in its aesthetic bias and idiosyncrasies for its imposing predecessor. The chapter on *Hamlet* furnishes a prime example of Hazlitt's own critical style.

'This is the true Hamlet'

Unlike Samuel Taylor Coleridge, who claimed, 'I have a smack of Hamlet', Hazlitt's equally notorious formulation came in the first person plural: 'It is *we* who are Hamlet' (4:232). Although this was primarily due to Hazlitt's indiscriminate use of 'we' in place of 'I' in his critical writings, the statement did reflect his view that Hamlet naturally combines the general ('the distresses of Hamlet are transferred, by the turn of his mind, to the general account of humanity') and the particular ('The character of Hamlet stands quite by itself', 4:233). In fact, Shakespeare's naturalism is not limited to the protagonist but pervades the whole play, as the plot and the sentiments of other characters also escape artificiality and arbitrariness:

> There is no attempt to force an interest: every thing is left for time and circumstances to unfold. The attention is excited without effort, the incidents succeed each other as matters of course, the characters think and speak and act just as they might do, if left entirely to themselves. There is no set purpose, no straining at a point. The observations are suggested by the passing scene – the gusts of passion come and go like sounds of music borne on the wind. (4:233)

At this point Hazlitt slightly varied the 'mirror up to nature' imagery and stretched his eulogy on Shakespeare's natural imitation to an extent that most Shakespeareans today would find hardly acceptable:

> The whole play is an exact transcript of what might be supposed to have taken place at the court of Denmark, at the remote period of time fixed upon, before the modern refinements in morals and manners were heard of. It would have been interesting enough to have been admitted as a by-stander in such a scene, at such a time, to have heard and witnessed something of what was going on. (4:233)

If Hazlitt had lived in the twenty-first century, he would have compared the play to a fly-on-the-wall reality television show, instead of using the awkward metaphor of 'exact transcript' and eavesdropping. He then enlarged on Shakespeare's psychological truth and immediacy:

> But here we are more than spectators. We have not only 'the outward pageants and the signs of grief'; but 'we have that within which passes shew'. We read the thoughts of the heart, we catch the passions living as they rise. Other dramatic writers give us very fine versions and paraphrases of nature; but Shakespear, together with his own comments, gives us the original text, that we may judge for ourselves. (4:233)

So far so good. For Hazlitt, a special difficulty arose when Shakespeare's lifelike dramatic characters were actually given a new life and reincarnated in the persons of particular actors. Up to this point the discussion had been based exclusively on the critic's reading experience:

> THIS is that Hamlet the Dane, whom we read of in our youth, and whom we may be said almost to remember in our after-years; he who made that famous

soliloquy on life, who gave the advice to the players ... who lived at the court of Horwendillus five hundred years before we were born, but all whose thoughts we seem to know as well as we do our own, because we have read them in Shakespear. (4:232)

The truth of Hamlet's speeches was 'in the reader's mind' and, for Hazlitt, 'this is the true Hamlet' (4:232–3). Stage realisations of the prince inevitably disappointed this dedicated reader: 'We do not like to see our author's plays acted, and least of all, HAMLET. There is no play that suffers so much in being transferred to the stage. Hamlet himself seems hardly capable of being acted' (4:237). This is a shockingly defeatist view from someone who established his journalistic career by contributing an excellent series of theatrical reviews to the *Morning Chronicle*, the *Champion* and other leading periodicals of the day. It is highly ironical, too, as Hazlitt's favourite metaphor of 'mirror up to nature' illustrates in its original context the ultimate goal of acting, not playwriting or painting: 'anything so o'erdone is from the purpose of playing, whose end, both at the first and now, was and is to hold as 'twere the mirror up to nature; to show virtue her feature, scorn her own image, and the very age and body of the time his form and pressure' (3.2.21–5). To examine Hazlitt's reader-oriented and private, as opposed to theatrical and communal, view of Shakespeare, and especially of *Hamlet*, let us visit Drury Lane on 26 January 1814, when his debut as drama critic coincided with the appearance of an astonishing tragedian in London.

2 READERS' *HAMLET*, ACTORS' *HAMLET*

A kindly proposal

Recalling the 1794 performance of *Macbeth* with John Philip Kemble and Sarah Siddons that opened the new Drury Lane theatre, Walter Scott recorded 'an especial reason' why the materialisation of the 'Black Spiritts, and white / Red Spiritts, and Gray' in the witches' den had to be given up: it was not only because there was 'little taste in rendering these aerial beings visible to the bodily eye'. In the group of the four-coloured boy actors, there was 'a blackeyed urchin, yclept *Edmund Kean*', who 'egged on' the other boys and made such confusion on the stage 'that Kemble was fain to dismiss them to the elements'.[13]

Edmund Kean, who was to threaten Kemble's histrionic supremacy in a more serious way just twenty years later, was born in 1787 as the illegitimate son of hawker and itinerant actress Ann Carey. His father is said to have been either Edmund or Aaron Kean, brothers whose third brother was the ventriloquist Moses Kean. Probably through the family connections, the infant Edmund made his way to the stage and played some minor parts. Deserted by his mother, he temporarily found shelter under Uncle Moses, who gave him lessons in elocution. After his uncle's death, he lived with Miss Tidswell (Aunt Tid), an insignificant actress at Drury Lane, who gave him 'further instruction for the stage, and – the sticks'. She endeavoured 'to withdraw his attention from acrobatic pursuits' and 'to awaken in his youthful mind a refined susceptibility to the numberless beauties of the great poet of nature'. Kean studied *Hamlet*, *King Lear*, *Macbeth* and *Othello*, 'each of which, both in conception and execution, opposed a direct contrast to Kemble's manner of doing them':

> Being a constant visitor behind the scenes at Drury-lane Theatre while the performance was going on, it was not difficult for him to detect the adventitious artifice resorted to by Kemble in his representations, and in the general dissonance of that actor's subordination to critical propriety with the unrestrained, unforced, and impulsive aspect of nature, arose that strict fidelity to truth and flexibility of conduct which displayed so beautiful a harmony with the fiery and glowing idea for which he was subsequently distinguished.[14]

Aunt Tid made Edmund say 'Alas! *poor uncle*' in preparation for the apostrophe 'Alas! poor Yorick', so that the lamented demise of Uncle Moses might 'impart to his utterance the requisite combination of pathos, tenderness, and regret'. He accomplished the trick so well that 'the boy himself was moved by the sad and touching melody of his voice as he gave out the words'.[15] In this way Kean grew up in a deeply theatrical ambience.

But triumph as a great tragedian proved hard to come by. After a moderate success as an infant prodigy, Kean endured many years of hardship and poverty as a strolling player. To earn a living he resorted to tightrope dancing, sparring with pugilists and other such acrobatics. He is even known to have accepted a costume role as 'Chimpanzee the Monkey'. Yet eventually, on 26 January 1814, Kean made his comeback to Drury Lane in the role of Shylock and, in spite of the inclement weather and the accordingly small audience, his innovative impersonation that evening instantly stormed the London theatrical world.

Theatre is a collaboration between actors and the audience. Acting premises an audience, and 'great' acting is possible only when the audience appreciates and responds to its greatness. Kean was not particularly successful in provincial theatres but he electrified the London audience. His acting did not change, as the actor himself attested, 'I have done all these things at country theatres, and perhaps better, before I was recognised as a great

London actor; but the applause I received never reached as far as London.'[16] Kean's good luck on the freezing debut evening was that, among the sparse spectators, there were two theatre critics, of whom one was the *Morning Chronicle*'s recruit, William Hazlitt.[17] It was his enthusiastic review ('Mr. Kean's Shylock') that propelled the actor to fame:

MR. KEAN ... last night made his appearance at Drury-Lane Theatre in the character of Shylock. For voice, eye, action, and expression, no actor has come out for many years at all equal to him ... in giving effect to the conflict of passions arising out of the contrasts of situation, in varied vehemence of declamation, in keenness of sarcasm, in the rapidity of his transitions from one tone and feeling to another, in propriety and novelty of action, presenting a succession of striking pictures, and giving perpetually fresh shocks of delight and surprise, it would be difficult to single out a competitor. (5:179)

Hazlitt was already 'a seasoned playgoer' when he started as a theatre critic.[18] He was only twelve when he first saw Kemble act 'admirably as an officer'.[19] The new critic was therefore quite ready to pass judgement on Kean's Richard III with reference to that of the late George Frederick Cooke (5:180–2, 401 note), and to compare Eliza O'Neill with the retired tragic queen Sarah Siddons (5:199). Another rich source of reference for Hazlitt, when it came to Shakespearean drama especially, was his lifelong reading experience. He examined the performance against his literary preconceptions. The encounter of the theatre prodigy Kean with this inveterate reader of Shakespeare necessarily created much tension, and the reviewer tried to reconcile, and make sense out of, the conflicting reading and theatrical experiences, especially in his early articles.

Kean performed his next part, Richard III, on 12 February. Hazlitt commented that 'Mr. Kean's manner of acting this part has one peculiar advantage; it is entirely his own, without any traces of imitation of any other actor [except where his ear had caught in passages the tone of the late Mr. Cooke]' (5:180, 401 note).[20] It was only with a certain reservation, however, that Hazlitt endorsed Kean's Richard, as it is 'possible to form a higher conception of this character (we do not mean from seeing other actors, but from reading Shakespear) than that given by this very admirable tragedian' (5:181). Hazlitt illustrated the 'higher' character of 'Shakespear's' Richard as follows:

The Richard of Shakespear is towering and lofty, as well as aspiring; equally impetuous and commanding; haughty, violent, and subtle; bold and treacherous; confident in his strength, as well as in his cunning; raised high by his birth, and higher by his genius and his crimes; a royal usurper, a princely hypocrite, a tyrant, and a murderer of the House of Plantagenet.

> 'But I was born so high;
> Our airy buildeth in the cedar's top,
> And dallies with the wind, and scorns the sun.' (5:181)

Incidentally, the three lines quoted by Hazlitt (1.3.263–5) were omitted in the Colley Cibber stage version that Kean performed in, but the critic insisted that the 'idea conveyed in these lines ... is never lost sight of by Shakespear, and should not be out of the actor's mind for a moment' (5:181). Little wonder that the actor's Richard failed to satisfy the critic.

This conflict between the literary and the theatrical Shakespeare became especially acute when Kean played his third role of Prince Hamlet. Hazlitt's long review of the performance of 12 March was neatly divided into two halves, the first of which scrutinised 'Shakespear's' characterisation in general and of 'his' Hamlet in particular. Shakespeare is like a good ventriloquist and makes his characters speak as if they were real people. A very case in point is *Hamlet*, which stands out 'for perfect dramatic truth' and whose lines are like 'an exact transcript of what might have taken place at the Court of Denmark five hundred years ago, before the modern refinements in morality and manners', an idea, as we have seen, that he would repeat in *Characters of Shakespear's Plays*. Hazlitt went on to comment on Prince Hamlet:

> The character of Hamlet is itself a pure effusion of genius. It is not a character marked by strength of passion or will, but by refinement of thought and feeling. Hamlet is as little of the hero as a man can well be; but he is 'a young and princely novice', full of high enthusiasm and quick sensibility – the sport of circumstances, questioning with fortune, and refining on his own feelings, and forced from the natural bias of his character, by the strangeness of his situation. (5:185–6)

Shakespeare's (or indeed Hazlitt's) Hamlet is not a stereotypical tragic hero and therefore 'probably of all others the most difficult to personate on the stage' (5:186). His character is 'quite remote from hardness and dry precision' and is spun 'to the finest thread, yet never loses its continuity'. It has 'the yielding flexibility of "a wave of the sea"' and is made up of 'undulating lines, without a single sharp angle' (5:187). While these characteristics sound too intangible to be at all actable, Hazlitt still appreciated Kean's Hamlet ('Yet, in spite of these difficulties, Mr. Kean's representation of the character had the most brilliant success') but once again not without reservation. The critic hastened to add, 'It did not indeed come home to our feelings, as Hamlet (the very Hamlet whom we read of in our youth, and seem almost to remember in our after-years), but it was a most striking and animated rehearsal of the part' (5:187). In Hazlitt's opinion, it was 'less perfect as a whole' though there were 'parts in it of a higher cast of excellence than any part of his Richard [III]'. Impressed as he was by the powerful theatrical moments that the actor created, Hazlitt still found 'his general delineation of the character wrong' (5:187).

After seeing Kean's Iago, Macbeth, Othello and Romeo with similar ambivalence, Hazlitt came up with some kindly advice to the newcomer, who was in fact a very old hand, in the final paragraph of his *Champion* review on 2 January 1815:

> We would, if we had any influence with him, advise him to give one thorough reading to Shakespeare, without any regard to the prompt-book, or to his own cue, or to the effect he is likely to produce on the pit or gallery. If he does this, not with a view to his profession, but as a study of human nature in general, he will, we trust, find his account in it, quite as much as in keeping company with 'the great vulgar, or the small'. (5:406 note)[21]

Hazlitt assured Kean that, by reading Shakespeare properly, he would find 'all that he wants, as well as all that he has: – sunshine and gloom, repose as well as energy, pleasure mixed up with pain, love and hatred, thought, feeling, and action, lofty imagination, with point and accuracy, general character with particular traits, and all that distinguishes the infinite variety of nature'. Kean would 'then', and only then, 'find that the interest of *Macbeth* does not end with the dagger scene, and that *Hamlet* is a fine character in the closet, and might be made so on the stage, *by being understood*'. Hazlitt concluded his proposal by encouraging the actor further: 'He may then hope to do justice to Shakespeare, and when he does this, he need not fear but that his fame will last' (5:406 note). This confrontation between Hazlitt's literary preconceptions and Kean's acting is thrown into clearer perspective when the latter's archrival Kemble comes into the picture.

Kemble's revision (serves two)

> Garrick's nature displaced Quin's formalism: and in precisely the same way did Kean displace Kemble ... It was as sure a thing as Nature against Art, or tears against cheeks of stone.[22]

John Philip Kemble was an extremely good-looking man. He was tall and dark, and his movement was solemn and controlled. 'My brother John', Siddons confided to a friend, 'in his most impetuous bursts, is always careful to avoid any discomposure of his dress or deportment; but in the whirlwind of passion, I lose all thought of such matters.'[23] According to Hazlitt, Kemble's acting 'had always something dry, hard, and pedantic in it', as his delivery was deliberate, slow and affected, 'but his monotony did not fatigue, his formality did not displease; because there was always sense and meaning in what he did' ('Mr. Kemble's Retirement', 5:378). Kemble studied and in many cases reedited his promptbooks carefully, and created his dramatic characters in a scholastic way.

Kean's only physical asset was his brilliant black eyes. Otherwise his physique was 'not only diminutive [at five feet four inches tall] but insignificant'.[24] His voice was so hoarse that the audience assumed that he was suffering from a cold at his London debut. As Kean himself attested, his acting was carefully calculated and premeditated, but it gave the impression of impulsiveness, suddenness, and what Coleridge called 'flashes of lightning' nonetheless.[25]

The partnership with his sister in *Macbeth* apart, Kemble's signature role was Coriolanus. It is not difficult to imagine how the actor's noble features, studied demeanour, and even unnaturalness and awkwardness would have contributed to a successful delineation of the Roman aristocrat who is haughty and aloof to the point of ridiculousness. Just as understandably, Kean's appearance in this role in January 1820 was dismal fare. Hazlitt commented:

> Mr. Kean's acting is not of the patrician order; he is one of the people, and what might be termed a *radical* performer. He can do all that may become a man 'of our infirmity', 'to relish all as sharply, passioned as we'; but he cannot play a God, or one who fancies himself a God, and who is sublime, not in the strength of his own feelings, but in his contempt for those of others, and in his imaginary superiority to them ... The intolerable airs and aristocratical pretensions of which he is the slave, and to which he falls a victim, did not seem *legitimate* in him, but upstart, turbulent, and vulgar. ('The Drama', 18:290)

Among non-Shakespearean characters, Kean's masterpiece was Sir Giles Overreach of Philip Massinger's comedy *A New Way to Pay Old Debts* (1633). His energetic portrayal of the dirty, upstart commoner who tries to wed his daughter to an aristocrat was 'received with shouts of applause' from his first performance in January 1816, and Hazlitt did not hesitate to declare, 'He was not at a single fault' (5:274). With uncharacteristic foolhardiness, Kemble countered his younger rival by playing the same role in May the same year, which proved a disaster. The concerned Hazlitt even suspected a managerial conspiracy against his old favourite ('No doubt, it is the Managers' doing, who by rope-dancing, fire-works, play-bill puffs, and by every kind of quackery, seem determined to fill their pockets for the present, and disgust the public in the end, if the public were an animal capable of being disgusted by quackery', 5:302). Somewhat miraculously, *Hamlet* provided both Kemble and Kean with an opportunity to exert their widely discrepant histrionic personalities. The two tragedians gave the Danish prince entirely different, but equally striking, stage lives. Kemble meddled with the script with typical studiousness: he published seven (slightly) different acting versions and left a promptbook (four copies: two for the theatre, one for his brother Charles, and one for himself) in which stage business and textual modifications were entered meticulously.[26] Kean was not bothered with textual details: Oxberry's 1818 edition citing the actor as Drury Lane's Hamlet followed Kemble's final version very closely.[27]

Unlike either *King Lear* or *Macbeth*, *Hamlet* was not drastically altered for performance in the post-Restoration period.[28] Theatre managers cut, but tended not to add to or rewrite, the promptbook that had derived ultimately from Q2.[29] Their abridgements followed a few basic guidelines. Professedly, they prioritised dramatic action over poetry and rhetoric by omitting 'such places as might be least prejudicial to the Plot or Sense' ('To The Reader', Hamlet 1676), and customarily cut Polonius's instructions to Leartes (1.3) and to Reynaldo (2.1), and Hamlet's reflections on the 'heavy-headed revel' (1.4), on the ideal acting style (3.2) and on Yorick's skull (5.1), along with the foreign issues. Hamlet's first soliloquy lost the repetitive, even obsessive, lamentation over his mother's hasty remarriage (1.2), while the stage ghost shed the droning self-pity and recounted the direful fratricide and incest in a crisp, businesslike fashion (1.5). From the practical viewpoint of stage management, Hamlet's theory of acting ('Speak the speech, I pray you ...', 3.2.1–46) was no doubt far more dispensable than the mundane business message ('How now, my lord? Will the King hear this piece of work?', 3.2.47–8).

While these seemingly neutral theatrical decisions vaguely reflected the neoclassical, even Aristotelian, preference for plot over characterisation,[30] other modifications more specifically responded to the many censures that literary critics hurled at the play's undignified characterisation and clumsy plotting. Jeremy Collier (in *A Short View of the Immorality and Prophaneness of the English Stage*, 1698) led the way by condemning the unseemly behaviour of the deranged 'young Virgin *Ophelia*',[31] to be followed by the anonymous author of 'Some Remarks on the *Tragedy of Hamlet*' (1736), most probably George Stubbes, who found Hamlet's revenge too slow, his wish to condemn Claudius to eternal damnation in the prayer scene too cruel, and his feigned, and Ophelia's real, madness incongruous with their supposed nobility.[32] Samuel Johnson's 'stricture' on *Hamlet* shared much of Stubbes's viewpoint, while George Steevens criticised Hamlet as not only a negligent revenger but also a thoughtless murderer of largely innocent people such as Polonius, Ophelia, and Rosencrantz and Guildenstern.[33] Steevens was especially repulsed by the prince's 'brutal' conduct towards Ophelia and his behaviour at her funeral ('[Hamlet] interrupts the funeral ... insults the brother of the dead, and boasts of an affection for his sister, which, before, he had denied to her face'). Hamlet certainly apologises later on but, as Johnson had also pointed out, he 'has availed himself of a dishonest fallacy' to excuse his rudeness to Laertes.[34]

While character critics such as William Richardson, Samuel Taylor Coleridge and Hazlitt would later counter these neoclassical censures, particularly on Hamlet's behaviour, by speculating on his deep psychology, adapters since William Davenant had long since taken care of the prince's supposed problems through discreet revisions of the promptbook. While eliminating religious words and tinkering with obscenity, Davenant abbreviated Hamlet's rude remarks to Ophelia in the play-within-the-play scene (after F1), and spared the deranged Ophelia both the lewdest lines of the Saint Valentine song ('Then up he rose, and donn'd his clo'es, / And dupp'd the chamber door, / Let in the maid that out a maid / Never departed more', 4.5.52–5), and the embarrassing dialogue of the 'By Gis and by Saint Charity' sequel, where the deserted girl complains, 'Before you tumbled me, You promis'd me to wed.' Only to be answered by her cruel lover, 'So would I a done, by yonder sun, / And thou hadst not come to my bed' (4.5.62–6). Jeremy Collier would have relished the adapter's efforts to preserve the modesty of his 'young Virgin *Ophelia*'. Hamlet's so-called 'cruelty' in the prayer scene also materially diminished when the three bloodiest lines ('Then trip him, that his heels may kick at heaven / And that his soul may be as damn'd and black / As hell, whereto it goes', 3.3.93–5) were cut. The actor Robert Wilks, in cooperation with the poet and editor John Hughes, revised the Davenant adaptation further by restoring Hamlet's two important speeches ('Angels and ministers of grace defend us! ...', 1.4.39–57; 'Speak the speech, I pray you ...', 3.2.1–46) while cutting the dumb show and the final appearance of Fortinbras. This Hughes-Wilks version, first printed in 1718, furnished the basis of most of the eighteenth-century promptbooks.

Garrick's stage version of 1772 departed from Hughes-Wilks but realised an equally, if not more, heroic conception of the Danish prince by editing away the gravediggers and most of Act 5.[35] Missing out on his trip to England, this new Hamlet returned immediately after Ophelia's final exit

(4.5.197; 'Garrick', 5.2.259), fought with Laertes and killed the intervening Claudius. Gertrude was shocked and rushed off stage. Hamlet ran upon Laertes's sword, exchanged forgiveness with him and died. Garrick's Hamlet certainly did '*sweep to my revenge*' ('Garrick', 5.2.62) without delay, cleverly avoiding, or at least downplaying, the deaths of the innocent Ophelia, Gertrude and Laertes.[36]

Kemble based his version on a more conventional theatrical text that had been in use from around 1751.[37] Adding to the Hughes-Wilks cuts, this stage version lost the '*Hic et ubique*' sequence (1.5.158–71) and thereby not only economised on stage business but also avoided Hamlet's unseemly 'levity' of calling his revered father 'truepenny' and 'old mole'.[38] Elements of cruelty, intrigue and violence were reduced and softened overall. The prayer scene lost Hamlet's bloody reflection ('Now might I do it pat ...', 3.3.73–96) along with Claudius's final exclamation ('My words fly up ...', 3.3.97–8). Claudius's wish to have Hamlet killed in England (4.3.62–71) was cut (after both Davenant and Hughes-Wilks) and was substituted by a single weak line ('Let it be testified in Hamlet's death'). Hamlet's description of Claudius's conspiracy against his life and of his own scheme to have Rosencrantz and Guildenstern killed (5.2.4–80) was also omitted.[39]

Let me also note an interesting minor omission in the fencing match. After Hamlet's 'another hit', the two young men played for the third time. (I indicate the cut by brackets.)

HAMLET	Come for the third, Laertes. You do but dally. I pray you pass with your best violence. I am afeard you make a wanton of me.
LAERTES	Say you so? Come on. (*They play.*)
[OSRICK	Nothing neither way.
LAERTES	Have at you now.] (*Laertes wounds Hamlet; then, in scuffling, they change rapiers.*)
KING	Part them; they are incensed. (5.2.303–9)

In this version Laertes was accorded the minimum fairness of wounding Hamlet during the match, not from behind his back when the judge had called for an interval.

While restoring Shakespeare's language to this conventional theatre version, Kemble created the most straightforward, and least problematic, text of *Hamlet* on record. His first published text (1796) dropped the discussion of the quarrel between Denmark and Norway (1.1.70–108) and streamlined the foreign business further. It also cut Hamlet's dubious apology for his rudeness to Laertes completely (instead of the conventional

partial cut, which I indicate by brackets) and eliminated what both
Johnson and Steevens had cited as an example of Hamlet's insincerity:

> This presence knows, and you must needs have heard,
> How I am punish'd with a sore distraction.
> What I have done
> That might your nature, honour, and exception
> Roughly awake, I here proclaim was madness.
> [Was't Hamlet wrong'd Laertes? Never Hamlet.
> If Hamlet from himself be ta'en away,
> And when he's not himself does wrong Laertes,
> Then Hamlet does it not, Hamlet denies it.
> Who does it then? His madness. If't be so,
> Hamlet is of the faction that is wrong'd;
> His madness is poor Hamlet's enemy.] (5.2.227–38)

In Kemble's 1800 playbook (Hamlet 1800), Hamlet's self-accusation beginning 'O what a rogue and peasant slave am I! . . .' (2.2.550–90) was cut entirely (instead of the predecessors' half cut). The new prince therefore resumed plotting his revenge after the exit of the players without meandering: ' – I have heard / That guilty creatures sitting at a play . . .' (2.2.590–607). Claudius's confession of his guilt ('O, my offence is rank, it smells to heaven', 3.3.36–72) was also eliminated and, as Hamlet's bloodthirsty soliloquy had been dropped already, the entire prayer scene disappeared. In the meantime, replacing the description of Hamlet's sea adventure (5.2.1–74), the following Folio lines were restored and added to the prince's respectability:

> But I am very sorry, good Horatio,
> That to Laertes I forgot myself;
> For by the image of my cause I see
> The portraiture of his. (5.2.75–8)

From Kemble's next version (Hamlet 1804) on, Hamlet even refrained from jumping into Ophelia's grave to fight with Laertes: it was now Laertes who, '*Springing out of the Grave, and seizing* HAMLET', cried, 'The devil take thy soul!' (5.1.257). Kemble's Hamlet actually did not have much reason to feel 'very sorry' any longer. In the Folger promptbook (but not repeated in the subsequent printed texts), Kemble saved the honour of Laertes by reassigning the nasty proposal to poison the rapier ('And for that purpose I'll anoint my sword . . .', 4.7.140–7) to Claudius ('To make all sure, your sword shall be anointed').[40] Thus, by discreet editing, Kemble provided the tragedy with rather respectable dramatis personae who would have silenced the most censorious of literary critics. This was the text that both Kemble and his rival Kean used to exert their respective geniuses.

The general and the particular in acting

It was not only James Boaden's biography of the actor that associated Kemble's acting with Reynolds's theory of generalisation. In a commemorative pamphlet published on Kemble's retirement, an anonymous contributor echoed Reynolds's *Discourses* and praised the actor's observance of the high artistic principle:

> Nature may be copied too closely, and she will then disgust ... The truth is, that the advocates for natural representation, forget that Mr. Kemble always bore in mind, that it is the best part of Nature only, which should be faithfully given; that stooping to represent the common defects of common life, either in person or action, degrades the character and the art, and only makes that too palpable, which even in reality had better be concealed.[41]

As John A. Mills pointed out, the 'best part of nature' that Kemble singled out for his Hamlet was melancholy. The actor fixed on this interpretation and sought 'to give a generalised and idealized portrait of that single trait': 'Sadness hung like a visible color over everything he said and did. Levity, anger, tenderness, intellectual pleasure – all were subordinated, suppressed, subsumed ... Kemble's mournfulness was as lofty as it was everlasting'.[42] Hazlitt's verdict on Kemble's Hamlet was negative, primarily because of the interpretation's lack of variations, details and accidents:

> In Hamlet ... Mr. Kemble in our judgment unavoidably failed from a want of flexibility, of that quick sensibility which yields to every motive, and is borne away with every breath of fancy, which is distracted in the multiplicity of its reflections, and lost in the uncertainty of its resolutions ... in Mr. Kemble's acting, 'there was neither variableness nor shadow of turning'. ('Mr. Kemble's Retirement', 5:377)

Hazlitt recognised Kemble's uniformity as his very strength in such roles as Coriolanus and Cato (5:376), but in Hamlet its monotonousness and languidness, if not quite melancholy, only detracted from the portrayal.

'If it was less perfect as a whole, there were parts in it of a higher cast of excellence than any part of his Richard.' This was Hazlitt's impression of Kean's first acting of Hamlet: 'We will say at once, in what we think his general delineation of the character wrong. It was too strong and pointed' (5:187).[43] Although their scripts were virtually identical, Kean's Prince of Denmark stood in striking contrast with Kemble's endlessly sullen version.

In fact, the actor's 'parts in it of a higher cast of excellence', or Coleridge's 'flashes of lightning', depended very little on the text he used.

Central to Kean's interpretation was Hamlet's tender affection towards his late father, Ophelia and even his incestuous mother and Laertes. While lengthy soliloquies were not this hoarse actor's particular strength, Kean illustrated Hamlet's relationship with these characters with great immediacy by subtle tone of voice, expressive eyes and, above all, ingenious stage business. The first encounter with the ghost was exemplary. Kean's Hamlet expressed filial love, not terror, from a very early stage, and triumphed as he spoke: 'I'll call thee Hamlet, King, *father*, royal Dane' (1.4.44–5; emphasis added). The tremulous tone in which Kean breathed the word 'father' aroused the whole house's sympathy and Hazlitt was moved by the 'impressive pathos of his action and voice' (5:188). (Kean must have conjured up the late Uncle Moses yet again to deliver the line.) To underscore the new interpretation, the actor pointed Hamlet's sword at the followers as he exited, unlike most of his predecessors, who pointed it menacingly at the ghost, or Kemble, who dragged it behind him.

The next climax was the nunnery scene. Like Garrick before him, Kemble's 'dry scholastic personage' harassed Ophelia with 'threatening of fists', 'ferocity of voice', 'stamping of feet' and 'clattering of doors' but (the *Examiner* reviewer assured his readers) 'not so Mr. KEAN'. After the soliloquy, Kean's Hamlet 'turns round and sees *Ophelia*: he is surprized and vexed to find that he has been overheard, but his thoughts are too much elevated for bitterness or paltry pique, and he addresses her as so pure a being ought to be addressed'. This unconventionally courteous encounter concluded with a new pantomime striking enough to rescue Hamlet from the charge of cruelty to Ophelia for aye: 'at the end as he was leaving her, afraid that even this treatment had been unkind, he returns to her with the humility of a man who thinks he has offended a virtuous being, and kisses her hand, at once to re-assure her and to vindicate himself'.[44] This 'noble touch' was 'hailed as it deserved' and Hazlitt sanctioned it wholeheartedly:

> whatever nice faults might be found in this scene, they were amply redeemed by the manner of his coming back after he has gone to the extremity of the stage, from a pang of parting tenderness to press his lips to Ophelia's hand. It had an electrical effect on the house. It was the finest commentary that was ever made on Shakespear. It explained the character at once (as he meant it), as one of disappointed hope, of bitter regret, of affection suspended, not obliterated, by the distractions of the scene around him! (5:188)

It is in fact highly debatable whether the new Hamlet's tenderness did justice to Shakespeare's nunnery scene.[45] To the dilettante critic John

Finlay, the overt expression of affection was superfluous and destroyed the agonising tension between Hamlet and Ophelia that the preceding dialogue had successfully portrayed:

> We think he did convey this [i.e. Hamlet's suppressed affection in the preceding dialogue] sufficiently, and therefore it becomes questionable whether he is authorized to superadd to the scene a pantomimical exhibition of repentance, which gives a direct contradiction to the language of the whole dialogue. When he returns in tenderness to Ophelia, he in fact turns upon Shakspeare, and gives his author a slap in the face.[46]

Moreover, Kean's kiss contradicted eavesdropper Claudius's observation: 'Love? His affections do not that way tend' (3.1.163). The audience adored the pantomime nonetheless. After the emotionally charged interview between the two former lovers, where the audience was left uncertain as to whether the protagonist 'did love you once' or 'loved you not', the kiss was clearly the consummation devoutly wished for. Kean certainly flashed his lightning with great success in defiance of the text and dramatic context.

No less sensational was his play-within-the-play. Hazlitt coyly refrained from giving the specifics of what had struck him as 'the most daring of any' acting, and noted only in general terms: 'Its extreme boldness "bordered on the verge of all we hate", and the effect it produced, was a test of the extraordinary powers of this extraordinary actor' (5:188). The *Herald* reporter overcame his modesty and gave us the details:

> During the mimic representation, Mr. Kean so far forgot that inalienable delicacy, which should eternally characterize a gentleman in his deportment before the ladies, that he not only exposed his *derrière* to his mistress, but positively crawled upon his belly towards the King like a wounded snake in a meadow, rather than a Prince openly indulging himself in moral speculation in the salon of a royal palace.[47]

The audience was greatly entertained. But, as the ever sensible Finlay observed, '[h]ad his uncle observed his ungallant position, he must have been convinced that he had some object for declining his place than merely that the lady was "metal more attractive"'.[48] Let me also add that, at least until halfway through *The Mousetrap*, Hamlet's attention should primarily be on Gertrude, not Claudius, as the prince's asides ('That's wormwood', 3.2.183; 'If she should break it now', 3.2.226) indicate. Kean neglected Hamlet's dilemma (he wants to observe but does not want to be observed), the text and dramatic context once again and created a dazzling theatrical moment. These two *coups de théâtre* aptly illustrate Hazlitt's oracular pronouncement on Kean's histrionic personality: 'in giving effect to the conflict of passions arising out of the contrasts of situation ... it would be difficult to single out a competitor' (5:179).

The closet scene misfired. Eva Maria Violetta Garrick, who liked to regard Kean as the immediate successor to her late husband David, regretted that the actor was not 'so severe with Gertrude in the closet scene' as Garrick used to be and was too gentle and affectionate to the incestuous mother.[49] The graveyard fight with Laertes also lacked impetuosity. Kean discarded Kemble's reticence to a certain degree and once again jumped into the grave to grapple with Laertes but, as Hazlitt complained, it 'had not the tumultuous and overpowering effect we expected from it' (5:187). It may not be a coincidence that Kean's text missed three lines (instead of Kemble's two, which I indicate by brackets) after Claudius's 'Pluck them asunder':

QUEEN	Hamlet! Hamlet!
[ALL	Gentlemen!
HORATIO	Good my lord, be quiet.] (5.1.263–5)

It apparently did not take all these people to dissuade the two well-behaved young men from fighting.

The final histrionic feat was Hamlet's death scene. The actor distinguished between the effects of the poison and of the cut that Hamlet had sustained, and decided that the former should kill the prince. He delineated the gradual action of the poison on Hamlet's body with great truth but, unfortunately, many of the spectators missed the point: the portrayal was too subtle to be at all discernible in a large commercial theatre. Leigh Hunt deplored that no criticism 'has done justice to the beauty and fidelity of the dying scenes':

What are the effects of such a poison? Intense internal pain, wandering vision, swelling veins in the temple. All this Kean details with awful reality: his eye dilates and then loses lustre; he gnaws his hand in the vain effort to repress emotion; the veins thicken in his forehead; his limbs shudder and quiver, and as life grows fainter, and his hand drops from between his stiffening lips, he utters a cry of expiring nature, so exquisite that I can only compare it to the stifled sob of a fainting woman, or the little wail of a suffering child.[50]

The brilliant Finlay secured a seat close enough to see this ingenious portrayal that 'occupied some minutes' but, once again, he was not convinced, and with terribly good reason: if the poison had taken effect, should not Hamlet have been the first to die, as he was poisoned before Laertes and Claudius? Kean's great genius was to create amazing theatrical moments even in defiance of the text and dramatic context. He worked up the spectators' emotion so powerfully that they would forget, for the moment at least, the absurdities and incongruities. In a paradoxical way, what Hazlitt regarded as Kean's fault ('we think his general delineation of the character wrong. It was too strong and pointed') and his strength ('there were parts in it of a higher cast of excellence') pointed to the same thing.

Concluding the *Hamlet* chapter of *Characters of Shakespear's Plays*, Hazlitt examined the theatrical viability of the tragedy by reusing excerpts from his theatrical reviews. First, he supplied three new sentences to introduce the paragraph. Let me quote again: 'We do not like to see our author's plays acted, and least of all, HAMLET. There is no play that suffers so much in being transferred to the stage. Hamlet himself seems hardly capable of being acted' (4:237). Now the denial of actability sounded final: no friendly proposal or suggestion was offered to the actors any longer. Quoting from his 1817 review ('Mr. Kemble's Retirement', 5:377), Hazlitt denounced Kemble's generalisation and Kean's idiosyncrasies in equal terms:

Mr. Kemble unavoidably fails in this character from a want of ease and variety ... Mr. Kemble plays it like a man in armour, with a determined inveteracy of purpose, in one undeviating straight line, which is as remote from the natural grace and refined susceptibility of the character, as the sharp angles and abrupt starts which Mr. Kean introduces into the part. Mr. Kean's Hamlet is as much too splenetic and rash as Mr. Kemble's is too deliberate and formal. (4:237)

Hazlitt then excerpted *only* the negative statements from his 1814 review of Kean's Hamlet: 'His manner is too strong and pointed. He throws a severity, approaching to virulence, into the common observations and answers' (4:237). But the audience, including Hazlitt himself, loved Kean's extraordinary effusion of energy. Hazlitt had also said that, for all the difficulties, 'Mr. Kean's representation of the character had the most brilliant success'. It seems that Hazlitt had changed his mind: 'There is nothing of this in Hamlet. He is, as it were, wrapped up in his reflections, and only *thinks aloud*' (4:237).The two representative tragedians of Hazlitt's day failed to combine the general and the particular and were therefore unable to hold the mirror up to nature, when the character of Hamlet 'is made up of undulating lines' and has the yielding flexibility of 'a wave o' th'sea'. As if to preclude further theatrical adulteration, Hazlitt defined the 'true' Hamlet as someone who could not possibly appear on stage:

There should therefore be no attempt to impress what he says upon others by a studied exaggeration of emphasis or manner; no *talking at* his hearers. There should be as much of the gentleman and scholar as possible infused into the part, and as little of the actor. A pensive air of sadness should sit reluctantly upon his brow, but no appearance of fixed and sullen gloom. (4:237)

Prince Hamlet had come a very long (and arguably very wrong, too) way indeed from being an Elizabethan revenge hero to become this delicate thing: 'He is full of weakness and melancholy, but there is no harshness in his nature. He is the most amiable of misanthropes' (4:237).

***

In preparing the 1818 version of *Hamlet*, Kean's editor – it is not known whether the actor himself was involved in the revision – made a rather inadvertent minor cut. As discussed earlier, Kemble eliminated Claudius's soliloquy at prayer (3.3.36–72) in 1800, but from the next 1804 edition restored two lines to him that had customarily been cut since Davenant. They come after Polonius's instruction to Ophelia to 'Read on this book' to 'sugar o'er / The devil himself':

> KING (*aside*) O 'tis too true.
> How smart a lash that speech doth give my conscience. (3.1.49–50)

Kemble seems to have realised that the audience should be convinced of Claudius's guilt in his own words at least once in the play. In tidying up the script, the 1818 editor dropped these two lines again and Claudius lost both of the two occasions to confess his tortured conscience as a result.

It probably did not matter much, as everyone knew that Claudius killed his brother. The secondary character's sense of remorse would have been marginal anyway on Kean's amazing stage. There was, however, one Romantic poet and critic to whose understanding of Hamlet's tragedy remorse was indeed central. In fact, this poet would compose his own tragedy of a usurper and younger brother using this sentiment of remorse at its dramatic core.

3 IN THE THEATRE OF REMORSE: COLERIDGE, HIS FRIEND AND HIS TRAGEDY

Edmund Burke was not the only witness of the phantom of the Revolution. From October to December 1792, William Wordsworth stayed in a Paris that was under the immediate influence of the September Massacres, and wandered past 'The prison where the unhappy monarch lay, / Associate with his children and his wife / In bondage' and 'The square of the Carousel, few weeks back / Heaped up with dead and dying'. All these spectacles were to the foreign poet like 'a volume whose contents he knows / Are memorable but from him locked up, / Being written in a tongue he cannot read'. But when he returned to his hotel room and began to read under a taper until late at night, 'The fear gone by / Pressed on me almost like a fear to come'. Wordsworth recalled several apocalyptic images to give an expression to the amorphous terror, 'Until I seemed to hear a voice that cried / To the whole city, "Sleep no more!"'.[51]

Urged by youthful idealism, Wordsworth once sympathised with what was believed to be the liberation of the French people and 'pushed without remorse / My speculations forward; yea set foot / On Nature's holiest places' (10:876–8). Did the grim realities of the Revolution make the poet think twice and repent his former opinions, just as Macbeth does after killing Duncan and his own sleep alike?

> Time may come
> When some dramatic story may afford
> Shapes livelier to convey to thee, my friend,
> What then I learned – or think I learned – of truth,
> And the errors into which I was betrayed
> By present objects, and by reasonings false
> From the beginning, inasmuch as drawn
> Out of a heart which had been turned aside
> From Nature by external accidents,
> And which was thus confounded more and more,
> Misguiding and misguided. (10:878–88)

The 'dramatic story' that Wordsworth promised, perhaps retrospectively, in this 1805 *Prelude* had materialised in 1796–7 in the form of his first play, *The Borderers*.[52] Revolutionary France had taught the poet that 'sin and crime are apt to start from their very opposite qualities', and 'it was while that knowledge was fresh upon my memory, that the Tragedy of "The Borderers" was composed'.[53] Set in the lawless borders of Scotland and England against the backdrop of the Crusade and the Barons' War, the tragedy presents the idealistic leader (Mortimer) of a band of borderers who is falsely led to believe by an Iago-like instigator (Rivers) that the elderly father of his lover (Matilda) is a villain. Mortimer deserts the infirm patriarch on the stormy heath and kills him, firmly convinced that he is administering justice in doing so. Rivers in his turn was duped by his evil peers when he was younger and killed another patriarchal figure ('Captain', also father of a young girl), in the belief that the old man had defiled his name. Rivers relives, and tries to deal with, his own trauma by making another young man make the same fatal mistake. When the innocence of

Matilda's father, together with Rivers's conspiracy, comes to light, the devastated Mortimer flees the borderland to seek death.

While Wordsworth was finishing off this dark story of compulsive repetitions of murder and remorse, 'my friend' was quite independently undertaking his own theatrical project. After receiving a flattering request from Richard Brinsley Sheridan to write a tragedy for Drury Lane, Samuel Taylor Coleridge began to work on *Osorio* in April 1797, having 'Siddons & Kemble in my mind'.[54] The scene of his Spanish tragedy was 'the reign of Philip II. shortly after the civil war against the Moors, & during the heat of the Persecution which raged against them'.[55] Like Wordsworth, Coleridge relied on Friedrich Schiller's *Robbers* (1781) for his portrayal of the bands of outlaws (the Moors in his case), as well as for the motif of sibling rivalry. Coleridge's villain-hero (Osorio) is therefore an oppressor of the Moors politically, while domestically he is the Marquez Velez's younger son who has attempted (but failed) to kill his elder brother (Albert) in a bid to seize both his fiancée (Maria) and his title.

The two Romantic poets knew each other from either August or September of 1795, but intimacy deepened in the first week of June 1797, when Coleridge visited the Wordsworths at Racedown in Dorset and spent most of the following months in their company. Interestingly, the very obscure *The Borderers* and *Osorio* were as vital an ingredient of their intercourse as the iconic *Lyrical Ballads* published the following year. Wordsworth's sister Dorothy recorded the memorable meeting: 'The first thing that was read after he came was William's new poem *The Ruined Cottage* with which he was much delighted; and after tea he repeated to us two acts and a half of his tragedy *Osorio*. The next morning William read his tragedy *The Borderers*.'[56] 'Wordsworth admires my Tragedy – which gives me great hopes,' wrote Coleridge, who in his turn believed that his friend's drama was 'absolutely wonderful' (1:325; To Joseph Cottle, [8 June 1797]). Coleridge sent his script to Drury Lane as planned, but after enduring a long wait and the rumours of 'some silly remarks of Kemble's', learnt that his work had been rejected on account of 'the obscurity of the three last acts'. Wordsworth's work was sent to, and rejected by, Covent Garden in a similar manner. The pair then considered joint publication of their tragedies. This project did not materialise either, as the publisher Joseph Cottle was not willing to pay the money the two playwrights required.

Insufficient and immature as tragedy, and completely abortive as either theatrical or literary ventures at this stage, the two plays anticipated, and complemented, *Lyrical Ballads*. To cite the most obvious coalescence, two of the four poems that Coleridge contributed to the collection ('The

Foster-Mother's Tale' and 'The Dungeon') were actually extracted from *Osorio*. He obviously saw much poetic merit in these pieces but somehow dropped both of them when the tragedy eventually reached the Drury Lane stage in 1813. Their playwriting was also directly related to the poetics of Romanticism as developed in the Preface to *Lyrical Ballads* and in *Biographia Literaria* (1817), and vitally informed Coleridge's *Hamlet* criticism. Let me start from Wordsworth's famous prolegomena.

Poetic and dramatic illusion

Incredible friendship between men of genius tends not to be everlasting. When the second edition of *Lyrical Ballads* was published in 1800 in two volumes, the precarious power relationship between the two poets was already painfully clear. With his *Christabel* having been rejected by Wordsworth, Coleridge added only a ninety-six-line poem ('Love') to this edition and supplied nothing to the new second volume.[57] *The Rime of the Ancyent Marinere*, which opened the 1798 edition, was relegated to a spot near the end of the first volume and was appended with his friend's patronising 'Note'.[58] Most crucially, Wordsworth's Preface to this second edition defined its 'principal object' as '[to make the incidents of common life interesting] by tracing in them, truly though not ostentatiously, the primary laws of our nature'.[59] Wordsworth went on to emphasise naturalism further by expanding on the phrase I bracketed ('to make ... interesting') from the next 1802 edition as follows:

to chuse incidents and situations from common life, and to relate or describe them, throughout, as far as was possible, in a selection of language really used by men; and, at the same time, to throw over them a certain colouring of imagination, whereby ordinary things should be presented to the mind in an unusual way; and, further, and above all, to make these incidents and situations interesting.[60]

With language going through the process of 'selection' and commonplace topics being heightened by 'a certain colouring of imagination', Wordsworth's poetry was certainly much more than a mere transcript of everyday conversation. However, his objectives were ultimately incompatible with the gothic balladry of *Christabel* and the gripping supernaturalism and mock archaism of *The Rime of the Ancyent Marinere*, which was very symbolically modernised to *The Ancient Mariner* from the 1800 edition onwards. Other additions to the Preface (including the long insertion beginning 'the language of such Poetry as I am recommending was, as far as is possible, a selection of the language really spoken by men') in the 1802 and subsequent editions also punctuated Wordsworth's viewpoint, quietly corroding the poetics of the co-author.[61]

Coleridge expressed uneasiness about his friend's prolegomena in private correspondence soon after the appearance of the second edition,[62] but it was not until the publication of *Biographia Literaria* in 1817 that his side of the story was made public. *Lyrical Ballads* was conceived on equal terms by the two poets and was to include 'a series of poems . . . of two sorts'. In the one, of which Coleridge was in charge, 'the incidents and agents were to be, in part at least, supernatural; and the excellence aimed at was to consist in the interesting of the affections by the dramatic truth of such emotions, as would naturally accompany such situations, supposing them real', while in the other, 'subjects were to be chosen from ordinary life; the characters and incidents were to be such, as will be found in every village and its vicinity, where there is a meditative and feeling mind to seek after them, or to notice them, when they present themselves'. Coleridge enlarged on the supernatural poetry: 'it was agreed, that my endeavours should be directed to persons and characters supernatural, or at least romantic; yet so as to transfer from our inward nature a human interest and a semblance of truth sufficient to procure for these shadows of imagination that willing suspension of disbelief for the moment, which constitutes poetic faith'[63].

In fact, Coleridge had developed this celebrated idea of 'willing suspension of disbelief', as distinct from the involuntary mistaking of the supernatural for the real, over many years, mainly in the field of drama criticism. (The phrase 'dramatic truth' used unguardedly in one of the above quotations gives away its original context.) In 'Critique of *Bertram*' (first published in the *Courier* in 1816 and later adapted into chapter 23 of *Biographia*), the insipid characters of Charles Maturin's tragedy were compared with the Shakespearean protagonists, such as Richard III, whose intellectual fortitude 'can bribe us into a voluntary submission of our better knowledge, into suspension of all our judgment derived from constant experience, and enable us to peruse with the liveliest interest the wildest tales of ghosts, wizards, genii, and secret talismans'. In this 'voluntary submission' consists dramatic probability: 'The poet does not require us to be awake and believe; he solicits us only to yield ourselves to a dream; and this too with our eyes open, and with our judgment *perdue* behind the curtain, ready to awaken us at the first motion of our will: and meantime, only, not to *dis*believe.'[64]

The same idea can be traced further back to an 1808 lecture note, 'Desultory Remarks on the Stage, & the present state of the Higher Drama', where stage illusion was distinguished from delusion and was likened rather to the experience of dreaming (as in the 'Critique of *Bertram*') and of seeing a picture: 'what Pictures are to little Children, Stage-Illusion is to Men, provided they retain any part of the Child's sensibility: except in the latter instance, this suspension of the Act of Comparison, which permits this sort of negative Belief, is somewhat more assisted by the Will, than in that of the Child respecting a Picture'.[65] French classicists' faith in, and Samuel Johnson's denouncement of, dramatic verisimilitude and delusion rested on the same misunderstanding of the nature of aesthetic illusion. The former's 'reasoning on it [stage illusion] as actual Delusion' and the latter's 'denying it altogether' seemingly represent very opposite views but 'as Extremes meet, would lead to the very same Consequences by excluding whatever would not be judged probable by us in <our> coolest state of feeling with all our faculties in even balance'.[66]

Patricia Jenkins collects Coleridge's references to stage illusion, alongside the associated ideas of poetry, supernaturalism, dream and painting, and traces its origin to a letter to Robert Southey written in 1799, where Coleridge contrasted the transient faith in poetic fiction with the 'awful realities' of the divinity.[67] But can we not push the date a little further back to 1797, when Coleridge actually composed a drama of his own in which practically every single dramatic character dreams and talks of dreams? A play in which a portrait and a history painting play a crucial role? A play in which Coleridge (as if to preclude Wordsworth's Preface to *Lyrical Ballads*) 'endeavoured to have few [presumably 'a few'] sentences which *might not* be spoken in conversation, avoiding those that are *commonly* used in conversation' (1:356; To William Lisle Bowles, 16 October 1797)? A play where a conjuror initiates a magical séance by saying, 'Doubt, but decide not'? My answer to all these queries would be in the affirmative, though I seriously question if Coleridge carried off these ideas successfully in dramatic terms.[68] My reasons are as follows.

'Doubt, but decide not!': Osorio

The erudite Coleridge turned to various materials for information and inspiration to write *Osorio*.[69] Robert Watson's *History of the Reign of Philip the Second, King of Spain* (1785) taught him about the persecutions of the Moors and the edict against the wearing of Moresco dress. (In Coleridge's play the suppressed Moors are forced to wear Christian robes, while the elder brother Albert returns to his native land in Moresco dress to disguise his identity.) As mentioned already, Schiller's *Robbers* supplied the plot of outlawry and sibling rivalry. (Younger brother Osorio commissions assassins to get rid of Albert and marry his fiancée.) Schiller's narrative, *The*

Ghost-seer (serialised from 1786 and published as a book in 1789), helped him to formulate the séance in which the ghost of the elder brother is conjured up to convince his fiancée of his death. Shakespeare's *Macbeth* and *Richard III* provided the archetype of the villain-hero Osorio whose emotional conflicts constitute the tragic core,[70] while Wordsworth's *The Borderers* influenced especially the latter half of the tragedy.[71] When Coleridge saved the life of Albert (unlike in either *The Robbers* or *The Ghost-seer*, where the elder brother is actually murdered) and made him perform his own séance, it seems that the metatheatrical Danish prince was the inspiration.

Discrediting the report of Albert's death, his fiancée Maria has long been refusing Osorio's proposal. The younger brother devises a fake séance, in the course of which a locket portrait of Maria, a love token she gave Albert six years ago, should mysteriously emerge to prove its owner's death. In fact, Osorio's assassins spared Albert's life and one of them (Ferdinand) brought the locket to Osorio to disguise the fact. Now Osorio employs a Moorish conjuror (the disguised Albert) to conduct the séance.

While Hamlet is a producer, 'a chorus', and a scriptwriter of 'a speech of some dozen or sixteen lines' of *The Mousetrap*, Albert is an accomplished amateur painter, or as his attendant Maurice puts it: 'You are a painter – one of many fancies – You can call up past deeds, and make them live On the blank Canvas' (2.2.19–21). By putting on *The Mousetrap* and reproducing the murder as described by the ghost, Hamlet intends to 'catch the conscience of the King', for:

> I have heard
> That guilty creatures sitting at a play
> Have, by the very cunning of the scene,
> Been struck so to the soul that presently
> They have proclaim'd their malefactions. (2.2.590–4)

Albert, on the other hand, has painted a very realistic picture of 'my assassination'. He is to substitute the painting for Maria's locket at the séance with a view to torturing his brother's conscience. Gazing at the locket just returned to him by Osorio for the séance, Albert outlines his agenda:

> Dear Image! rescued from a Traitor's keeping,
> I will not now prophane thee, holy Image!
> To a dark trick! That worst bad Man shall find
> A picture which will wake the Hell within him,
> And rouse a fiery Whirlwind in his Conscience! (2.2.159–63)

The séance takes place in '*A Hall of Armory, with an altar in the part farthest from the stage*'. Osorio has prepared 'incense and music' to heighten the stage effect. Maria is unwilling to attend this heathen ritual but Albert's conjuror assures her:

> O high-soul'd Maiden and more dear to me
> Than suits the Stranger's name, I swear to thee,
> I will uncover all concealed things!
> Doubt, but decide not! (3.1.7–10)

At the time of the composition of the tragedy, Coleridge had just reviewed various gothic stories for the *Critical Review* ('the Monk, the Italian, Hubert de Sevrac, &&c &&c') and grown tired of 'dungeons and old castles, & solitary Houses by the Sea Side, & Caverns, & Woods, & extraordinary characters, & all the tribe of Horror and Mystery' (1:318; To William Bowles, [16 March 1797]). It seems that Coleridge deliberately avoided the facile 'Horror and Mystery' potential of this séance and opted for some metaphysical and metatheatrical effects. In the first place, everybody is a 'doubter' in the scene: none of the participants actually believes in the séance.[72] As soon as she enters, Maria flatly pronounces, 'My heart approves it not! 'tis mockery!' (3.1.3). Velez, the father, 'scent[s] it from the first' that it is an 'excellent scheme, and excellently manag'd' by Osorio to 'blow away' Maria's doubts as to Albert's death, which he has long accepted as sad truth (3.1.150–1). And of course, neither Albert nor Osorio believes in the séance as such: they are utilising the occasion for their own ends. The ritual begins with solemn instrumental music, an incantation and a doleful song. After a short exchange between Albert and Osorio, the assassination picture emerges out of an overwhelming mixture of music, fire, smoke and lightning:

> (*The whole Orchestra crashes into one Chorus.*)
> Wandring Daemon! hear the spell
> Lest a blacker charm compel!
> (*A Thunder Clap – The Incense on the Altar takes fire suddenly.*)
> (3.1.111–12)

The painting is a lifelike representation of the assassination that has never materialised. Velez marvels at its ingenious portrayal later in the same scene:

> VELEZ (*looking intently at the picture*)
> Calm, yet commanding! how he [i.e. Albert] bares his breast,
> Yet still they [i.e. the assassins] stand with dim uncertain looks,
> As Penitence had run before their crime –
> A crime too black for aught to follow it
> Save blasphemous Despair! See *this* man's face –

> With what a difficult toil he drags his soul
> To do the deed. (3.1.202–8)

The effect of Albert's painting on the guilty brother and other attendants is, unfortunately, not as unequivocal as in the case of *The Mousetrap* and Claudius. What is most problematic, or Coleridge would say 'metaphysical', is that the assassination picture is so small (presumably not much larger than Maria's locket) that most of the dramatis personae, let alone the audience, cannot actually see what is painted in it. Velez is the only lucky one to get to the altar to see it, but he simply exclaims, 'Hah! / A Picture!' (3.1.115–16), and *'takes and conceals the Picture in his robe'* (3.1.120 SD) to spare Maria the agony of seeing the portrayed atrocity. Maria does not even register the appearance of the picture at first, 'Yet my weak Fancy, and these bodily creepings, / Would fain give substance to the shadow' (3.1.114–15). Then, at Velez's exclamation ('A Picture!'), she inexplicably jumps to the wrong conclusion that it must be her locket ('O God! *my* picture!' 3.1.116) and swoons. Osorio still believes that Maria's portrait has been displayed: it is only when everyone retires and Osorio reenters with his father that he learns that the scheme has gone wrong ('Dup'd – dup'd – dup'd!' 3.1.185). This failure leaves the usurper increasingly confused, violent and agonised towards the end of the tragedy.

All this is very interesting intellectually. Coleridge is clearly weaving a complex tissue of seeing and not seeing, reality and representation, belief and disbelief, innocence and guilt, and so on, in this mock-supernatural centrepiece. However, this conjuring sequence simply does not work in the theatre. Most crucially, the audience is left uncertain throughout the séance as to which picture has been displayed in the end. Coleridge was aware of the problem and entered the following additional explanation in the margin of his manuscript copies: 'Instead of Maria's Portrait Albert places on the Alter a small picture of his attempted assassination.'[73] Unfortunately, a dramatist cannot whisper this essential information into the ears of the audience while the show is going on. The picture's visibility to respective dramatic characters is not properly indicated either, and the significance of their different responses to it would therefore be lost on the audience. Again Coleridge entered an explanation in the manuscripts: 'Velez [who sees it] supposes the *picture*, which represents the attempt to assassinate Albert, to have been a mere invention, contrived by Osorio, with the most innocent intentions. *Osorio* [who does not see it] supposes it of course to be the *portrait* of Maria which he had restored to Albert.'[74] Of course? I find it highly debatable.

According to Coleridge, learning the failure of the séance later in the same scene, 'Osorio immediately supposes that this Wizard[,] whom Ferdinand had recommended to him, was in truth an accomplice of Ferdinand's to whom the whole Secret had been betrayed.' As a friend pointed out to the playwright, 'I doubt how an audience will receive this reasoning.' Coleridge's metaphysical and poetic hypersophistication confused the plot and destroyed the intensity of the conjuring sequence: 'The Scene is not wholly without *poetical* merit / but it is miserably undramatic, or rather untragic.'[75]

More than two years after Sheridan's rejection, Coleridge reflected on his unsuccessful theatrical effort yet again in a letter to Daniel Stuart (15 July 1800). As an inexperienced playwright, he did not intend to stick to the initial draft but, on the contrary, expected Sheridan to alter it to make it actable ('When I sent my play to him [Sheridan], I gave at the same time expressly to him the whole & absolute power of alteration, addition, & omission'). Neither Sheridan nor the members of his troupe provided the necessary assistance. Coleridge certainly defended the play against a friend's criticism but it was 'only as a *metaphysician*; never supposing myself to have any voice or suffrage, or even *opinion*, as to what was or was not suited for representation'. His confidence in his dramatic talent was seriously shaken: 'After all, I never blamed Mr Sheridan for not bringing my play on the stage. God knows my inmost heart, & knows that I never for an hour together thought it likely to succeed ... I am convinced, I have no Talents for so arduous a species of composition as the Drama' (1:604). The next section explores how Coleridge revised the metaphysical 'untragic' tragedy over the years and made it actable in the end.

'To act, to do, to perform': Remorse *on stage*

Being a good drama critic, if not a good dramatist, Coleridge had a clear view as to what had gone wrong with his own tragedy. To aggravate the 'metaphysical' confusion as exemplified in the incantation scene, he had failed to incorporate in the speeches some vital background information ('it *presupposes* a long story – & this long story, which yet is necessary to the complete understanding of the Play, is not half-told'): 'Albert had sent a letter informing his family, that he should arrive about such a time by ship – he was shipwrecked – & wrote a private Letter to Osorio, informing *him* alone of this accident, that he might not shock Maria – Osorio destroyed the letter & sent Assassins to meet Albert.'[76] Missing these crucial premises, the tragedy simply fell apart. Even worse, the character of the villain-hero was not developed adequately. In an important lecture note ('The Character of Hamlet'), Coleridge speculated on Shakespeare's characterisation: 'Shakespear's mode of conceiving characters out of his own intellectual & moral faculties, by conceiving any one intellectual or moral faculty in morbid excess and then placing himself thus mutilated and diseased under given circumstances.'[77] Unlike Ben Jonson, Francis Beaumont and John Fletcher, and Philip Massinger, who wrote 'just as a man might fit together a quarter of an orange, a quarter of an Apple, and the like of a Lemon and of a Pomegranate, and make it look like one round diverse colored fruit', Shakespeare 'worked in the spirit of Nature, by evolving the Germ within by the imaginative Power according to an Idea'.[78] In his literary lectures Coleridge defended Hamlet's apparent cruelty in the prayer scene with recourse to his 'Germ of a character' and refuted Samuel Johnson.[79] In *Osorio* he would have put the theory into theatrical use by developing the 'Germ' of the villainous brother. The conception ('a man who from his childhood had mistaken constitutional abstinence from Vices for strength of character – thro' his pride duped into guilt – & then endeavouring to shield himself from the reproaches of his own mind by misanthropy') was forceful enough. Coleridge only failed to cultivate it within the economy of drama: 'Worse than all – the growth of Osorio's character is no where explained – & yet I had most clear & psychologically accurate ideas of the whole of it.' Through Osorio, Coleridge learnt 'one important Lesson – namely – that to have conceived strongly does not always imply the power of successful Execution'.[80]

When Coleridge resumed work on the script with a view to Drury Lane once again, it seems that Hamlet's vicious uncle gave him a hint. For Coleridge, the prayer scene was significant not only in terms of Hamlet's 'Germ of a character': Claudius's speeches that precede and follow the prince's soliloquy gave him a good insight into the psychology of guilt and its dramatic expression. Referring to the usurper's 'O, my offence is rank, it smells to heaven . . .' (3.3.36–72): 'The King's Speech well marks the difference between Crime and Guilt of Habit. The Conscience is still admitted to Audience. Nay, even as an audible soliloquy, it is far less improbable than is supposed by such as have watched men only in the beaten road of their feelings.'[81] Claudius's transient optimism, seen in 'All may be well' (3.3.72), attracted the critic's particular attention: 'a degree of Merit [is] attributed by the self-flattering Soul to its own struggle, tho' baffled – and to the indefinite half-promise, half-command, to persevere in religious Duties. The divine Medium of the Christian Doctrine of Expiation – in the – Not what you have done, but what you *are*, must determine – Metanoia.'[82]

The Greek word *metanoia* is usually translated as 'repentance', but unlike 'remorse' that dwells in and tortures the offender's mind, it is '*the Passing into a new mind*, into a new and contrary Principle of Action' and 'volunteer *Transmentation*'.[83] Coleridge's meaning here would be that, bidding for his salvation and getting on his knees to pray, Claudius temporarily believes in an expiation of his crime, *metanoia*, and a thorough restart. But the usurper's wilful wish is soon shattered. Coleridge went on to analyse Claudius's muted prayer that coincides with Hamlet's soliloquy ('Now might I do it pat ...'): 'But the interval taken up by Hamlet's Speech is truly awful! And then – "My words fly up" – O what a lesson concerning the essential difference between Wishing & Willing: and the folly of all motive-mongering, while the individual Self remains.'[84] Coleridge attended to this psychology of guilt and the (im)possibility of *metanoia*, which is nowhere developed in Schiller's *Robbers* or *The Ghost-seer*, when he revised *Osorio* into a new tragedy of *Remorse*: 'By REMORSE I mean the Anguish & Disquietude arising from the Self-contradiction introduced into the Soul by Guilt – a feeling, which is good or bad according as the Will makes use of it ... & Remorse is every where distinguished from virtuous Penitence' (3:433–4; To Robert Southey, 8 [9] February 1813).[85] Osorio (now renamed Ordonio) is a Claudius who has failed to kill his elder brother, while Albert (now Alvar) is both ghost Hamlet and young Hamlet, who looks not to revenge but to remorse. The revenge plot is taken over by a Moorish woman (Alhadra) whose husband (Ferdinand, now Isidore) Ordonio actually murders. The Gertrude figure (Maria, now Teresa) remains resolutely loyal to her first love.

It is not known when the fundamental rewriting of the tragedy took place. Coleridge worked on the play (or at least claimed that he was revising it) in 1800–1 and 1806–8, and the play was retitled and the characters renamed probably during the latter period. The Bollingen editor J. C. C. Mays argues, however, that substantial carpentry on the drama was carried out only after the tragedy was accepted by the new Drury Lane committee late in 1812, when Coleridge began to visit the theatre daily to oversee the rehearsals.[86] A close working partnership was forged between him and the stage manager and actors:

> James Wallack [who played one of the Moors] was present among the other actors in the Green-room of Drurylane theatre when Coleridge read to them his tragedy of Remorse, and gave them particular directions how certain passages were to be delivered. His reading was a sort of high musical chant; and his ideas of stage-effect were so exquisitely ridiculous, that the actors had great difficulty in listening to him without bursting out into laughter.[87]

This 'exquisitely ridiculous' closet playwright not only agreed to whatever cuts were suggested by the actors but even pleaded 'strenuously for more & more excisions'. 'The Foster-Mother's Tale' and 'The Dungeon' were dropped in the process.[88] This 'anomalous' behaviour earned him the nickname *'the Amenable Author'* in the greenroom (3:427–8; To John Rickman, 25 January 1813). In all probability, Coleridge's insights into the psychology of guilt and remorse were given theatrical expression with a great deal of practical help from the members of Drury Lane.

The stage version clarifies its moral imperative through a new opening dialogue between Alvar and his servant Zulimez (former Maurice). While the original Albert returns to his native Granada with only a vague wish to see Maria, the new Alvar is fully determined from the outset to make Ordonio face his own wickedness. He is urged by Zulimez to reclaim his title as the first son of Valdez (former Valez):

ALVAR   The more behoves it, I should rouse within him [i.e. Ordonio]
        REMORSE! that I should save him from himself.
ZULIMEZ REMORSE is as the heart, in which it grows:
        If that be gentle it drops balmy dews
        Of true repentance, but if proud and gloomy,
        It is a poison-tree, that pierced to the inmost
        Weeps only tears of poison! (1.1.18–24)

Zulimez's five lines were cited as an epigram when the play was published. The rest of the new opening scene explains the storyline that is 'not half-told' in *Osorio*.

The revised final scene recapitulates the theme of remorse. Replacing Alhadra's denouncement of the 'Lord of the Oppressor's' in *Osorio* (5.2.205), Alvar moralises on Ordonio's iniquities and his resulting death at the hand of the revenger:

> In these strange dread events.
> Just Heaven instructs us with an awful voice,
> That Conscience rules us e'en against our choice.
> Our inward Monitress to guide or warn,
> If listened to; but if repelled with scorn,
> At length as dire REMORSE, she reappears,
> Works in our guilty hopes, and selfish fears!
> Still bids, Remember! and still cries, Too late!
> And while she scare us, goads us to our fate. (5.1.214–22)

The playwright's message could not be clearer. Sandwiched by these two expository statements, the intervening events are placed in a much clearer perspective and made far easier to follow.

The impossible metaphysical crux of the conjuring scene, which had thrown the dramatic characters and the dramatist alike into sheer confusion in *Osorio*, dissolved miraculously when an ingenious idea of hanging a big – instead of small – assassination picture struck either Coleridge or one of his new showbiz friends. The difficulty solved, the incantation provides a sensational spectacle:

> [*The whole Music clashes into a Chorus.*]
> CHORUS.
> Wandering Demon hear the spell!
> Lest a blacker charm compel –
> [*Gong sounds & the incense on the altar takes fire suddenly, and an illuminated picture of* ALVAR*'s assassination is discovered, and having remained a few seconds is then hidden by ascending flames.*] (3.2.99–100)

Stage effect is similarly heightened in the final scene. While the original Osorio is unceremoniously dragged off the stage by the revengeful Moors to his probable death, the new Ordonio is stabbed on stage by Alhadra and dies in palpable remorse ('Forgive me, Alvar! – / Oh! – couldst thou forget me!', 5.1.206).[89]

The tragedy proved a box-office smash, achieving an honourable run of twenty performances.[90] The reviews were mixed, but the audience was entertained.[91] For Coleridge, it was the single most profitable venture in his entire literary career.[92]

Flushed with theatrical success, the playwright cited 'the simplicity and the Unity of the Plot' and 'the variety of metres' as the two prominent merits of his tragedy. The dramatic unity was achieved by the 'all-pervading, all-combining, Principle' of Ordonio's remorse: 'As from a circumference to a centre, every Ray in the Tragedy converges to Ordonio' (3:433–4; To Robert Southey, 8 [9] February 1813). Coleridge also managed to communicate the 'long story' underlying the dramatic action by inserting the explanatory dialogue before the equally expository original first scene between Teresa and Valdez. (Coleridge wrote, with slight self-mockery, in the margin of the presentation copy to Sara Hutchinson: 'This Tragedy has a particular Advantage – it has two *first* Scenes, in which Prologue plays Dialogue with Dumby [dummy].')[93] The Moorish subplot, which was little more than crude revolutionary propaganda in *Osorio*, was neatly pruned to contrast Alvar's toleration with Ordonio's persecution, and remorse (which is Alvar's objective) with revenge (which is Alhadra's). The séance and Ordonio's onstage death supplied spectacles, and Alvar's final statement reinforced the tragic theme. We might even say (with Joseph Donohue) that Coleridge succeeded in placing 'human emotions more securely within a well-conducted dramatic action' than in the first version.[94]

But is this the tragedy Coleridge always wanted to write? Stripped of the metaphysical complications and excessive poetry, the final product looked suspiciously like the kind of run-of-the-mill gothic story that Coleridge despised.

The dubious dramatic achievements aside, playwriting taught Coleridge to appreciate the greatness of the author of *Hamlet*. In a quiet moment of reflection twenty years after the performance, Coleridge sent a tribute to Shakespeare by misquoting from Claudius: 'There's such a divinity doth hedge our Shakespeare round, that we cannot even imitate his style. I tried to imitate his manner in the *Remorse*, and, when I had done, I found I had been tracking Beaumont and Fletcher and Massinger instead. It is really very curious.'[95] The frantic revisions reduced Coleridge's purportedly Shakespearean tragedy to the rank of the particoloured fruits of his lesser contemporaries.

There was another regret. In a paradoxical way, Coleridge's tragedy, especially in the unactable original version, premised great acting: his dramatic signification, psychological portrayal especially, depended heavily on actors. For example, the stage directions in the original séance demand that the Osorio actor be seen '*struggling with his feelings*' when confronting the disguised Albert. He has to be '*in a state of stupor*' then subsequently '*rousing himself*' when the altar catches fire. Indeed, the Osorio actor has to achieve the height of histrionic sophistication to justify Maria's later recollection of the scene:

> Saw you [i.e. Velez] his countenance?
> How rage, remorse, and scorn, and stupid fear,
> Displac'd each other with swift interchanges?
> If this were all assum'd, as you believe,
> He must needs be a most consummate Actor;
> And hath so vast a power to deceive me,
> I never could be safe. And why assume
> The semblance of such execrable feelings? (4.2.109–16)

In the long course of revisions, Coleridge learnt to translate the characters' feelings into speeches and dramatic action to a certain degree, but even in the revised stage version Ordonio must be seen '*With affected gravity*', '*vacantly repeating the words*', '*with frantic wildness*', '*with a countenance of at once awe and terror*' and '*fiercely recollecting himself*' in the final scene alone.

Unfortunately, when the play reached the stage in January 1813, Drury Lane was short on tragic talents. John Philip Kemble and Sarah Siddons, whom Coleridge had originally in mind, had transferred to the rival Covent Garden already. Although Coleridge included a courteous tribute to the actors in the preface to the tragedy,[96] he was terribly let down by their acting. Alexander Rae's Ordonio was particularly disappointing.

> Poor Rae (why poor? for Ordonio has almost made his fortune) did the best in his power – & is a good man – ... & is an honest man, a moral, & affectionate Husband & Father – But Nature has denied him Person, & all volume & depth of Voice – so that the blundering Coxcomb, Elliston [who played Alvar], by mere dint of Voice & Self-conceit out-dazzled him (3:436–37; To Thomas Poole, [13 February 1813])

Begun in 1797, Coleridge's tragedy was very slow indeed to reach the stage and, as Southey lamented, it was a shame that he was not given the opportunity to develop his playwriting skills much earlier.[97] From a histrionic point of view, however, the performance materialised a year too early. In January the following year, a tragedian was to appear on the Drury Lane stage who was neither 'honest' nor 'moral' but would have realised Coleridge's tragic intentions and expressed 'at once awe and terror' to the fullest extent. Lord Byron, then a committee member of Drury Lane, wrote to the disappointed playwright on 31 March 1815: 'In Kean, there is an actor worthy of expressing the thoughts of the characters which you have every power of embodying; and I cannot but regret that the part of Ordonio was disposed of before his appearance at Drury Lane.'[98] The next section considers another Romantic 'playwright' whose theatrical ambitions were fired *after* seeing Kean's consummate acting and who tailored a tragic role specifically for him.

4 FABLES OF IDENTITY: KEATS, KEAN AND *OTHO THE GREAT*

Poetics of the street fight

It is comforting to learn that the consumptive poet of the Grecian urn and the nightingale did not simply cough away the whole of his twenty-five-year life. In 1878 Charles Cowden Clarke recalled a small boy who had attended his father's school in Enfield, Middlesex, from the 'dark backward and abysm' of seventy-odd years. John Keats was remembered as a boy who had 'a brisk, winning face, and was a favourite with all, particularly my mother'. Apart from 'a determined and steady spirit in all his undertakings', the schoolboy did not distinguish himself by any 'extraordinary indications of intellectual character' just yet. What Clarke remembered most clearly was the immense energy that lay hidden in Keats's diminutive body, which would erupt from time to time in flamboyant bust-ups:

> It has just been said that he was a favourite with all. Not the less beloved was he for having a highly pugnacious spirit, which, when roused, was one of the most picturesque exhibitions – off the stage – I ever saw ... Upon one occasion, when an usher, on account of some impertinent behaviour, had boxed his brother Tom's ears, John rushed up, put himself in the received posture of offence, and, it was said, struck the usher – who could, so to say, have put him into his pocket.[99]

The biographer associated the fire and intensity of the future poet with another vertically challenged luminary of the 1810s: 'One of the transports of that marvellous actor, Edmund Kean – whom, by the way, he [i.e. Keats] idolized – was its nearest resemblance; and the two were not very dissimilar in face and figure.' Clarke's casual identification of poet Keats and actor Kean takes on a further significance when the former himself defines his ambition in playwriting in terms of emulating the contemporary theatrical sensation: 'One of my Ambitions is to make as great a revolution in modern dramatic writing as Kean has done in acting.'[100]

The following is an appraisal of Keats's attempted dramatic revolution, as seen first in his periodical review of Kean's acting and second in a tragedy (*Otho the Great*) that the poet tailored to the actor, and of the issues of self-identity and identification in playwriting and acting. In fact, Clarke's anecdote about the childhood fight has already helped us to reach the inmost core of Keatsian poetics, as the poet himself explained: 'Though a quarrel in the streets is a thing to be hated, the energies displayed in it are fine; the commonest Man shows a grace in his quarrel – By a superior being our reasoning[s] may take the same tone – though erroneous they may be fine – This is the very thing in which consists poetry' (2:80–1; To George and Georgiana Keats, 19 March 1819). Did Keats, and his alter ego Kean, successfully translate the sheer energy and flare of the street fight into tragic language and performance? Let us listen to Keats's verdict on Kean first.

Keats on Kean: the Champion *review*

While Keats's admiration for Leigh Hunt, his mentor and ally in the so-called Cockney School, quickly gave way to coolness, William Hazlitt remained his all-time critical hero.[101] Keats attended Hazlitt's lectures

('On the English Poets') regularly, read and annotated his publications (*Principles of Human Action*, *Characters of Shakespear's Plays* and *Round Table*, among others),[102] and even counted his 'depth of taste', along with William Wordsworth's *Excursion* and B. R. Haydon's pictures, among the 'three things to rejoice at in this Age' (1:203; To B. R. Haydon, 10 January 1818). So when asked to review Kean's comeback performances in *Richard III* and in James Bland Burges's *Riches* (1810), an adaptation of Philip Massinger's *City Madam* (1632?), for the *Champion* (21 December 1817), the poet naturally turned to the critical vocabulary of the foremost Keanite. Keats's review set Kean's impassioned acting against the background of political oppression, as symbolised by the controversial suspension of habeas corpus, and the cultural complacency of the Regency: ' "In our unimaginative days" – *Habeas Corpus'd* as we are, out of all wonder, uncertainty and fear; – in these fireside, delicate, gilded days, – these days of sickly safety and comfort, we feel very grateful to Mr. Kean for giving us some excitement by his old passion in one of the old plays.'[103] Keats went on to examine Kean's merit as Shakespearean actor by relying on two of Hazlitt's pet concepts: 'hieroglyphics' and 'gusto'. Like a painter, Hazlitt saw Shakespeare's language as 'hieroglyphical', as it 'translates thoughts into visible images'.[104] Keats distinguished two stages in dramatic communication: 'spiritual' written words and their 'sensual' vocal realisations. Shakespeare was responsible for the first 'spiritual' stage: 'A melodious passage in poetry is full of pleasures both sensual and spiritual. The spiritual is felt when the very letters and prints of charactered language show like the hieroglyphics of beauty; – the mysterious signs of an immortal freemasonry! "A thing to dream of, not to tell!" ' (530).

Unlike in Hazlitt's formulation, Keats's hieroglyphics were not a set of readily discernible 'visible images' but 'mysterious signs' of beauty. Kean's superb elocution would take the poetry on to the second 'sensual' stage and deliver the mysterious signs to the audience: 'The sensual life of verse springs warm from the lips of Kean, and to one learned in Shakespearian hieroglyphics, – learned in the spiritual portion of those lines to which Kean adds a sensual grandeur: his tongue must seem to have robbed "the Hybla bees, and left them honeyless" ' (530). Keats then explained Kean's powerful elocution in terms of 'gusto' in art. According to Hazlitt, gusto is the 'power or passion defining any object' and conveys its 'truth of character from the truth of feeling' to the outside world (*Round Table*, 4:77). Keats continued: 'There is an indescribable gusto in his voice, by which we feel that the utterer is thinking of the past and the future, while speaking of the instant. When he says in Othello "put up your bright swords, for the dew will rust them", we feel that his throat had commanded where swords were as thick as reeds' (530). Like a good student of a character critic, Keats appreciated the continuity and consistency in Kean's characterisation ('the past ... the future ... the instant') that the gusto made possible. The architectonics of the drama, on the other hand, was greatly played down. Keats praised, rather than criticised, the fact that Kean 'delivers himself up to the instant feeling, without a shadow of a thought about any thing else', when other actors are 'continually thinking of their sum-total effect throughout a play'.[105] In *Richard III*, '[a]lthough so many times he has lost the battle of Bosworth Field, we can easily conceive him really expectant of victory, and a different termination of the piece'. Keats marvelled at the actor's rich emotional resource and compared him to the representative Romantic of the day: 'He feels his being as deeply as Wordsworth, or any other of our intellectual monopolists' (531).

Published at the end of 1817, Keats's tribute to Kean was not particularly new in its insights, as the tragedian had presided over the London stage for nearly four years and his histrionic excellence had long been established. Nevertheless, this theatrical criticism was to trigger a crucial series of associations in the poet's mind on its day of publication.

'Negative Capability'

Celebrated as it is, and widely regarded as the quintessence of Keatsian poetics, the phrase 'Negative Capability' is used only once in the poet's writings. In a letter to his brothers dated 22 December 1817, Keats recalled an evening out with Charles Brown and Charles Wentworth Dilke. They were on their way back from a Christmas pantomime:

> I had not a dispute but a disquisition with Dilke, on various subjects; several things dovetailed in my mind, & at once it struck me, what quality went to form a Man of Achievement especially in Literature & which Shakespeare pos[s]essed so enormously – I mean *Negative Capability*, that is when man is capable of being in uncertainties, Mysteries, doubts, without any irritable reaching after fact & reason. (1:193)

Unfortunately, the 'various subjects' of the 'disquisition' with Dilke were not recorded, and the 'several things' that dovetailed in the poet's mind were not specified. Researchers have discussed Keats's Negative Capability extensively, in terms especially of the inconclusiveness of his poems and of the development of his artistic theories as seen in various other letters.[106]

The events and ideas mentioned in this letter deserve particular attention in relation to Keats's dramatic theory and playwriting, as they revolved around the same themes of dogmatism and negativity, along with their corollary question of intensity and 'gusto', as in the theatrical review, before finally crystallising into the famous manifesto. And, once again, Hazlitt's critical acumen stimulated Keats's thinking throughout.

Before writing the letter, Keats had sent out a copy of the *Champion* to his younger brothers with another journal, the *Examiner*, 'in which you will find very proper lamentation on the obsolation of christmas Gambols & pastimes' (1:191). For all its righteous contentions, the *Examiner* essay ('Christmas and other old National Merry-makings', 21, 28 December 1817) was tarnished by the perverse dogmatism of its author Hunt, or as Keats himself put it: 'it was mixed up with so much egotism of that drivelling nature that pleasure is entirely lost'. After referring to the trial of the radical journalist William Hone and the issue of censorship, which is dogmatism taken into a political arena, Keats criticised a history painting by Hunt's elderly friend, Benjamin West: 'I spent Friday evening with Wells & went the next morning to see *Death on the Pale horse*. It is a wonderful picture, when West's age is considered; But there is nothing to be intense upon; no women one feels mad to kiss; no face swelling into reality' (1:192). Keats's formulation echoed Hazlitt's demonstration of the 'gusto' of Correggio and Raphael ('Whenever we look at the hands of Correggio's women or Raphael's, we always wish to touch them', *Round Table*, 4:78) simultaneously with the critic's recent attack on West's faulty 'hieroglyphics' in *Death on the Pale Horse* (18:138).[107] In clear contrast with West's inept visualisation of the idea of death, Shakespeare's *King Lear* sublimates tragic motifs into a profound aesthetic sensation. Keats continued: 'the excellence of every Art is its intensity, capable of making all disagreeables evaporate, from their being in close relationship with Beauty & Truth – Examine King Lear & you will find this exemplified throughout; but in this picture we have unpleasantness without any momentous depth of speculation excited, in which to bury its repulsiveness' (1:192). Unlike in the *Champion* review, Keats's discussion was limited to the first 'spiritual' hieroglyphics in this passage, as *King Lear* was banned from the stage for the period 1810–20 owing to George III's mental disorder. (It was no accident that the poet sat down 'to Read *King Lear* Once Again' in the famous sonnet.) While intensity and gusto were not necessarily tragic, Keats found their artistic consummation in the Shakespearean tragedy, where 'all disagreeables', 'unpleasantness' and 'repulsiveness' evaporate into beauty and truth.

Keats next explored the comical manifestation of gusto, and lack of it, in the forms of 'humour' and 'wit'. The insight dawned on him on a boring social evening:

I dined too . . . with Horace Smith & met his two Brothers with Hill & Kingston & one Du Bois, they only served to convince me, how superior humour is to wit in respect to enjoyment – These men say things which make one start, without making one feel, they are all alike; their manners are alike; they all know fas[h]ionables; they have a mannerism in their very eating & drinking, in their mere handling a Decanter. (1:192–3)

The self-complacency and snobbery of the fashionable men repelled Keats and, like Hunt's Christmas essay, taught him to distinguish between egotism and true intensity. In the meantime, Kean's notorious drinking club ('The Wolf Club') was buying notoriety in town.[108] The polite society grimaced at Kean's binge sessions and licentious behaviour, of which street fights formed a very notable part. Keats exclaimed, '[Smith and his friends] talked of Kean & his low company – Would I were with that company instead of yours said I to myself!'

Finally, we are back to the Christmas pantomime night and the Negative Capability, with a clearer idea of what dovetailed in Keats's mind during the 'disquisition' with Dilke. Kean's acting and Hunt's criticism, libel and censorship, West's *Death* and Shakespeare's *King Lear*, the dinner with the snobs and Kean's 'low company': all these episodes illustrate true intensity, 'gusto' and Negative Capability, as opposed to egotism and complacency, in various artistic, personal and social contexts. If we are still short on illustration, we can also turn to Keats's later comment on his friend Dilke's personality:

That Dilke was a Man who cannot feel he has a personal identity unless he has made up his Mind about every thing. The only means of strengthening one's intellect is to make up ones mind about nothing – to let the mind be a thoroughfare for all thoughts. Not a select party. The genus is not scarce in population. All the stubborn arguers you meet with are of the same brood – They never begin upon a subject they have not preresolved on. They want to hammer their nail into you and if you turn the point, still they think you wrong. Dilke will never come at a truth as long as he lives; because he is always trying at it. (2:213; To George and Georgiana Keats, 24 September 1819)

Now let me quote the crucial paragraph from that letter to his brothers in full:

I had not a dispute but a disquisition with Dilke, on various subjects; several things dovetailed in my mind, & at once it struck me, what quality went to form a Man of Achievement especially in Literature & which Shakespeare pos[s]essed so enormously – I mean *Negative Capability*, that is when man is capable of being in uncertainties, Mysteries, doubts, without any irritable reaching after fact & reason – Coleridge, for instance, would let go by a fine isolated verisimilitude caught from the Penetralium of mystery, from being incapable of remaining content with half knowledge. This pursued through Volumes would perhaps take us no further than this, that with a great poet the sense of Beauty overcomes every other consideration, or rather obliterates all consideration.

Keats's aesthetics of negativity was to find a slightly modified expression in a letter to Richard Woodhouse (27 October 1818), where the true poetical character (as represented by Keats himself and once again by Shakespeare) was defined not against Samuel Taylor Coleridge's restless reaching after truth but against the more self-assured egotism of his onetime best friend, Wordsworth. Correspondingly, the poetical character became even more 'negative' than before: now he was not 'capable' of negativity but was negativity itself.

As to the poetical Character itself, (I mean that sort of which, if I am any thing, I am a Member; that sort distinguished from the wordsworthian or egotistical sublime; which is a thing per se and stands alone) it is not itself – it has no self – it is every thing and nothing – It has no character – it enjoys light and shade; it lives in gusto, be it foul or fair, high or low, rich or poor, mean or elevated – It has as much delight in conceiving an Iago as an Imogen. What shocks the virtuous philosop[h]er, delights the c[h]amelion Poet . . . A Poet is the most unpoetical of any thing in existence; because he has no Identity. (1:386–7)

After scrutinising the Negative Capability letter, we encounter the same combination of Shakespeare, 'gusto' and Wordsworth's egotism as noted in Keats's theatrical review. But with one important difference. In the review article Kean was a man of gusto and the perfect theatrical realisation of Shakespearean tragedy. *And* he felt 'his being as deeply as Wordsworth, or any other of our intellectual monopolists'. Kean's gusto shone when he delivered 'himself up to the instant feeling', and this firmly premised the actor's 'himself'. In the letter just quoted, on the other hand, Keats asserted that the true poetic character should be *unlike* Wordsworth and be devoid of selfhood.

The two statements may not be as contradictory as they first appear. In the theatrical review Keats's attitude to Wordsworth's selfhood and 'intellectual monopoly' was fairly negative already: he praised the deep selfhood of the thespian very much at the expense of the poetic giant and his allies. After all, Keats did not say that Kean was the same as Wordsworth: the tragedian may feel, and achieve, *more* than the egotistical poet. Even so, this small logical loop in Keats does posit an important question concerning artistic expression and the artist's identity. Is it really possible for an artist to create a strong expression by becoming nothing himself? Is Keatsian negativity capable of intensity or gusto? Keats's own tragedy, the largely unsuccessful *Otho the Great* (1819), will afford an invaluable insight into these difficult questions.

Scene by scene

In 1819 Keats was seriously short of cash and was considering 'a situation with an Apothecary'. He had lost access to his late father's estate in Chancery, over which the widow of his uncle had brought a lawsuit. Charles Brown offered help first by lending him some money and second by proposing what sounded like a financially beneficial literary venture: a joint authorship of a tragedy for the popular stage. Keats gratefully complied with his friend's suggestion, as he had long regarded playwriting as his 'chief attempt'. The idea was that Brown, whose comic opera (*Narensky*, 1814) had once reached the Drury Lane stage, would provide the narrative for each scene, which Keats would then turn into speeches in blank verse. Retreating to Shanklin on the Isle of Wight, the pair worked together on the first four acts of the tragedy in July and early August. Keats then finished the last act on his own in Winchester in about ten days.

Their tragedy is set in the reign of Otho the Great, the first Holy Roman Emperor, and his hot-tempered son, Ludolph, is the protagonist. Young Ludolph once rebelled against the emperor out of antipathy to his domineering nature. They also clashed over Ludolph's wish to marry the temptress Auranthe, as his father wanted him to choose the virtuous Erminia. When the play opens, however, the situation has changed. Ludolph has always loved Otho at heart, and secretly supported his father during a battle against the Huns by disguising himself as a valiant Arab. Otho is indeed a doting father and, seeing through his son's disguise, has much appreciated his valour. Erminia, in the meantime, has fallen from grace with the emperor, as her allegedly lewd behaviour – a beau was rumoured to have entered her room in the night by climbing up a ladder to her window – has been disclosed. (Needless to say, this was a conspiracy of Auranthe, in cooperation with her ambitious brother Conrad, to disguise her own rendezvous.) Otho and Ludolph are now reunited, and the son marries his beloved. Only then is Auranthe's true nature disclosed. The betrayed Ludolph goes mad and dies in a frenzy.

Critics' verdicts on Keats's only completed tragedy, when they make one at all on this largely neglected work, have never been favourable. Francis Jeffrey regarded it as a 'great failure' and Amy Lowell called it 'dull beyond belief'.[109] For them, it is a 'mere hack work' and 'primarily for money'.[110] Recent critics have been slightly more kind to Keats and attribute the disaster to the awkward way in which he worked with Brown. Their 'curious' procedure was recorded by the co-author:

> At Shanklin he [i.e. Keats] undertook a difficult task: I engaged to furnish him with the fable, characters, and dramatic conduct of a tragedy, and he was to embody it into poetry. The progress of the work was curious; for, while I sat opposite to him, he caught my description of each scene, entered into the characters to be brought forward, the events, and every thing connected with it. Thus he went on, scene after scene, never knowing nor inquiring into the scene which was to follow, until four acts were completed.[111]

Critics sympathise with the cash-strapped genius who had to work with the less talented sponsor, and agree that the piecemeal versification crippled Keats's poetic imagination. Thomas McFarland's comment is representative: 'Brown was the villain – if that be not too strong a word for a most well-intentioned friend – of the whole dramatic misadventure, which violated in its very inception Keats's own understandings of how poetry should be generated.'[112]

I certainly agree that *Otho the Great* is not among Keats's masterpieces: it is at best a failed attempt at Shakespearean tragedy. I do question, however, whether Keats was quite as passive and submissive in the compositional procedure. Brown's memoir continues:

> It was then he required to know, at once, all the events which were to occupy the fifth act. I explained them to him; but, after a patient hearing, and some thought, he insisted on it that my incidents were too numerous, and, as he termed them, too melodramatic. He wrote the fifth act in accordance with his own view; and so enchanted was I with his poetry, that, at the time, and for a long time after, I thought he was in the right.[113]

This indicates that if Keats had wanted to know the whole story, Brown would have obliged him willingly, and that the poet could return a negative to his friend's proposals when necessary. To express strong tragic feeling 'never knowing nor inquiring into the scene which was to follow' certainly sounds like a challenge, but did Keats not admire how Kean threw himself up to the passion of the moment as if he knew nothing about the future storyline ('Other actors are continually thinking of their sum-total effect throughout a play. Kean delivers himself up to the instant feeling, without a shadow of a thought about any thing else')? The similarity between Keats's analysis of Kean's acting and his own playwriting procedure seems more than a coincidence, as the poet was tailoring the part of young Ludolph specifically for his favourite tragedian ('There is no actor can do the principal character besides Kean'). I would argue that Keats was far more conscious and deliberate about the composition of *Otho the Great* than critics have ever believed. The poet experimented, though unsuccessfully, with some daring methods to create tragic intensity.

Tragic flaw: Acts 1 to 4

Written in mock-Shakespearean (or 'sub-Shakespearean', as Andrew Motion has more happily put it) blank verse, Keats's tragedy encompassed various echoes and verbal borrowings from the Bard's canon.[114] The opening monologue of the scheming Conrad is redolent of that of Shakespeare's famous hunchback, while Otho's visit to the siblings' castle in the next scene reminds critics of King Duncan in *Macbeth*. Albert, the sometime beau of Auranthe, learns of her vicious intrigue against Erminia and soliloquises his tortured conscience *à la* Hamlet:

> O that the earth were empty, as when Cain
> Had no perplexity to hide his head!
> Or that the sword of some brave enemy
> Had put a sudden stop to my hot breath,
> And hurl'd me down the illimitable gulph
> Of times past, unremember'd![115]

And Erminia's alleged midnight rendezvous and the ladder to her window obviously owe much to *Much Ado About Nothing*.[116]

Staying in Shanklin with his good friend Brown, Keats apparently enjoyed playwriting a great deal, discussing (or joking about) various ideas to enliven the drama:

Brown and I are pretty well harnessed again to our dog-cart. I mean the Tragedy which goes on sinkingly – We are thinking of introducing an Elephant [presumably for Otho's entry at Act 1 scene 2] but have not historical reference within reach to determine us as to Otho's Menagerie. When Brown first mention'd this I took it for a Joke; however he brings such plausible reasons, and discourses so eloquently on the dramatic effect that I am giving it a serious consideration. The Art of Poetry is not sufficient for us. (2:135; To C. W. Dilke, 31 July 1819)

The audacity of some of Keats's own proposals stunned the co-author, likewise. Regarding the scene to follow Ludolph and Auranthe's offstage wedding (3.2), he noted: 'Keats is very industrious, but ... obstinately monstrous. What think you of Otho's threatening cold pig to the new married couple? He says the Emperor must have a spice of drollery.'[117] Eric Partridge's slang dictionary informs that to give cold pig is 'to awaken by sluicing with cold water or by pulling of the bed-cloth'. Keats apparently did not have sufficient 'historical reference within reach' as to the protocol of the Holy Roman Empire, either. The poet made another unruly suggestion regarding Ludolph's response to Auranthe's betrayal (4.2): 'K.'s introduction of Grimm's adventure, lying three days on his back for love, though it spoils the unity of time is not out of the way for the character of Ludolph, so I have consented to it.'[118] According to editor Jack Stillinger, Brown's reference was to F. M. Grimm's *Historical Literary Memoirs*, in which the baron's experience of being jilted and falling 'into a sort of catalepsy which continued for several days' is told. The unfortunate lover then suddenly recovered from the coma and 'never thought more of his chaste Lucretia'.[119] The story is certainly interesting, but hardly tragic: if the hero just swoons at the apex of agony, sleeps right through, and forgets the trauma as he awakens, there would not be much scope for Edmund Kean to display his legendary whirlwind of passions.

Somewhat disappointingly, these colourful details are missing from the final product. *Otho the Great* as we have it today is a boringly regular tragedy that French classicists would be proud of. The three unities are preserved, if we overlook a short scene set in a distant Hungarian camp (2.2). Otho is devoid of the spicy naughtiness and appears as a dignified monarch and affectionate father throughout. The play is very uneventful especially in the early acts, as potentially powerful episodes are kept offstage: Ludolph's revolt against Otho, his Arab disguise during the Hungarian warfare, and the alleged midnight dating of Erminia (in fact Auranthe) have all happened before curtain-up. Keats's dramatic characters recall, report and comment on the past incidents in scene after scene.

Tragic momentum was also in short supply. The potentially catastrophic tension between Otho and Ludolph is resolved during their very first interview (2.1), where Otho forgives the son's past rebellion and thanks him for his support during the war. In fact, the play could end very happily at the end of Act 4, as in Keats's source story *Much Ado About Nothing*, when Erminia's innocence and Auranthe's intrigue come to light. The only impetus to drive Ludolph to madness and subsequent death in the final act is his personality and, for this, Keats owed much to Shakespeare or, to be more precise, to contemporary character criticism of Shakespeare.

Character criticism, when it is applied to tragedy especially, is liable to a curious inversion. With the protagonist's mindset prioritised over the dramatic action he is in, the play is deemed tragic not on account of what happens to the hero but of the character of the hero. According to Coleridge's 'Character of Hamlet', Shakespeare inflated a certain aspect of his own intellectual or moral property 'in morbid excess' and placed himself 'thus mutilated and diseased under given circumstances' to create his characters. Coleridge applied this theory to Hamlet:

> In Hamlet I conceive him [i.e. Shakespeare] to have wished to exemplify the moral necessity of a due Balance between our attention to outward objectives, and our meditation on inward Thoughts – a due Balance between the real and the imaginary World – In Hamlet this Balance does not exist – his Thoughts Images & Fancy far more vivid than his Perceptions, and his very Perceptions instantly passing thro' the medium of his contemplations, and acquiring as they pass, a form and color not naturally his own. Hence great enormous intellectual activity, and a consequent proportionate aversion to real action, with all its symptoms and accompanying qualities.[120]

According to this explanation, Hamlet's meditativeness is 'in morbid excess', 'mutilated' and 'diseased' even before he is placed 'under given circumstances'. Hamlet is tragic not because Claudius killed his father and whored his mother, but because he is obsessed with his inner world and is unable to act. In other words, the Prince of Denmark is tragically flawed from the start. It was therefore no accident that Coleridge associated him with Wordsworth's villain Rivers and referred to the following passage in the same lecture note:

> RIVERS
> Action is transitory, a step, a blow –
> The motion of a muscle – this way or that –
> 'Tis done – and in the after vacancy
> We wonder at ourselves like men betray'd.
> Suffering is permanent, obscure and dark,
> And has the nature of infinity. (*The Borderers*, 3.5.60–5)

The dramatic situations that Hamlet and Rivers are in are completely different. Rivers has acted villainously (he has killed an old man and trapped Mortimer into killing another old man) and is now remorseful of what he has done. Hamlet's regret is lack of action. However, from Coleridge's character-based point of view, Hamlet is just as responsible for the tragedy of *Hamlet* as Rivers is for *The Borderers*.

This tragic flaw also defines Keats's protagonist. Ludolph goes mad and dies not simply because the vicious Auranthe betrayed him but, more crucially, because his character is flawed. Keats underscored Ludolph's excessive pride and lack of balance from before the revelation of Auranthe's intrigues. The prince has helped his father in the war but refuses to let him know of the fact. His confidant Sigifred is puzzled:

SIGIFRED   My lord, forgive me that I cannot see
            How this proud temper with clear reason squares.
            What made you then, with such an anxious love,
            Hover around that life, whose bitter days
            You vext with bad revolt? Was't opium,
            Or the mad-fumed wine – ? (1.3.30–5)

When Ludolph marries Auranthe, his extreme rapture surprises the ladies of the court:

FIRST LADY   How deep she has bewitch'd him!
FIRST KNIGHT   Ask you for her receipt for love philtres.
                . . .
FIRST LADY   He soars!
SECOND LADY   Past all reason. (3.2.14–15; 37)

Ludolph goes on to gush even more about his feelings for Auranthe (3.2.38–44) and worries his doting father:

OTHO.   This is a little painful; just too much.
         Conrad, if he flames longer in this wise,
         I shall believe in wizard-woven loves
         And old romances. (3.2.45–8)

In short, the protagonist is 'a little painful' and 'just too much' even before destiny throws him into profound disillusionment and dismay. Keats would single-mindedly develop the emotional turmoil of this flawed protagonist in the final act in a bid to flash Kean's lightning.

'Whirlwind of your passion': Act 5

> Is it not monstrous that this player here,
> But in a fiction, in a dream of passion,
> Could force his soul so to his own conceit
> That from her working all his visage wann'd,
> Tears in his eyes, distraction in his aspect,
> A broken voice, and his whole function suiting
> With forms to his conceit? And all for nothing!
> For Hecuba! (*Hamlet*, 2.2.551–8)

Acting is a mystery. Actors fascinate, and even puzzle, the spectators by the extraordinary range and force of emotions they express. Do the actors feel their characters' feeling or do they just pretend they do by histrionic expertise? And if they do, does the feeling derive from the actors' sympathetic identification with the dramatic character and the situation he or she is in or do they dig up some appropriate emotion from their own real-life experiences and use it on stage? Various actors and critics have addressed the enigma. Colley Cibber noted that, in *Hamlet*, the ruddy Betterton would 'thro' the violent and sudden Emotions of Amazement and Horror, turn instantly on the Sight of his Father's Spirit, as pale as his Neckcloth, when every Article of his Body seem'd to be affected with a Tremor inexpressible'. Does this suggest that Betterton actually felt the emotion? And does it follow that the feeling was really his, or was it Hamlet's? Cibber continued, 'had his [i.e. Betterton's] Father's Ghost actually risen before him; he could not have been seized with more real Agonies'.[121]

As was discussed in chapter 1, David Garrick mastered Lear's emotion by observing a deranged neighbour. Did he sympathise with the madman's misery or did he just imitate his facial expressions and bodily movements? Garrick's own explanations were contradictory. He emphasised his 'feelings' when he confronted Samuel Johnson, who regarded him as a mindless Punch, but demonstrated to the *philosophe* Denis Diderot that he could express any feeling without actually feeling it. Diderot recorded a curious experiment:

Garrick will put his head between two folding-doors, and in the course of five or six seconds his expression will change successively from wild delight to temperate pleasure, from this to tranquillity, from tranquillity to surprise, from surprise to blank astonishment, from that to sorrow, from sorrow to the air of one overwhelmed, from that to fright, from fright to horror, from horror to despair, and thence he will go up again to the point from which he started. Can his soul have experienced all these feelings, and played this kind of scale in concert with his face? I don't believe it.[122]

Sarah Siddons's tragic acting reached its zenith when consumption claimed the lives of her teenage daughters, and there was a rumour that John Philip Kemble's acting was mechanical and emotionless because he had no child. It was no accident either that Johnson, who 'had thought more upon the subject of acting than might be generally supposed', found his ally in the latter tragedian:

Talking of it one day to Mr. Kemble, he [Johnson] said, 'Are you, Sir, one of those enthusiasts who believe yourself transformed into the very character you represent?' Upon Mr. Kemble's answering that he had never felt so strong a persuasion himself; 'To be sure not, Sir, (said Johnson;) the thing is impossible. And if Garrick really believed himself to be that monster, Richard the Third, he deserved to be hanged every time he performed it.'[123]

Kean remembered his late Uncle Moses when he needed to glamorise his tragic acting, but he also said that 'real' feeling was evoked in him on stage only when his partner was an attractive young actress. According to another theatrical legend, Kean observed 'the deaths of the Cato Street conspirators' and declared, 'I mean to die like Thistlewood tonight; I'll imitate every muscle of that man's countenance.'[124]

These confused and contradictory testimonies on tragic impersonation find their exact parallel in the discussions of Shakespeare's characterisation. It is a critical commonplace, from Margaret Cavendish on, to marvel at the variety and depth of Shakespeare's dramatic characters and to applaud the Protean mutability of the dramatist.[125] Did Shakespeare infuse himself into and feel with different characters, or were they all different aspects of the dramatist's own vast personality? Or maybe it was simply a matter of playwriting technique? In his Preface Johnson maintained his no-nonsense approach to theatrical art and dispensed with the drollery of empathy and feeling. For him, Shakespeare was a great observer of the way of the world and was a master of assigning everyday speeches to appropriate characters ('The choice is right, when there is reason for choice'). It was strictly in this sense that 'his drama is the mirrour of life':

> This therefore is the praise of Shakespeare ... that he who has mazed his imagination, in following the phantoms which other writers raise up before him, may here be cured of his delirious extasies, by reading human sentiments in human language; by scenes from which a hermit may estimate the transactions of the world, and a confessor predict the progress of the passions. (*On Shakespeare*, 65)

Elizabeth Montagu's view in her *Essay* was not quite as sobering. Shakespeare's tragic lines 'open to us the internal state of the person interested, and never fail to command our sympathy', all thanks to his magical identification with dramatic characters and situations: 'Shakespear seems to have had the art of the Dervise, in the Arabian tales, who could throw his soul into the body of another man, and be at once possessed of his sentiments, adopt his passions, and rise to all the functions and feelings of his situation' (13). Coleridge regarded Shakespeare's characters as punctuated and distorted segments of the dramatist's own personality. To Hazlitt, Shakespeare was quite devoid of specific character and was really a master of becoming somebody else ('He was the least of an egotist that it was possible to be. He was nothing in himself; but he was all that others were, or that they could become'). Hazlitt, however, did not necessarily believe in Shakespeare's sympathetic fusion with his dramatis personae:

> [Shakespeare] was like the genius of humanity, changing places with all of us at pleasure, and playing with our purposes as with his own. He turned the globe round for his amusement, and surveyed the generations of men, and the individuals as they passed, with their different concerns, passions, follies, vices, virtues, actions, and motives . . . The dreams of childhood, the ravings of despair, were the toys of his fancy. (*Lectures on the English Poets*, 5:47)

To create various characters, including tragic ones, was Shakespeare's 'amusement', and 'the dreams of childhood' and 'the ravings of despair' were equally 'toys' for the gigantic genius and nothing more. In short, Shakespeare enjoyed, rather than suffered, the agonies of the tragic characters.

Keats's explanation of the 'poetical Character', of which Shakespeare was the model, echoed Hazlitt's denunciation of egotism but emphasised the pure aesthetic joy and 'delight', not playful 'toys' or 'amusement', of playwriting: '[The poetical character] enjoys light and shade . . . It has as much delight in conceiving an Iago as an Imogen. What shocks the virtuous philosop[h]er, delights the c[h]amelion Poet.' From around the time of *Otho the Great*'s composition, however, letters recorded a very different side to this aesthetic hedonist. Referring to the misery of the English men of letters, Keats wrote, 'One of the great reasons that the english have produced the finest writers in the world; is, that the English world has ill-treated them during their lives and foster'd them after their deaths. They have in general been trampled aside into the bye paths of life and seen the festerings of Society' (2:115; To Sarah Jeffrey, 9 June 1819). Now it was the real-life misery, not aesthetic joy, that had helped the writers create literature, and Shakespeare was no exception: 'The middle age of Shakspeare was all c[l]ouded over; his days were not more happy than Hamlet's who is perhaps more like Shakspeare himself in his common every day Life than any other of his Characters' (2:115–16). Keats's theory of Shakespeare's 'unhappiness' may refer to the death of the dramatist's son (Hamnet) whose name was interchangeable with that of the Danish prince,[126] but the association between the playwright's private agony and his tragic characterisation was no doubt strengthened by the hardship that Keats himself went through in 1819.[127]

After a prolonged illness, the poet's beloved brother Tom had died of tuberculosis in December the previous year. Financial difficulties prevented Keats from marrying his half-official fiancée, Fanny Brawne, for whom he nurtured an obsessive jealousy ('My greatest torment since I have known you has been the fear of you being a little inclined to the Cressid', 2:256; To Fanny Brawne, February 1820?). It is believed that the sojourn on the Isle of Wight in July was Keats's self-imposed exile from the agony of the unconsummated relationship. While composing Act 4, in which Auranthe's infidelity is revealed, Keats wrote to Fanny, 'I leave this minute a scene in our Tragedy and see you (think it not blasphemy) through the mist of Plots speeches, counterplots and counter speeches – The Lover is madder than I am – I am nothing to him – he has a figure like the Statue of Maleager and double distilled fire in his heart. Thank God for my diligence! were it not for that I should be miserable' (2:137; 5 August 1819). Critics agree that a great deal of Ludolph's agony was painfully studied from Keats's own experience. However, this self-identification was not simply a by-product of an unfortunate love affair but a means that the poet consciously employed, especially in the final act, to delineate strong tragic passions. As already noted, the scene-by-scene versification was abandoned at Act 4, when Keats demanded that Brown give 'at once, all the events which were to occupy the fifth act' and, finding the incidents 'too numerous, and . . . too melodramatic', completed the play on his own. Brown did not list the 'events' that Keats had found 'too numerous', but they probably included the love between Erminia and the Hungarian prince Gersa and an onstage confrontation between Albert and Conrad. These minor characters and subplots omitted, the final act was devoted entirely to Ludolph's growing jealousy and desperation.

After capturing the eloped Auranthe, Ludolph goes mad and 'fills the arched rooms / With ghastly ravings' (5.3.15–16). He holds a wedding feast during which he intended to kill the duplicitous woman (Auranthe commits suicide offstage and is discovered dead in the end). Deeply concerned about his son's derangement, Otho has requested all the guests to 'obey / The Prince from A to Z' (5.5.5–6). With other characters acting as the prince's puppets, Ludolph overwhelmingly dominates the last scene, where he raves and dies.

To portray the protagonist's frenzy, the usually 'selfless' Keats made the most of his own tormented mental state. On the Isle of Wight, Fanny's features haunted the distanced poet, who complained, 'Why may I not speak of your Beauty, since without that I could never have lov'd you – I cannot conceive any beginning of such love as I have for you but Beauty . . . So let me speak of you[r] Beauty' (2:127; 8 July 1819). The betrayed Ludolph frantically remembers Auranthe's face, which bears a noticeable resemblance to that of the poet's fiancée:

> Deep blue eyes, semi-shaded in white lids,
> Finish'd with lashes fine for more soft shade,
> Completed by her twin-arch'd ebon brows;

> White temples, of exactest elegance,
> Or even mould, felicitous and smooth;
> Cheeks fashion'd tenderly on either side,
> So perfect, so divine, that our poor eyes
> Are dazzled with the sweet proportioning,
> And wonder that 'tis so, – the magic chance!
> Her nostrils, small, fragrant, fairy-delicate;
> Her lips – I swear no human bones e'er wore
> So taking a disguise; – you shall behold her! (5.5.61–72)[128]

Living away from home and being insecure about his financial future, Keats was constantly threatened by the idea of Fanny's betrayal, which was, as far as can be seen from biographical evidences, almost entirely unfounded. Keats's anxiety was recorded in many letters:

> indeed if I thought you felt as much for me as I do for you at this moment I do not think I could restrain myself from seeing you again tomorrow for the delight of one embrace. But no – I must live upon hope and Chance. In case of the worst that can happen, I shall still love you – but what hatred shall I have for another! (2:123; To Fanny Brawne, 1 July 1819)

The ambiguous final word ('another!') is clarified by Keats's subsequent misquotation from Massinger's *Duke of Milan* (1623) (1.3.203–6): 'To see those eyes I prize above mine own / Dart favors on another – / And those sweet lips (yielding immortal nector) / Be gently press'd by any but myself – '. Keats's reference was 'another man'. It is as if the poet was even afraid of verbalising his worst anxiety. In *Otho the Great* betrayal, separation and consequent desperation are expressed forthrightly:

> LUDOLPH   A barrier of guilt! I was the fool,
> She was the cheater! Who's the cheater now,
> And who the fool? The entrapp'd, the caged fool,
> The bird-lim'd raven? She shall croak to death!
> Secure! Methinks I have her in my fist,
> To crush her with my heel! (5.5.104–9)

One of Keats's fantasies of this period was an aesthetic fusion of love and death. He wrote to Fanny that 'I have two luxuries to brood over in my walks, your Loveliness and the hour of my death. O that I could have possession of them both in the same minute' (25 July 1819; 2:133). Love and death are firmly united in the catastrophe of the tragedy, when the sight of the lifeless Auranthe finally kills the deranged lover:

> LUDOLPH   She's gone! I am content – nobles, good night!
> Where is your hand, father? – what sultry air!

> We are all weary – faint – set ope the doors –
> I will to bed! – To-morrow [*Dies.*] (5.5.192–5)

Researchers regret that Keats's tragedy did not realise the Shakespearean 'Negative Capability'. The poet is condemned as being far from selfless, as his 'violent agitation about Fanny is the thinly disguised theme of his most impressive scenes, and also the reason why the play as a whole is a failure'.[129] *Otho the Great* is certainly a failed tragedy but, quite significantly, Keats himself was happy with the final product and attributed the supposed success to his very egotism. Immediately after the completion of the tragedy, Keats wrote to the publisher John Taylor on 23 August 1819:

> I feel every confidence that if I choose I may be a popular writer; that I will never be; but for all that I will get a livelihood – I equally dislike the favour of the public with the love of a woman . . . You will observe at the end of this if you put down the Letter 'How a solitary life engenders pride and egotism!' True: I know it does but this Pride and egotism will enable me to write finer things than any thing else could – so I will indulge it. (2:144)[130]

The same misgivings over the world outside and the strong sense of egotism reappear in a letter to J. H. Reynolds written the following day:

> The more I know what my diligence may in time probably effect; the more does my heart distend with Pride and Obstinacy – I feel it in my power to become a popular writer – I feel it in my strength to refuse the poisonous suffrage of a public – My own being which I know to be becomes of more consequence to me than the crowds of Shadows in the Shape of Man and women that inhabit a kingdom. The Soul is a world of itself and has enough to do in its own home . . . I have nothing to speak of but myself – and what can I say but what I feel? (2:146–7)

Otho the Great no doubt failed the Shakespearean ideal of Negative Capability, but it was Keats's intention to infuse his suppressed anxiety and aggression into Ludolph especially in the final scene, and he did succeed in this. The only problem is that the poet's empathy with the protagonist does not evoke the reader's (and if it is performed, the spectator's) emotions in a strong way.

Keats was just as confident about the suitability of the part of Ludolph for his idol Kean, the only concern being the actor's rumoured departure for an American tour ('I had hoped to give Kean another opportunity to shine. What can we do now? There is not another actor of Tragedy in all London or Europe', 2:149; To Fanny Keats, 28 August 1819). In Keats's mind Kean's acting and his playwriting were to ensure each other's success: 'If he should [stay in England] I have confident hopes of our Tragedy – If he smokes the hotblooded character of Ludolph – and he is the only actor that can do it – He will add to his own fame, and improve my fortune' (2:217; To George and Georgiana Keats, 27 September 1819).

In the end, Kean stayed in London, and Keats's tragedy was accepted by Drury Lane to be produced in the following season. According to Brown, Kean even 'desired to play the principal character'.[131] Unfortunately, Brown and Keats were desperate for cash and could not endure the one-year wait. They retracted the script from Drury Lane and sent it to the rival Covent Garden to be considered for a ready production. Covent Garden returned the script without even opening the parcel. And this was the (appropriately) unclimactic end of Keats's theatrical enterprise.

A symposium

It is time to remember James Northcote, the disciple and biographer of Joshua Reynolds who recorded such interesting anecdotes on *Count Ugolino and His Children* and the Shakespearean pictures. (He also modelled as one of the sons of Ugolino – the young man clutching his hand to his face – for his master.) He developed into a fairly capable history and portrait painter and established himself as a Royal Academician. By a curious coincidence, he found a good friend in his old age in Hazlitt, who deeply admired the senior painter and recorded his conversations with the octogenarian in the style of James Boswell's *Life of Samuel Johnson* (*Boswell Redivivus* (1826–30); also known as *Conversations of James Northcote*). Their second conversation took place while Northcote was working on his self-portrait. Hazlitt regretted that, lacking in pictorial invention, he could never have painted history, though he had managed portraiture. Northcote then explained the relations between history painting and portraiture for his younger companion, and their discussion subsequently spilled over into the issue of good and bad acting.

Keats, we might conclude, was a good lyric and narrative poet but clearly failed as a playwright. He composed several masterly poems around the themes of fatal attraction, betrayal and disillusionment ('La Belle Dame Sans Merci', *Lamia* and 'The Cap and Bells; or, The Jealousies', for example), but when he dramatised the same set of motifs, the result was less than satisfactory.

To end this chapter on Romantic acting and playwriting, let Keats join Northcote and Hazlitt and see if he finds any means to transfer his poetic skills to playwriting from their aesthetic conversation. (Aristotle and Dr Johnson might also deign to give some odd comments.)[132]

***

NORTHCOTE	I wanted to ask you about a speech you made the other day: you said you thought you could have made something of portrait, but that you never could have painted history. What did you mean by that?
HAZLITT	Oh! all I meant was, that sometimes when I see a fine Titian or Rembrandt, I feel as if I could have done something of the same kind with the proper pains, but I have never the same feeling with respect to Raphael. My admiration is there utterly unmixed with emulation or regret. In fact, I see what is before me, but I have no invention.
KEATS	It was the opinion of most of my friends that I should never be able to write a scene – I will endeavour to wipe away the prejudice – One of my ambitions is to make as great a revolution in modern dramatic writing as Kean has done in acting. (2:139; To Benjamin Bailey, 14 August 1819)
NORTHCOTE	You do not know till you try. There is not so much difference as you imagine. Portrait often runs into history, and history into portrait, without our knowing it. Expression is common to both, and that is the chief difficulty. The greatest history-painters have always been able portrait-painters. How should a man paint a thing in motion, if he cannot paint it still?
KEATS	My having written that argument [of *Endymion*] will perhaps be of the greatest service to me of any thing I ever did – It set before me at once the gradations of happiness even like a kind of pleasure thermometer – and is my first step towards the chief attempt in the drama – the playing of different natures with joy and sorrow. (1:218–19; To John Taylor, 30 January 1818)
NORTHCOTE	But the great point is to catch the prevailing look and character: if you are master of this, you can make almost what use of it you please. If a portrait has force, it will do for history; and if history is well painted, it will do for portrait. This is what gave dignity to Sir Joshua: his portraits had always that determined air and character that you know what to think of them as if you had seen them engaged in the most decided action.
JOHNSON	I should grieve to see Reynolds transfer to heroes and to goddesses, to empty splendor and to airy fiction, that art which is now employed in diffusing friendship, in reviving tenderness, in quickening the affections of the absent, and continuing the presence of the dead.[133]
NORTHCOTE	No! if you can give the *look*, you need not fear painting history. Yet how difficult that is, and on what slight causes it depends! It is not enough that it is seen, unless it is at the same time felt. How odd it seems, that often while you are looking at a face, and though you perceive no difference in the features, yet you

	find they have undergone a total alteration of expression! What a fine hand then is required to trace what the eye can scarcely be said to distinguish!
JOHNSON	(*aside*) 'Tis vain, says the satirist, to set before any Englishman the scenes of landscape, or the heroes of history; nature and antiquity are nothing in his eye; he has no value but for himself, nor desires any copy but his own form.[134]
NORTHCOTE	(*Continues.*) So I used to contend against Sir Joshua that Raphael had triumphed over this difficulty in *The Miracle of Bolsena*, where he has given the internal blush of the unbelieving priest at seeing the wafer turned into blood – the colour to be sure assists, but the look of stupefaction and shame is also there in the most marked degree. Sir Joshua said it was my fancy, but I am as convinced of it as I am of my existence; and the proof is that otherwise he has done nothing. There is no story without it; but he has trusted to the expression to tell the story, instead of leaving the expression to be made out from the story.
ARISTOTLE	Without action there could be no tragedy, but without character there could be: in fact, the works of most of the recent poets are lacking in character, and in general there are many such poets, as with Zeuxis's relationship to Polygnotus among painters: Polygnotus is a fine depicter of character, while Zeuxis's painting contains no character. Plot is the first principle and, as it were, soul of tragedy, while character is secondary. (*Poetics*, 51, 53)
KEATS	Other actors are continually thinking of their sum-total effect throughout a play. Kean delivers himself up to the instant feeling, without a shadow of a thought about any thing else. Although so many times he has lost the battle of Bosworth Field, we can easily conceive him really expectant of victory, and a different termination of the piece. He feels his being as deeply as Wordsworth.
HAZLITT	And don't you think, Sir, that this explains the difficulty of fine acting, and the difference between good acting and bad – that is, between face-making or mouthing and genuine passion? To give the last, an actor must possess the highest truth of imagination, and must undergo an entire revolution of feeling.
JOHNSON	(*aside*) Punch has no feelings. Ask Reynolds whether he felt the distress of Count Hugolino when he drew it.
HAZLITT	(*Continues.*) Is it wonderful that so many prefer an artificial to a natural actor, the mask to the man, the pompous pretension to the simple expression? Not at all; the wonder rather is that people in general judge so right as they do, when they have such doubtful grounds to go upon; and they would not, but they trust less to rules or reasoning than to their feelings.

NORTHCOTE	You must come to that at last. The common sense of mankind (whether a good or a bad one) is the best criterion you have to appeal to. You necessarily impose upon yourself in judging of your own works. Whenever I am trying at an expression, I hang up the picture in the room and ask people what it means, and if they guess right, I think I have succeeded.
KEATS	I feel it in my strength to refuse the poisonous suffrage of a public – My own being which I know to be becomes of more consequence to me than the crowds of shadows in the shape of man and women that inhabit a kingdom. The soul is a world of itself, and has enough to do in its own home. (2:146; To J. H. Reynolds, 24 August 1819)
NORTHCOTE	You yourself see the thing as you wish it, or according to what you have been endeavouring to make it. When I was doing the figures of Argyll in prison and of his enemy who comes and finds him asleep, I had a great difficulty to encounter in conveying the expression of the last – indeed I did it from myself – I wanted to give a look of mingled remorse and admiration; and when I found that others saw this look in the sketch I had made, I left off. By going on, I might lose it again. There is a point of felicity which, whether you fall short of or have gone beyond it, can only be determined by the effect on the unprejudiced observer.
KEATS	I feel every confidence that if I choose I may be a popular writer; that I will never be – I equally dislike the favour of the public with the love of a woman – they are both a cloying treacle to the wings of independence. I shall ever consider them (people) as debtors to me for verses, not myself to them for admiration. (2:144; To John Taylor, 23 August 1819)
NORTHCOTE	You cannot be always with your picture to explain it to others: it must be left to speak for itself.
KEATS	The little dramatic skill I may as yet have, however badly it might show in a drama, would I think be sufficient for a poem – I wish to diffuse the colouring of *St Agnes's Eve* throughout a poem in which character and sentiment would be the figures of such drapery – Two or three such poems, if God should spare me, written in the course of the next six years, would be a famous *gradus ad Parnassum altissimum* – I mean they would nerve me up to the writing of a few fine plays – my greatest ambition – when I do feel ambitious. I am sorry to say that is very seldom. (2:234; To John Taylor, 17 November 1819)

***

Needless to say, Keats was neither to live another 'six years' – he died in Rome in 1821 – nor to compose 'a few fine plays': all we have after *Otho the Great* is some two hundred lines of the first act of *King Stephen*.

The symposium continued. (If you have found it frustrating that the interlocutors are not responding to each other's opinions correctly and that the dialogue is not progressing as logically as it should, please remember that these artists are a bunch of egotists, after all.)

Conclusion: Kean's farewell

The preceding chapters traced the incessant exchange of ideas and inspirations between artists and critics as they were engaged in various Shakespearean enterprises. The parties concerned were highly conscious of each other's activities and their works came into being not independently but in response to other people's acting, criticism, playwriting and painting. Their artistic identities were both defined against each other and merged into each other to such an extent that we cannot discuss their respective works without addressing the company they kept.

In the meantime, the metaphor of 'dialogue' which I used in the Introduction to describe the negotiations between them now requires much correction and qualification. Consciously or unconsciously, the artists and their critics responded to each other's works with alarming inaccuracy and impropriety, misquotation, misreading and misuse (or even abuse) being the rule rather than the exception. The prevalence of authorship misattribution was yet another symptom of their tricky relationship. People liked to ascribe David Garrick's Jubilee Ode (mistakenly) to Elizabeth Montagu and his Jubilee oration (with some truth) to Edmund Burke.[1] Montagu's *Essay* in its turn was misattributed to various male writers including Joseph Warton, whose *Adventurer* essays on Lear's madness were discussed in chapter 1.[2] Joshua Reynolds's *Discourses* was rumoured to have been ghost-written by either Burke or Samuel Johnson, the latter of whom did have a part in the composition, as can be seen in the manuscript copy of the treatise that bears corrections made in his hand.[3]

Some of their negotiations were compounded by a greater measure of accidents and hidden objectives than in the cases of simple misattribution. Arthur Murphy, for one, made a terrible *faux pas* when he poached 'a very pretty oriental tale' from a French magazine for the *Gray's-Inn Journal*,[4] which turned out to be a French translation from Johnson's *Rambler* article.[5] Murphy was horrified when he realised the blunder and immediately 'waited upon Johnson, to explain this curious incident. His talents, literature, and gentleman-like manners, were soon perceived by Johnson, and a friendship was formed which was never broken.'[6] Murphy was also rumoured to have been paid by the publicity-conscious Garrick for publishing favourable articles in his journal. He even fought a duel with the lawyer and minor playwright Macnamara Morgan to prove his integrity.[7]

The chaotic dealings of these individuals resist monolithic explanations. Their wilful exploitation of each other's critical and artistic discourse lacks an acute sense of otherness and falls short of constituting a fair dialogic exchange, let alone subscribing unconditionally to the epistemology of post-Enlightenment reason. Their colourful renditions of Shakespearean tragedy keep upsetting the reader's and spectator's horizon of expectations, while the Stratford Jubilee defies a strategic and political understanding of Shakespeare's afterlife by having been wrecked by a freak downpour.

The composition of my chapters, with their respective focus on the three generations of tragic actors, might also have caused readers to form the mistaken impression that the artistic and critical dialogues were conducted only synchronically and were confined to contemporary London. The repercussion of their conversation in fact reached wider and farther, to which two memorials attest. Sir George Beaumont built a cenotaph to Reynolds twenty years after the painter's death in 1792. The memorial bore an inscription by Beaumont's protégé William Wordsworth and was flanked by two busts, one of Michelangelo (left) and the other Raphael (right), as can be seen in John Constable's famous painting (see figure 20). A descendant of the Jacobean playwright Francis Beaumont, Beaumont was not only a great patron of art and literature but an accomplished amateur painter who trained under Reynolds. In fact, Samuel Taylor Coleridge's aristocratic painter Alvar in *Remorse* was modelled on this country gentleman.[8]

The later fortunes of the memorial statue for Garrick in the Poets' Corner of Westminster Abbey were tinged with a little irony. Erected at Burke's suggestion some fifteen years after the thespian's death in 1779, and inscribed by one Samuel Jackson Pratt with a verse ending 'Shakespeare and Garrick, like twin-stars shall shine, / And earth irradiate with a beam divine', this monument was to earn the dubious honour of prompting Charles Lamb to write the notorious antitheatrical essay 'On the Tragedies of Shakespeare, Considered with Reference to Their Fitness for Stage Representation' (1812).[9]

It was not only friendship that lingered through generations. Born in 1795, John Keats had no personal correspondence with Elizabeth Montagu,

20 John Constable, *The Cenotaph*.

who died in 1800 aged eighty. This did not stop the poet abhorring the Queen of the Blues:

The world, and especially our England, has within the last thirty year's [*sic*] been vexed and teased by a set of Devils, whom I detest so much that I al<ways> hunger after an acherontic promotion to a Torturer, purposely for their accom[m]odation; These Devils are a set of Women, who having taken a snack or Luncheon of Literary scraps, set themselves up for towers of Babel in Languages Sapphos in Poetry – Euclids in Geometry – and everything in nothing. Among such the Name of Montague has been preeminent. (1:163; To J. H. Reynolds, 21 September 1817)

This antipathy to the Bluestocking women crucially defined Keats's artistic objectives, of which one was 'to make as great a revolution in modern dramatic writing as Kean has done in acting', as we saw in chapter 3, while the other was 'to upset the drawling of the blue stocking literary world' (2:139; To Benjamin Bailey, 14 August 1819).

Artistic and critical dialogues continued even after personal amity, or enmity, had ceased. The controversy over Garrick's natural acting, for instance, was resumed by such Victorian theatre critics as G. H. Lewes, whose essay 'On Natural Acting' rejoined Henry Fielding's rendition of Garrick's Hamlet in *Tom Jones*,[10] and William Archer, who collected various testimonies on theatrical emotions from actors and actresses in *Masks or Faces?* as a way to refute Denis Diderot's *Paradoxe sur le comédien*, which was itself a reply to Antoine-Fabio Sticotti's *Garrick ou les acteurs anglois* (1769). Diderot's antiemotionalist interpretation of Garrick's acting was to exert a direct influence on the theatrical theories of V. E. Meyerhold and Konstantin Stanislavski in the twentieth century.[11]

My three chapters, within their very limited scope, tried to capture the moments of tragic effusion in the intimate interactions among the players, critics, painters and playwrights of contemporary London. But why are we moved by tragedy – staged, printed or painted – at all? Is it because the artistic representation reminds us of the calamities in real life or is it because we forget the reality and sympathise with the tragic fiction? Do the actors express tragic passion on the stage by resorting to their personal sorrow, or do they forget themselves and assume the dramatic personality completely? An anecdote on Kean's very last stage appearance will provide a suitable finale to my deliberations.[12]

***

Binge drinking and a life of licence took its toll. Towards the end of his career, Edmund Kean was cursed by ill health and poverty. He was so fragile that, when he acted, he was not sure if he would live through the part. It was a choice between courting death and starving to death.

In February 1833, when the Drury Lane management declined his request for an advance payment of £500, Kean transferred to the rival Covent Garden, where his estranged son Charles was contracted. On 21 March he made a successful debut appearance there as Shylock, and was billed to play Othello opposite his son's Iago on 25 March. This sparked wide and general interest among playgoers, as it would be the first time that father and son had acted together on the London stage.

Kean was very pale and shivering when he was driven to the theatre that afternoon. In the dressing room he told his son that he was very ill and afraid that he should not be able to act, but the manager, who was also present, cheered him up. Having drunk some hot brandy-and-water,

Kean declared he was much better. He changed his clothes and blackened his face. Even so, from time to time he still shivered and complained of feeling cold. His vitality was clearly at a low ebb. It was a pitiful sight.

The overture ended and the curtain rose. Charles was warmly greeted on entering as Iago in the first scene, but the spectators were evidently impatient for a sight of their old favourite. When Kean came onstage with Charles in the second scene, the whole house received them with warmest acclamations. Tears welled in Kean's eyes. The veteran actor bowed again and again, and then suddenly, as if remembering himself, turned towards his son. He took him by the hand and led him a few steps forward. It was as if he was presenting his heir to the public. The enthusiasm of the house redoubled. Hats and handkerchiefs were waved and cheers rent the air. The father and the son stood hand in hand, bowing repeatedly.

Kean struggled feebly through the first two acts. His voice was so weak at times that it sank almost to a whisper, and his pauses were longer than usual. He was not pleased with himself but he was proud of his son. He remarked to someone in the wings, 'Charles is getting on tonight, he is acting very well. I suppose that is because he is acting with me.' When the drop curtain fell at the close of the second act, the father warned, 'Mind, Charles, that you keep before me. Don't get behind me, in this act. I don't know that I shall be able to kneel; but if I do, be sure that you lift me up.'

The climactic third act began. Kean struggled through the earlier part of the act with great resolution, but his weakness was greater than his will. On 'What! False to me', he was scarcely able to walk across the stage. He held up, however, until the celebrated 'farewell' speech, which he uttered with all his emotional energy:

> O now for ever
> Farewell the tranquil mind, farewell content!
> Farewell the plumed troops and the big wars
> That makes ambition virtue! O farewell,
> Farewell the neighing steed and the shrill trump,
> The spirit-stirring drum, th'ear-piercing fife,
> The royal banner, and all quality,
> Pride, pomp and circumstance of glorious war!
> And, O you mortal engines whose rude throats
> Th'immortal Jove's dread clamours counterfeit,
> Farewell: Othello's occupation's gone. (3.3.350–60)

He delivered the lines with his usual melancholy sweetness and more than his customary feeling. The audience was so touched by the sobbing tone of the last line that they burst into stormy applause that lasted some minutes.

'Farewell: Othello's occupation's gone.' With this line Kean had dwarfed J. B. Booth, Edwin Forrest, W. C. Macready and all the other Iagos who had ever crossed his path. This was the line to herald Kean's terrific explosion, beginning, 'Villain, be sure thou prove my love a whore.'

But now Kean stood motionless and fixed, his chin resting on his breast, his eyes riveted on the ground. A deathlike silence fell upon the house. Kean raised his head, and looked round with dimmed sight. He advanced a few steps to Iago and would have continued his part, but a deep mist was blotting out his vision and a wracking pain was paralysing his limbs. Kean tottered towards his son, flung himself on his neck, and with a faint and faltering voice cried out, 'O God, I am dying. Speak to them for me, Charles.' Then he fell unconscious.

***

'Farewell: Othello's occupation's gone.' This was the final line that the great tragedian Kean ever delivered on stage. Did the agony conveyed by the farewell speech belong to Othello or to Kean? Whose tragedy was it that the audience saw that evening, Othello's or Kean's? Or possibly Shakespeare's? Kean's finale spawned more questions than it answered, but to answer was not important for the tragedian or the spectators, his mission being to move and theirs to be moved. Both parties succeeded in this in a spectacular manner. As for me, I am just as moved speechless as anyone who witnessed Kean's dramatic exit from the Shakespearean stage at Covent Garden that night. (It is about time I stopped writing, too.)

Notes

INTRODUCTION: GARRICK'S PROLOGUE

1. Samuel Johnson, 'Prologue Spoken at the Opening of the Theatre in Drury-Lane, 1747', ll. 1–8, in Johnson, *Poems*, ed. by E. L. McAdam, Jr, The Yale Edition (New Haven: Yale University Press, 1964). Further references to this edition are given after quotations in the text.
2. George Birbeck Hill, ed., *Johnsonian Miscellanies*, 2 vols. (Oxford: Clarendon Press, 1897), 2:314.
3. Michael Dobson, *The Making of the National Poet: Shakespeare, Adaptation and Authorship, 1660–1769* (Oxford: Clarendon Press, 1992), and Jean I. Marsden, *The Re-Imagined Text: Shakespeare, Adaptation, and Eighteenth-Century Literary Theory* (Lexington: University Press of Kentucky, 1995).
4. Margreta De Grazia, *Shakespeare Verbatim: The Reproduction of Authenticity and the 1790 Apparatus* (Oxford: Clarendon Press, 1991).
5. Jonathan Bate, *Shakespeare and the English Romantic Imagination* (Oxford: Clarendon Press, 1986), and *Shakespearean Constitutions: Politics, Theatre, Criticism, 1730–1830* (Oxford: Clarendon Press, 1989).
6. Michael Bristol, *Big-Time Shakespeare* (London: Routledge, 1996), and Gary Taylor, *Reinventing Shakespeare: A Cultural History from the Restoration to the Present* (London: Hogarth, 1989).
7. Jean E. Howard and Marion F. O'Connor, eds., *Shakespeare Reproduced: The Text in History and Ideology* (New York: Methuen, 1987); Jean I. Marsden, ed., *The Appropriation of Shakespeare: Post-Renaissance Reconstructions of the Works and the Myth* (Hemel Hempstead: Harvester Wheatsheaf, 1991); Christy Desmet and Robert Sawyer, eds., *Shakespeare and Appropriation* (London: Routledge, 1999); and Peter Holland, ed., '*Macbeth* and Its Afterlife', *Shakespeare Survey* (Special Issue) 57 (2004), 1–195.
8. For the quotations, see respectively Taylor, *Reinventing Shakespeare*, 372; De Grazia, *Shakespeare Verbatim*, 1; Dobson, *National Poet*, 8; Bate, *Shakespearean Constitutions*, 2; and Marsden, *Appropriation*, 1.
9. Dobson, *National Poet*, 13 (emphases added).
10. Walter Benjamin, 'Eduard Fuchs, Collector and Historian', in Benjamin, *Selected Writings*, trans. Edmund Jephcott et al., ed. Marcus Bullock and Michael W. Jennings, 4 vols. (Cambridge, MA: Belknap Press of Harvard

University Press, 1996–2003), 3:267. See also 'On the Concept of History', ibid., (4:392) for a later formulation of the same idea.
11. See Nancy Maguire, 'Nahum Tate's *King Lear*: "The King's Blest Restoration"', in Marsden, *Appropriation*, 29–42, and Dobson, *National Poet*, 80–85.
12. Nahum Tate, 'To My Esteemed Friend, Thomas Boteler, Esq.', in Spencer 1965. Further references to Tate's *Lear* (designated as 'Tate') are to this edition and are given after quotations in the text.
13. Sandra Clark, ed., *Shakespeare Made Fit: Restoration Adaptations of Shakespeare* (London: Dent, 1997), lxix.
14. James Boswell, the Elder, *Life of Johnson: Together with Boswell's Journal of a Tour to the Hebrides and Johnson's Diary of a Journey into North Wales*, ed. George Birkbeck Hill, 2nd edn, rev. L. F. Powell, 6 vols. (Oxford: Clarendon Press, 1934, 1950), 1:96–103.
15. Walter Jackson Bate, *Samuel Johnson* (New York: Harcourt Brace Jovanovich, 1977), 82, 217.
16. [John Genest], *Some Account of the English Stage, from the Restoration in 1660 to 1830*, 10 vols. (Bath: H. E. Carrington, 1832), 4:231.

1 WINDING UP 'TH'UNTUNED AND JARRING SENSES': GARRICK, *KING LEAR* AND CONTEMPORARY THEATRICAL/LITERARY CRITICISM

1. See John Hawkesworth et al., eds., *The Adventurer*, 2 vols. (London: J. Payne, 1753–4), 2:253–8, 271–6, 307–12, and Arthur Murphy ('Charles Ranger'), ed., *The Gray's Inn Journal*, 2nd edn, 2 vols. (London: P. Vaillant, 1756), 2:73–80, 82–8. Further references to these editions are given after quotations in the text.
2. This article is dated '15 June 1754', but was in fact newly written for the 1756 edition (2:219–25).
3. The revisionist theory about the Q1 and F1 texts has made it extremely controversial to talk about 'Shakespeare's' *King Lear*. Nahum Tate himself used a Folio (edition unidentified) for his copy text and occasionally referred to Q1. See Sonia Massai, 'Tate's Critical "Editing" of His Source-Text(s) for *The History of King Lear*', *Analytical and Enumerative Bibliography* 9.4 (1995), 168–96. My analysis is based on R. A. Foakes's conflated Arden text, but important variants in Q1 and F1 will be noted.
4. Tate's political motives are discussed by Maguire ('Nahum Tate's *King Lear*') and Dobson (*National Poet*, 80–85).
5. [Francis Gentleman], *The Dramatic Censor*, 2 vols. (London: J. Bell and others, 1770), 1:353.
6. Two theatrical texts (Bell 1774; Lear 1786) respectively record certain stages of Garrick's cumulative restoration. J. S. Bratton identifies a contemporary promptbook in the British Library (c.119.dd.22; Lear 1756) as Garrick's (Bratton, *King Lear*, Plays in Performance (Bristol: Bristol Classical, 1987), xviii), but the relationship between this text and Garrick's staging is not clear.

While the cuts made in the copy text (1756 edition of Tate's *Lear*) anticipate Garrick's later acting versions, textual restoration is limited to 2.2.442–7 and 466–70. According to Warton's article, Garrick had restored the line, 'O me, my heart! My rising heart! But down!' (2.2.313) by 1753. The promptbook, however, does not record the restoration.

7. George W. Stone, 'Garrick's Production of *King Lear*: A Study in the Temper of the Eighteenth-Century Mind', *Studies in Philology* 45.1 (1948), 89–104 (91). See also George W. Stone, Jr. and George M. Kahrl, *David Garrick: A Critical Biography* (Carbondale: Southern Illinois University Press, 1979), 261.
8. Arthur John Harris, 'Garrick, Colman, and *King Lear*: A Reconsideration', *Shakespeare Quarterly* 22 (1971), 57–66.
9. George C. D. Odell, *Shakespeare from Betterton to Irving*, 2 vols. (London: Constable, 1920–1), 1:377.
10. *King Lear: A Tragedy* (1.2.23; 42–4) in David Garrick, *Plays*, ed. Harry William Pedicord and Frederick Louis Bergmann, 7 vols. (Carbondale: Southern Illinois University Press, 1980–2). Further references to Garrick's adaptations (designated as 'Garrick') and plays are to this edition unless otherwise specified and are given after quotations in the text. Important variants in Lear 1756, Bell 1774 (in vol. 2, dated 1773) and Lear 1786 will also be noted. Tate's aside is kept in Lear 1756. Line 1.2.23 is dropped in Lear 1786.
11. William Cooke, *Memoirs of Charles Macklin, Comedian*, 2nd edn (London: J. Asperne, 1806), 105.
12. Ibid., 107.
13. Here I summarise Stone and Kahrl's useful survey of eighteenth-century acting in *David Garrick*, 30–5.
14. *Prompter*, 7 October 1735. The most recent performance of *Lear* was at Drury Lane, 27 September 1735, starring James Quin.
15. Alan S. Downer, 'Nature to Advantage Dressed: Eighteenth-Century Acting', *PMLA* 58 (1943), 1002–37. For a historical survey of the theatrical expression of tragic passion, see also Joseph R. Roach, *The Player's Passion: Studies in the Science of Acting* (Newark: University of Delaware Press, 1985), 23–57.
16. Cited in R. D. Hume, ed., *The London Theatre World, 1660–1800* (Carbondale: Southern Illinois University Press, 1980), 165–6.
17. Cooke, *Memoirs of Macklin*, 100.
18. Roach, *Player's Passion*, 56.
19. Thomas Davies, *Memoirs of the Life of David Garrick, Esq.*, 2 vols. (London: For the author, 1780), 1:44.
20. David Garrick, *Letters*, ed. David M. Little and George M. Kahrl, 3 vols. (London: Oxford University Press, 1963), 1:92 (To the Rev. Peter Whalley, 15 March [1748]).
21. Garrick, *Letters*, 1:350 (To Hall Hartson, 24 January [17]62).
22. Arthur Murphy, *The Life of David Garrick, Esq.*, 2 vols. (London: J. Wright, 1801), 1:45.
23. [Samuel Foote], *A Treatise on the Passions* (London: C. Corbet, 1747), 17–18.

24. *An Examen of the New Comedy, Call'd 'The Suspicious Husband'* (London: J. Roberts, 1747), 27. For Foote's reply to this anonymous critic, see also Samuel Foote, *The Roman and English Comedy Consider'd and Compar'd* (London: T. Waller, 1747), 4–5.
25. Garrick, *Letters*, 1:53 ([*post* 10 October 1745]).
26. Hayman followed most of Garrick's suggestions in the frontispiece (see figure 2), but somehow dropped the Fool, bringing the illustration even closer to the actor's staging.
27. Murphy, *Life of David Garrick*, 2:28–9.
28. Ibid., 2:29–30.
29. Ibid., 2:27–8.
30. James Boaden, ed., *The Private Correspondence of David Garrick, with the Most Celebrated Persons of His Time*, 2 vols. (London: H. Colburn and R. Bentley, 1831–2), 1:539 (27 May 1773).
31. Samuel Johnson, *Letters*, ed. Bruce Redford, The Hyde Edition, 5 vols. (Princeton: Princeton University Press, 1992–94), 1:67 (8 March 1753).
32. For the authorship attribution of the *Adventurer* essays, see David Fairer, 'Authorship Problems in *The Adventurer*', *RES* 25 (1974), 137–51.
33. Charles Harold Gray, *Theatrical Criticism in London to 1795* (1931; New York: B. Blom, 1964), 115–16.
34. Cited in Stone and Kahrl, *David Garrick*, 39.
35. Interestingly, Foote had made the same point regarding the cause of Lear's madness in his appraisal of Garrick's acting (Foote, *Passions*, 20–1).
36. Johnson, *Letters*, 1:77 (8 March 1754).
37. The bracketed words are inserted in the 1756 edition.
38. Cited in Gray, *Theatrical Criticism*, 113. Hill does not identify the actor 'of whom the World supposes me too fond'. The context seems to suggest Garrick's archrival James Quin or someone of the old-fashioned declamatory school.
39. Stone (in 'David Garrick's Significance in the History of Shakespearean Criticism: A Study of the Impact of the Actor Upon the Change of Critical Focus During the Eighteenth Century', *PMLA* 65 (1950), 183–97) emphasises the relations between Garrick's acting and the vogue of character criticism, while Brian Vickers (in 'The Emergence of Character Criticism, 1774–1800', *Shakespeare Survey* 34 (1981), 11–21) defines character criticism as a full-length study of a single dramatic character and sees the last quarter of the eighteenth century as the crucial period of its development.
40. Boaden, *Private Correspondence*, 1:1–2.
41. Ibid., 1:2 (2 March 173[7]).
42. Boswell, *Life of Johnson*, 2:92.
43. Samuel Johnson, *Johnson on Shakespeare*, ed. A. Sherbo, The Yale Edition, 2 vols. (New Haven: Yale University Press, 1968), 104. Further references to Johnson's Shakespeare criticism are to this edition and are given after quotations in the text. Important variants in his Shakespeare editions (Johnson 1765; Johnson-Steevens 1773) will be noted.

44. Arthur Sherbo, *Samuel Johnson, Editor of Shakespeare, with an Essay on* The Adventurer (Urbana: University of Illinois Press, 1956), 56.
45. Jesse Foot, *The Life of Arthur Murphy, Esq.* (London: J. Faulder, 1811), 59–60.
46. *Letters*, 1:350–1 (27 September 1770).
47. Sherbo, *Johnson*, 47. Johnson's remark is also cited by Sherbo.
48. Ibid., 58. See also Henry Home, Lord Kames, *Elements of Criticism*, 2nd edn, 3 vols. (Edinburgh: A. Millar and others, 1763), 3:305–6. Further references to the *Elements* are to this edition and are given after quotations in the text.
49. Boswell, *Life of Johnson*, 1:392.
50. Ibid., 1:393 note.
51. Ibid., 2:92.
52. Joan E. Klingel, 'Backstage with Dr. Johnson: "Punch Has No Feelings"', *Studies in Philology* 77 (1980), 300–18 (301–2).
53. Hester Lynch Piozzi (Thrale), *Dr Johnson by Mrs Thrale: The 'Anecdotes' of Mrs Piozzi in Their Original Form*, ed. Richard Ingram (London: Chatto & Windus, 1984), 28. Arthur Murphy also records this episode in his 'Essay on Johnson's Life and Genius', in Hill, *Johnsonian Miscellanies*, 1:355–488 (1:457).
54. Piozzi, *Dr Johnson*, 28.
55. James Boswell, the Elder, *Journal of a Tour to the Hebrides with Samuel Johnson*, ed. Frederick A. Pottle and Charles H. Bennett (London: W. Heinemann, 1936), 207.
56. See Garrick, *Letters*, 2:460, and Johnson, *Letters*, 1:252.
57. Boswell, *Life of Johnson*, 2:192.
58. Boswell, *Tour to the Hebrides*, 208.
59. [Elizabeth Montagu], *An Essay on the Writings and Genius of Shakespear* (London: J. Dodsley and others, 1769), a2.
60. Elizabeth Montagu, *Letters*, ed. Matthew Montagu, 4 vols. (London: T. Cadell and W. Davies, 1809–13), 4:7–8 (18 November 1755).
61. Elizabeth Eger, ed., *Elizabeth Montagu*, Bluestocking Feminism: Writings of the Bluestocking Circle, 1738–1785 (London: Pickering and Chatto, 1999), 12. Further references to Montagu's *Essay* and letters are to this edition unless otherwise specified and are given after quotations in the text.
62. For Voltaire's comparison of the two plays, see Theodore Besterman, ed., *Voltaire on Shakespeare* (Genève: Institut et Musée Voltaire, 1967), 92. His translation of *Julius Caesar* is also in this edition (93–156).
63. Reginald Blunt, ed., *Mrs. Montagu, 'Queen of the Blues': Her Letters and Friendships from 1762 to 1800*, 2 vols. (London: Constable, [1923]), 2:144 (24 October 1765). Blunt collects many letters relating to Montagu's response to Johnson's edition (2:140–67).
64. Ibid., 2:144.
65. Norma Clarke, *Dr Johnson's Women* (London: Hambledon and London, 2000), 138–43.
66. Blunt, *Montagu*, 2:146.
67. Clarke, *Dr Johnson's Women*, 145.

68. Blunt, *Montagu*, 2:147 (To Elizabeth Carter, [no date]).
69. Ibid., 2:147–8 (To Elizabeth Carter, [no date]).
70. Boswell, *Life of Johnson*, 2:53.
71. Blunt, *Montagu*, 1:154. See also Eger, *Montagu*, 226–7 note.
72. For Voltaire's 1764 review of *Elements of Criticism*, see Besterman, *Voltaire on Shakespeare*, 85–9.
73. Blunt, *Montagu*, 1:312.
74. Voltaire's letter is cited in Besterman, *Voltaire on Shakespeare*, 186–209.
75. Blunt, *Montagu*, 1:332.
76. Ibid., 1:334 (To Elizabeth Carter, 26 September 1776).
77. Boaden, *Private Correspondence*, 2:183.
78. Ibid., 2:188.
79. Ibid., 2:189.
80. Three comprehensive surveys of the Jubilee were published on the 400th anniversary of Shakespeare, to which I am indebted: Christian Deelman, *The Great Shakespeare Jubilee* (London: Michael Joseph, 1964); Martha Winburn England, *Garrick's Jubilee* (Columbus: Ohio State University Press, 1964); and Johanne M. Stochholm, *Garrick's Folly: The Shakespeare Jubilee of 1769 at Stratford and Drury Lane* (London: Methuen, 1964). Dobson regards Garrick's festival as the culmination of Shakespeare's 'nationalisation' (*National Poet*, 214–22).
81. This poem is cited in Garrick, *Plays*, 2:332–3 note.
82. England, *Garrick's Jubilee*, 17–25.
83. *Public Advertiser*, 23 August 1769.
84. See Stone and Kahrl, *David Garrick*, 338–53 for an overview of Garrick's relationship with contemporary journalism. Specimens of contemporary pamphlets on Garrick are collected in 'Poetical Tracts Relating to Garrick' (644.k.18) and 'Tracts Relating to Mr. Garrick' (641.f.8) in the British Library.
85. Ian McIntyre, *Garrick* (London: Penguin, 1999), 314 note. See also Frederick W. Hawkins, *The Life of Edmund Kean*, 2 vols. (London: Tinsley, 1869), 1:209.
86. David Garrick, *Poetical Works*, ed. George Kearsley, 2 vols. (London: G. Kearsley, 1785), 1:50.
87. Ibid., 1:52.
88. Charles Dibdin, *The Professional Life of Mr. Dibdin, Written by Himself*, 4 vols. (London: For the author, 1803), 1:74.
89. Garrick, *Poetical Works*, 1:57.
90. *Public Advertiser*, 16 September 1769.
91. Dibdin, *Professional Life*, 1:76–7.
92. Benjamin Victor, *The History of the Theatres of London and Dublin from the Year 1730 to the Present Time*, 3 vols. (London: T. Davies and others, 1761–71), 3:217. The oration is reproduced in Brian Vickers, ed., *Shakespeare: The Critical Heritage*, 6 vols. (London: Routledge, 1974), 5:355–60. Critics disagree as to the procedure of the ceremony and variously argue that the Ode was followed by: the oration-Macaroni-the address to the Ladies (Stochholm, *Garrick's Folly*, 82–93); or the address to the Ladies-Macaroni-the oration

(England, *Garrick's Jubilee*, 51–7). Deelman believes that the oration was not delivered at all, and that the Ode was followed only by the Macaroni episode and Garrick's address to the Ladies (*Great Shakespeare Jubilee*, 231–3).
93. Victor, *History of the Theatres*, 3:219–20.
94. Ibid., 3:220.
95. Stochholm, *Garrick's Folly*, 88.
96. Victor, *History of the Theatres*, 3:220–2.
97. Garrick's draft for King's interlude is preserved at the Folger Shakespeare Library ('Garrick Attack on Shakespeare', W b. 460).
98. England, *Garrick's Jubilee*, 57.
99. Victor, *History of the Theatres*, 3:222. For Garrick's reference to the so-called Shakespeare Ladies' Club that lobbied for the Westminster monument, see Emmett L. Avery, 'The Shakespeare Ladies Club', *Shakespeare Quarterly* 7 (1958), 153–8.
100. *Public Advertiser*, 16 September 1769.
101. Deelman, *Great Shakespeare Jubilee*, 227.
102. Blunt, *Montagu*, 1:225.
103. Ibid., 1:224 (To Lord Lyttleton, [October 1769]).
104. 'Advertisement', in David Garrick ('D. G.'), *An Ode Upon Dedicating a Building and Erecting a Statue to Shakespeare, at Stratford upon Avon* (London: T. Becket and P. A. de Hondt, 1769). Further references to this edition are given after quotations in the text.
105. For an overview of the relationship between Garrick and Voltaire, see Frank A. Hedgcock, *A Cosmopolitan Actor: David Garrick and His French Friends* (London: S. Paul, [1912]), 77, 186–8.
106. Boswell, *Life of Johnson*, 2:69.
107. In fact, Johnson made his third involuntary appearance as a copywriter for a Jubilee souvenir, the multicolour 'Shakspearian ribbands', whose advertisement, quoted from the same Drury Lane prologue, read: 'Each change of *many-colour'd* life he drew'(Boswell, *Life of Johnson*, 2:69). As Boswell observed elsewhere, 'I dare say Mr. Samuel Johnson never imagined that this fine Verse of his would appear on a Bill to promote the Sale of Ribbands' (*Public Advertiser*, 16 September 1769).
108. The Latin epigram is from Lucan's *Pharsalia*, III. 138–40, which Nicholas Rowe translates as: 'Nor time, nor chance breed such confusions yet, / Nor are the mean so rais'd, nor sunk the great; / But laws themselves would rather chuse to be / Suppress'd by Caesar, than preserved by thee.'
109. The poem is cited in Ann Thompson and Sasha Roberts, eds., *Women Reading Shakespeare, 1660–1900: An Anthology of Criticism* (Manchester: Manchester University Press, 1997), 22–3.
110. Garrick, *Letters*, 2:669 ([September–October 1769]).
111. England, *Garrick's Jubilee*, 220.
112. Ibid., 259.
113. Victor, *History of the Theatres*, 3:231–2.
114. Garrick, *Letters*, 2:675 (To the Rev. Evan Lloyd, 4 December 1769).

115. *The Devil upon Two Sticks*, cited in Deelman, *Great Shakespeare Jubilee*, 272. Foote's barbs against Garrick's Jubilee are cited in Philip H. Highfill, Jr, Kalman A. Burnim and Edward A. Langhans, *A Biographical Dictionary of Actors, Actresses, Musicians, Dancers, Managers, and Other Stage Personnel in London, 1660–1800*, 16 vols. (Carbondale: Southern Illinois University Press, 1973–93), under 'Foote, Samuel'.

2 'WHO DARES DO MORE': KEMBLE, SIDDONS AND THE QUESTION OF SUBLIMITY IN *MACBETH*

1. Donald F. Bond, ed., *The Spectator*, 5 vols. (Oxford: Clarendon Press, 1965), 3:239–42 (no. 335), (3:239, 241). Further references to this edition are given after quotations in the text.
2. Henry Fielding, *The History of Tom Jones: A Foundling*, ed. Fredson Bowers and Martin C. Battestin, Wesleyan Edition, 2 vols. (Oxford: Clarendon Press, 1974), 2:852. Further references to this edition are given after quotations in the text.
3. As Anthony J. Hassall points out, Fielding either deliberately or inadvertently changes the sequence of the play by putting the closet scene before the play-within-the-play. See his 'Fielding and Garrick's *Hamlet*', in R. F. Brissenden and J. C. Eade, eds., *Studies in the Eighteenth Century* (Canberra: Australian National University, 1979), 147–65.
4. John Allen Stevenson offers an interesting analysis of the metatheatrical and metafictional structure of this scene, though his analogy between *The Mousetrap* and the 1745 Scottish rebellion seems a little strained. See his 'Fielding's Mousetrap: Hamlet, Partridge, and the '45', *SEL* 37 (1997), 553–71.
5. Joshua Reynolds, *Discourses on Art*, ed. Robert R. Wark, 3rd edn (New Haven: Yale University Press for the Paul Mellon Centre for Studies in British Art, 1997), 84. Further references to this edition are given after quotations in the text.
6. Reynolds apparently borrowed the Latin epigram (which translates as 'What is more preposterous than to copy theatres in real life?') from Francis Bacon's *Advancement of Learning* (Book 2, 23).
7. Odell, *Shakespeare from Betterton to Irving*, 2:91–2.
8. *Covent Garden Journal*, cited in Thomas Campbell, *Life of Mrs. Siddons*, 2 vols. (London: E. Wilson, 1834), 2:327 note.
9. Campbell, *Life of Siddons*, 2:337.
10. James Boaden, *Memoirs of Mrs. Siddons*, 2 vols. (London: H. Colburn, 1827), 2:382–7.
11. Stanley Wells and Gary Taylor, eds., *William Shakespeare: A Textual Companion* (Oxford: Clarendon Press, 1987), 543.
12. Thomas Davies, *Dramatic Mi[s]cellanies*, 3 vols. (London: For the author, 1780), 2:166. Garrick's version was published in Bell 1774 (vol. 1, dated '1773'). For the 'authenticity' of the actor's restoration, see George W. Stone, 'Garrick's Handling of *Macbeth*', *Studies in Philology* 38 (1941), 609–28, and Stephen Orgel, 'The Authentic Shakespeare', *Representations* 21 (1988), 1–25.

13. Davies, *Miscellanies*, 2:118–19. Davies personally supported Garrick's comical interpretation of the witches, not only because of theatrical necessity ('the tragedians are all employed in various parts of the drama ... so that none but the comic actors are left to wear gowns, beards, and coifs') but because there is 'something odd and peculiar, and approaching to what we call humour' in Shakespeare's witches themselves.
14. John Philip Kemble ('J. P. K.'), *Macbeth Reconsidered* (London: T. and J. Egerton, 1786), 35. Further references to this edition are given after quotations in the text.
15. Joseph Donohue, 'Kemble and Mrs. Siddons in *Macbeth*: The Romantic Approach to Tragic Character', *Theatre Notebook* 22 (1968), 65–86 (76, 86).
16. [Thomas Whately], *Remarks on Some of the Characters of Shakespeare* (London: T. Payne, 1785), 2, 25. Further references to this edition are given after quotations in the text.
17. See also Donohue's excellent survey of this critical tradition in his *Dramatic Character in the English Romantic Age* (Princeton: Princeton University Press, 1970), 189–215.
18. Donohue, 'Kemble and Mrs. Siddons in *Macbeth*', 71, 75.
19. James Boaden, *Memoirs of the Life of John Philip Kemble, Esq.*, 2 vols. (London: Longman and others, 1825), 1:263–4.
20. A. B. G. (Augustus Bonville Granville?), *Critical Observations on Mr. Kemble's Performance* (1811), cited in Dennis Bartholomeusz, *Macbeth and the Players* (London: Cambridge University Press, 1969), 130.
21. In 1794 L. Lownes published two editions of *Macbeth* 'as represented by their Majesties servants, on opening the Theatre Royal Drury Lane on Monday, April 21st, 1794'. My analysis is based on the second edition (Macbeth 1794b), which records some significant additional cuts that presumably reflect the staging. Important variants will be noted. William Perdue Halstead 1977–83 mistakenly cites J MC49 (British Library 11763.e.23) as the first edition and J MC50 (British Library 1344.f34) as the second (when it is the other way round) and notes that the two editions are 'identical'. See Halstead, ed., *Shakespeare as Spoken: A Collection of 5000 Acting Editions and Promptbooks of Shakespeare*, Monograph Publishing on Demand, Sponsor Series, 12 vols. (Ann Arbor: UMI for American Theatre Association).
22. This passage is still kept in Macbeth 1794a. It is restored in Macbeth 1814.
23. This passage is still kept in Macbeth 1794a. The first exchange only (5.3.33–4) is restored from Macbeth 1803 onwards.
24. For Kemble's use of 'cowardice' and 'cowardly', see *Macbeth Reconsidered*, 4, 11, 15, 19, 34.
25. Campbell, *Life of Siddons*, 2:35–6.
26. Ibid., 2:36.
27. Cited in Linda Kelly, *The Kemble Era: John Philip Kemble, Sarah Siddons, and the London Stage* (London: Bodley Head, 1980), 134.
28. Sarah Siddons, *The Reminiscences of Sarah Kemble Siddons, 1773–1785*, ed. William Van Lennep (Cambridge: Widener Library, 1942), 14.

29. Anna Brownell Jameson, *Characteristics of Women, Moral, Poetical, and Historical*, 2nd edn, 2 vols. (London: Sounders and Otley, 1833), 1:319 note. Scholarly texts also fluctuate in the treatment of this line. F1 prints 'We fail?', which Rowe 1709 modifies to 'We fail!'. From Capell [1768] onwards, many texts print simply 'We fail.' Kemble's 1794 editions print 'We fail.' and 'We fail!' respectively.
30. Campbell, *Life of Siddons*, 2:55.
31. Donohue, 'Kemble and Mrs. Siddons in *Macbeth*', 66–7.
32. Campbell, *Life of Siddons*, 2:21–2.
33. Boaden, *Memoirs of Siddons*, 2:138–9.
34. Campbell, *Life of Siddons*, 2:22–4.
35. Ibid., 2:27.
36. Ibid., 2:28.
37. H. C. Fleeming Jenkin, ed., *Mrs. Siddons as Lady Macbeth and as Queen Katharine*, Papers on Acting, 2nd series (New York: Columbia University Dramatic Museum, 1915), 60 note.
38. Jenkin, *Mrs. Siddons*, 62 note.
39. Ibid., 64 note.
40. Ibid., 65 note.
41. Ibid.
42. Campbell, *Life of Siddons*, 2:30–1.
43. Jameson, *Characteristics*, 1:331 note. For other contemporary references to Siddons's reaction to Banquo's ghost, see Marvin Rosenberg, *The Masks of Macbeth* (Berkeley: University of California Press, 1978), 470 note.
44. See also Johnson's note on the cauldron scene (4.1) in the Shakespeare edition where he tried to show 'with how much judgment Shakespeare has selected all the circumstances of his infernal ceremonies, and how exactly he has conformed to common opinions and traditions' (*On Shakespeare*, 783–6).
45. I learnt about the technical details of the production from Joseph Donohue's 'Kemble's Production of *Macbeth* (1794): Some Notes on Scene Painters, Scenery, Special Effects, and Costumes', *Theatre Notebook* 21 (1967), 63–74.
46. W. C. Oulton, *The History of the Theatres in London*, 2 vols. (London: Martin and Bain, 1796), 2:139–40.
47. This song is reproduced in Macbeth 1997 (270).
48. *Quarterly Review* 34 (1826), 196–248 (227).
49. Donohue, 'Kemble's Production of *Macbeth*', 70.
50. *Quarterly Review* 34 (1826), 196–248 (227).
51. Interestingly, Davenant's adaptation gives a stage direction of 'A shriek like an Owl' not here but in the first witch scene (1.1.7), which may reflect Jacobean stage business (Spencer 1965, 404 note).
52. There was a tendency among nineteenth-century critics to regard Banquo's ghost as a hallucination of the beholder. See Madeleine Doran, 'That Undiscovered Country: A Problem Concerning the Use of the Supernatural in *Hamlet* and *Macbeth*', *Philological Quarterly* 20 (1941), 413–27 (420). Kemble's cut was probably under the influence of such critical trends.

53. Campbell, *Life of Siddons*, 2:185–7.
54. Cited in Donohue, *Dramatic Character*, 265. See also 263–5 for other supporters of Kemble's new direction.
55. See also Jenkin, *Mrs. Siddons*, 67 note. In an 1816 interpretation of the assassination scene, Siddons bended towards the door and listened for the sounds of the murder as she said, 'He is about it' (2.2.4) to coalesce the dramatic action and the Lady's hallucination further (Bartholomeusz, *Macbeth*, 111). It is not known, however, if she acted it this way already in 1794.
56. Campbell, *Life of Siddons*, 2:38–9.
57. Arthur Colby Sprague, *Shakespearian Players and Performances* (London: A. & C. Black, 1954), 67.
58. Campbell, *Life of Siddons*, 2:32.
59. G. B. Hill, *Johnsonian Miscellanies*, 2:248.
60. James Northcote, *The Life of Sir Joshua Reynolds*, 2nd edn, 2 vols. (London: H. Colburn, 1819), 1:279.
61. Cited in Nicholas Penny, ed., *Reynolds*, Exhibition Catalogue (London: Royal Academy of Arts, 1986), 251.
62. Northcote, *Life of Sir Joshua Reynolds*, 1:279.
63. Penny, *Reynolds*, 252.
64. Northcote, *Life of Sir Joshua Reynolds*, 1:14–15.
65. Jonathan Richardson, *Two Discourses*, 2 vols. in 1 (London: W. Churchill, 1719), 2:26–34. The sculpture that Richardson refers to as by Michelangelo is believed to be Pierino da Vinci's relief in the Ashmolean Museum, Oxford. See Carol Gibson Wood, *Jonathan Richardson: Art Theorist of the English Enlightenment* (New Haven: Yale University Press, 2000), 200–1, 250 note. For the influence of Richardson's essay on various English renditions of the Ugolino story, see Frances A. Yates, 'Transformation of Dante's Ugolino', *Journal of the Warburg and Caultauld Institute* 14 (1951), 92–117. Martin Postle also examines the relations between Richardson and Reynolds in *Sir Joshua Reynolds: The Subject Pictures* (Cambridge: Cambridge University Press, 1995), 148–50.
66. Northcote, *Life of Sir Joshua Reynolds*, 1:282–3.
67. For Reynolds's other studies of White, see David Mannings, ed., *Sir Joshua Reynolds: A Complete Catalogue of His Paintings*, 2 vols. (New Haven: Yale University Press for the Paul Mellon Centre for Studies in British Art, 2000), nos. 2030, 2066, 2134, 2135, 2136, 2138, 2141.
68. Cited in Postle, *Subject Pictures*, 141.
69. Ibid., 143, and Charles Le Brun, *The Conference ... upon Expression, General and Particular*, trans. J. Smith (London: J. Smith, E. Cooper and D. Mortier, 1701), figure 11.
70. The relationship between Le Brun's textbook and eighteenth-century histrionics has been extensively discussed. See, among others, Roach, *Player's Passion*, and Shearer West, *The Image of the Actor: Verbal and Visual Representation in the Age of Garrick and Kemble* (New York: St Martin's Press, 1991), 90–106.
71. *Quarterly Review* 34 (1826), 196–248 (218–19).
72. Ibid., 219.

73. Northcote, *Life of Sir Joshua Reynolds*, 2:226.
74. The connection between the Shakespeare Gallery and the contemporary London stage is discussed negatively in Richard D. Altick, *Paintings from Books: Art and Literature in Britain, 1760–1900* (Columbus: Ohio University Press, 1985), and positively in Frederick Burwick, 'John Boydell's Shakespeare Gallery and the Stage', *Shakespeare Jahrbuch* 133 (1997), 54–76. Stuart Sillars argues that 'a realist, personal narrative' predominates over theatrical elements in many Boydell pictures. See his *Painting Shakespeare: The Artist as Critic, 1720–1820* (Cambridge: Cambridge University Press, 2006), 261.
75. *New Monthly Magazine*, May 1831, cited in Nicolas Powell, *Fuseli: 'The Nightmare'* (London: Allen Lane, 1973), 19.
76. Penny, *Reynolds*, 322.
77. Cited in Postle, *Subject Pictures*, 258.
78. *Analytical Review*, 1789, 4:106.
79. Cited in Postle, *Subject Pictures*, 260.
80. Ibid., 264.
81. Northcote, *Life of Sir Joshua Reynolds*, 2:229.
82. Ibid., 2:230.
83. Ibid., 2:230–1. Henry Repton (alias 'The Bee') made a similar point when he wrote: 'the BEE almost despaired of finding any fault [with *The Death of Cardinal Beaufort*]; till at length, peeping from behind the bolster, he saw the *Devil*, in the Character of a *Chimney-Sweeper*, waiting for Beaufort's soul, without a *soot-bag* to put it in. This conceit is beneath the dignity of the Subject and the Artist.' See Repton, *The Bee; or, A Companion to the Shakespeare Gallery* (London: T. Cadell, 1789), 41.
84. *Analytical Review*, 1789, 4:111; 1790, 4:330.
85. Fuseli painted this scene several times. For his later versions, see Gert Schiff, ed., *Johann Heinrich Füssli, 1741–1825*, Oeuvrekataloge Schweizer Kunstler, 2 vols. (Zurich: Berichthaus, 1973), nos. 1204, 1260 and 1282.
86. For the modification of the fiend, see Penny, *Reynolds*, 320; Postle, *Subject Pictures*, 264–5; and Mannings, *Sir Joshua Reynolds* (text), 525.
87. Penny, *Reynolds*, 326.
88. Northcote, *Life of Sir Joshua Reynolds*, 2:227.
89. Henry Fuseli, *Life and Writings*, ed. J. Knowles, 3 vols. (London: Colburn and Bentley, 1831), 2:225–6. See also his Aphorism 58 (3:81) for a similar statement.
90. Fuseli painted this scene several times. For his earlier versions, see Schiff, *Füssli*, nos. 457, 458.
91. James Knowles, *The Life of Henry Fuseli*, in Fuseli, *Life and Writings*, 1:189–90.
92. Siddons, *Reminiscences*, 19.
93. Boaden, *Memoirs of Siddons*, 2:146.
94. For a discussion of the pictorial and linguistic implications of this 'as', see Joel Weinsheimer, 'Mrs. Siddons, the Tragic Muse and the Problem of *As*', *Journal of Aesthetic and Art Criticism* 36 (1978), 317–28.
95. Cited in Heather McPherson, 'Picturing Tragedy: *Mrs. Siddons as the Tragic Muse* Revisited', *Eighteenth-Century Studies* 33 (2000), 401–30 (403).

96. Critics have long discussed this problem of the general and the particular in Reynolds. For a convenient summary of the dispute, see Walter John Hipple, Jr, 'General and Particular in the *Discourses* of Sir Joshua Reynolds: A Study in Method', *Journal of Aesthetic and Art Criticism* 11 (1953), 231–47.
97. Cited in Penny, *Reynolds*, 324–5.
98. Ibid., 325.
99. Siddons, *Reminiscences*, 17.
100. Boaden, *Memoirs of Kemble*, 1:155–6. Recent critics point to *Isaiah* (figure 18), not *Joel*, in the Sistine Chapel as the most important source of Reynolds's composition.
101. Boaden, *Memoirs of Siddons*, 2:90.
102. Ibid., 2:187.
103. I learnt about the picture's compositional process from Shelly Bennett and Mark Leonard, '"A Sublime and Masterly Performance": The Making of Sir Joshua Reynolds's *Sarah Siddons as the Tragic Muse*', in Robyn Asleson, ed., *A Passion for Performance: Sarah Siddons and Her Portraitists* (Los Angeles: John Paul Getty Museum, 1999), 97–140.
104. Siddons, *Reminiscences*, 18. This episode is also recorded in Northcote, *Life of Sir Joshua Reynolds*, 1:246.
105. This passage with the three lines from Milton's *Paradise Lost* is quoted from Fitzgerald Molloy, *Sir Joshua and His Circle*, 2 vols. (London: Hutchinson, 1906), 2:621.
106. Edmund Burke, *Correspondence*, ed. Thomas W. Copeland et al., 10 vols. (Cambridge: Cambridge University Press, 1958–78), 1:70 (25, 31 July 1746).
107. 'Punch's Petition' is reproduced in F. P. Lock, *Edmund Burke*, 2 vols. (Oxford: Clarendon Press, 1998–2006), 1:176–7 (figure 3).
108. Edmund Burke, *Writings and Speeches*, gen. ed. Paul Langford, 9 vols. (to date) (Oxford: Clarendon Press, 1981–), 1:65. Further references to the *Reformer* are to this edition and are given after quotations in the text.
109. For the attribution of the *Reformer* articles, see Lock, *Edmund Burke*, 1:56–9. Burke wrote another theatrical essay around 1761 ('Hints for an Essay on the Drama'), which remained unpublished during his lifetime. The calendar of Smock Alley is in Esther Keck Sheldon, *Thomas Sheridan of Smock-Alley, Recording His Life as Actor and Theatre Manager in Both Dublin and London; and Including a Smock-Alley Calendar for the Years of His Management* (Princeton: Princeton University Press, 1967).
110. In fact, Garrick visited Sheridan's Smock Alley in the winter of 1745–6, and played Macbeth on 7 January. The cast list suggests that the Davenant version was performed on this occasion. See Sheldon, *Thomas Sheridan*, 436.
111. Boswell, *Life of Johnson*, 2:88.
112. Ibid., 2:90.
113. Ibid.
114. D. N. Smith, ed., *Eighteenth-Century Essays on Shakespeare*, 2nd edn (Oxford: Clarendon Press, 1963), 13.

115. For the controversial date and authorship of this famous treatise, see Donald Russell's introduction to the Loeb Classical Library edition (145–8; see note 120).
116. John Dennis, *Critical Works*, ed. Edward Niles Hooker, 2 vols. (Baltimore: Johns Hopkins University Press, 1939–43), 1:355–63.
117. Ibid., 1:517 note. For Dennis's theory of sublimity, see also Samuel H. Monk, *The Sublime: A Study of Critical Theories in XVIII-Century England*, Modern Language Association of America, General Series (New York: Modern Language Association of America, 1935), 54, and W. P. Albrecht, *The Sublime Pleasures of Tragedy: A Study of Critical Theory from Dennis to Keats* (Lawrence: University of Kansas Press, 1975), 17–18.
118. Smith in fact translated from Boileau-Despréaux's French version. See John W. Draper, 'Aristotelian Mimesis in Eighteenth-Century England', *PMLA* 36 (1921), 372–400 (380–1 note).
119. For a discussion of the relationship between tragedy and sublimity, see Albrecht, *Sublime Pleasures*, 1–11.
120. Longinus, *On the Sublime*, in Aristotle, *Poetics*, ed. and trans. Stephen Halliwell; Longinus, *On the Sublime*, trans. W. H. Fyfe, rev. Donald Russell; Demetrius, *On Style*, ed. and trans. W. Rhys Roberts, Loeb Classical Library, 2nd edn (Cambridge, MA: Harvard University Press, 1995), 143–307 (215, 217). Textual references to Longinus are to this edition and are given after quotations in the text. Important variants in Smith's translation will be noted.
121. [Dionysius Longinus], *On the Sublime*, trans. William Smith (London: W. Innys and R. Manby, 1739), 146 note. Further references to this edition are given after quotations in the text. Faulty footnote numbering is silently corrected with reference to the subsequent editions.
122. Burke, *Correspondence*, 1:78.
123. Burke, *Writings and Speeches*, 1:216. Further references to *The Sublime and the Beautiful* are to this edition and are given after quotations in the text.
124. For the mimetic explanation of the pleasure of tragedy, see, for example, Aristotle: 'we enjoy contemplating the most precise images of things whose actual sight is painful to us, such as the forms of the vilest animals and of corpses' (*Poetics*, 37, 39).
125. Lock, *Edmund Burke*, 1:124.
126. Thomas Paine, *The Rights of Man*, ed. Henry Collins (Harmondsworth: Penguin, 1969), 81. Further references to this edition are given after quotations in the text.
127. Edmund Burke, *Reflections on the Revolution in France*, ed. J. C. D. Clark (Stanford: Stanford University Press, 2001), 154. Further references to the *Reflections* are to this edition and are given after quotations in the text.
128. See Paul Hindson and Tim Gray, *Burke's Dramatic Theory of Politics*, Avebury Series in Philosophy (Aldershot: Avebury, 1988), 41, and Tom Furniss, 'Stripping the Queen: Edmund Burke's Magic Lantern Show', in Steven Blakemore, ed., *Burke and the French Revolution: Bicentennial Essays* (Athens: University of Georgia Press, 1992), 69–96.

129. Hindson and Gray, *Burke's Dramatic Theory*. See also Mary Jacobus, '"That Great Stage Where Senators Perform": *Macbeth* and the Politics of Romantic Theatre', *Studies in Romanticism* 22 (1983), 353–87; Frans de Bruyn, 'Theater and Counterheater in Burke's *Reflections on the Revolution in France*', in Blakemore, *Burke and the French Revolution*, 28–68; Furniss, 'Stripping the Queen'; and Linda M. G. Zerilli, 'Text/Woman as Spectacle: Edmund Burke's "French Revolution"', *The Eighteenth Century* 33 (1992), 47–72.
130. Burke, *Correspondence*, 7:344 (27 January 1793). For Burke's similar response to the death of Marie-Antoinette, see also his letter to William Windham (7:461; [24 October 1973]) and onwards.
131. Marilyn Butler, ed., *Burke, Paine, Godwin, and the Revolution Controversy* (Cambridge: Cambridge University Press, 1984), 49.
132. Edmund Burke, *Four Letters on the Proposals for Peace with the Regicide Directory of France*, *Select Works*, ed. E. J. Payne, 2nd edn, 4 vols. (Oxford: Clarendon Press, 1878), vol. 3, 4. Further references to the *Four Letters* are to this edition and are given after quotations in the text.

3   'SPEAK THE SPEECH, I PRAY YOU': KEAN, *HAMLET* AND THE ROMANTIC 'PLAYWRIGHTS'

1. William Blake, 'A Pitiful Case', in Blake, *Complete Poems*, ed. W. H. Stevenson, 2nd edn (London: Longman, 1989).
2. Blake owned Edmond Malone's second (1798) edition of Reynolds's writings in three volumes but annotated only the first volume, containing the first eight *Discourses*.
3. For the antagonism between Reynolds and Blake, see Hazard Adams, 'Revisiting Reynolds's *Discourses* and Blake's Annotations', *Blake in His Time*, ed. Robert N. Essick and Donald Ross Pearce (Bloomington: Indiana University Press, 1978), 128–44, and Aileen Ward, '"Sr Joshua and His Gang": William Blake and the Royal Academy', *Huntington Library Quarterly* 52 (1989), 75–95.
4. Cited in Reynolds, *Discourses*, 284–319 (284). Further references to Blake's marginalia are to this edition and are given after quotations in the text. Bibliographical and textual information is supplied in William Blake, *Writings*, ed. G. E. Bentley, Jr, 2 vols. (Oxford: Clarendon Press, 1978), 2:1450–1500, 1747–9 note.
5. Blake's marginalia on Francis Bacon's *Essays* survive but they are mainly on the philosopher's religious views. See Blake, *Writings*, 2:1425–46, 1745–6 note.
6. Needless to say, 'ideas', with their necessarily Platonic implications, are different from the more empirical 'generalisations'. Reynolds was not scrupulous about the distinction between them. See Leonard M. Trawick III, 'Hazlitt, Reynolds, and the Ideal', *Studies in Romanticism* 4 (1965), 240–7.
7. A list of his known paintings is given in P. P. Howe, *The Life of William Hazlitt*, 3rd edn (London: H. Hamilton, 1947), 395.

8. References to Hazlitt's writings are to William Hazlitt, *Complete Works*, ed. P. P. Howe, 21 vols. (London: J. M. Dent, 1930–4) and are given after quotations in the text.
9. See, among others, 'On Certain Inconsistencies in Sir Joshua Reynolds's *Discourses*' (*Table-Talk*, in *Works*, 8:122–45); and 'Character of Sir Joshua Reynolds' (*Works*, 18:51–62), where Reynolds's Shakespearean pictures are discussed. For twentieth-century assessments of the controversy, see also Elizabeth Schneider, *The Aesthetics of William Hazlitt: A Study of the Philosophical Basis of His Criticism* (Philadelphia: University of Pennsylvania Press, 1933), 43–69, and Eugene Clinton Elliot, 'Reynolds and Hazlitt', *Journal of Aesthetic and Art Criticism* 21 (1962), 73–9.
10. Ernst Gombrich discusses the relations between Reynolds's theory of artistic imitation and his paintings in 'Reynolds's Theory and Practice of Imitation', in Gombrich, *Norm and Form: Studies in the Art of the Renaissance* (London: Phaidon, 1966), 129–34.
11. Hazlitt mistakenly cites Whately as 'Mason'. Stanley Wells points out that Hazlitt's 'characters' refers not only to individual dramatis personae but also to the overall characteristic of each play. See Wells, 'Shakespeare in Hazlitt's Theatre Criticism', *Shakespeare Survey* 35 (1982), 43–55. Hazlitt's interest in dramatic structure is also emphasised by John Kinnaird, 'Hazlitt and the "Design" of Shakespearean Tragedy: A "Character" Critic Reconsidered', *Shakespeare Quarterly* 28 (1977), 22–39.
12. Hazlitt's use of pictorial analogies and metaphors in his critical writings is extensively surveyed by Roy Park in *Hazlitt and the Spirit of the Age: Abstraction and Critical Theory* (Oxford: Clarendon Press, 1971), 138–58. Schneider (in *Aesthetics*) also emphasises the relations between Hazlitt's aesthetics and his literary theory.
13. *Quarterly Review* 34 (1826), 196–248 (227–8). This episode is also recorded in Hawkins, *Life of Kean*, 1:8–11.
14. Hawkins, *Life of Kean*, 1:28–9.
15. Ibid., 1:41–2.
16. Ibid., 1:209.
17. Hazlitt's first theatrical review appeared in the *Morning Chronicle* on 1 October 1813. However, he apparently regarded this Kean review as his own virtual 'debut' and omitted the earlier articles from *A View of the English Stage*.
18. Wells, 'Hazlitt's Theatre Criticism', 43.
19. William Hazlitt, *Letters*, ed. Herschell Moreland Sikes et al. (London: Macmillan, 1978), 50–1 (To the Rev. William Hazlitt, [July 1790]).
20. Hazlitt omitted quite a few passages of the original articles when he compiled *A View of the English Stage* in 1818. I supply the deleted passages from the notes of Howe's edition in brackets.
21. This paragraph was dropped when the article was reprinted in *A View of the English Stage*.
22. Leigh Hunt, 'Kemble and Kean', in Hunt, *Dramatic Essays*, ed. William Archer and Robert W. Lowe (London: W. Scott, 1894), 222.

23. Cited in William Archer, *Masks or Faces?*, in *The Paradox of Acting* and *Masks or Faces?*, ed. Lee Strasberg (New York: Hill and Wang, 1957), 73–226 (197–8).
24. [Genest], *Some Account*, 8:413.
25. Kean reportedly complained to Mrs Garrick, 'Because my style is easy and natural they [i.e. critics] think I don't study, and talk about the "sudden impulse of genius". There is no such thing as impulsive acting; all is premeditated and studied beforehand' (Hawkins, *Life of Kean*, 1:208).
26. Kemble's stage versions were published in 1796 (reprinted 1797), 1800, 1804, 1808, 1811 and 1814. I personally inspected Hamlet 1800; 1804; 1814; Inchbald 1808 (in vol. 1), along with the Folger promptbook (Shattuck 1974, in vol. 2), where the 1804 playbook is annotated by Kemble.
27. See Hamlet 1818. In fact, Kean was given 'a rather free hand' in modifying the text and is believed to have revised *Richard II*, *The Bride of Abydos* and *De Montfort* personally. See Harry R. Beaudry, *The English Theatre and John Keats* (Salzburg: University of Salzburg, 1973), 77.
28. For a detailed account of the theatrical versions of the Restoration and the eighteenth century, see Reiko Oya, 'A Dream of Passion: Representation and Reception of Shakespearean Tragedy in the Age of Garrick to Kean', PhD (University of London, 2003), 175–89.
29. The use of the Folio texts, which derived ultimately from F1 and probably echoed the promptbook of the King's Men, was limited. The pattern of the abridgements certainly echoed F1, but the coincidence may have been due to theatrical tradition rather than specific textual reference. Q1, presumably a pirated and mangled stage version, remained virtually unknown until its 'rediscovery' in 1823. See Philip Edwards's introduction to Hamlet 1985, 62–3.
30. According to Aristotle's famous definition, tragedy 'is mimesis of an action which is elevated, complete and of magnitude', and 'it is not in order to provide mimesis of character that agents act; rather, their characters are included for the sake of their actions' (*Poetics*, 47, 51).
31. David Farley-Hills, ed., *Critical Responses to Hamlet 1600–1900*, The Hamlet Collection, 4 vols. (New York: AMS, 1997–2006), 1:19.
32. Ibid., 1:98–131 (117–21).
33. Ibid., 1:222–9 (227–8).
34. Ibid., 1:228. See also Johnson, *On Shakespeare*, 1010.
35. Garrick's new version is studied extensively by George W. Stone, Jr in 'Garrick's Long Lost Alteration of *Hamlet*', *PMLA* 49 (1934), 890–921. For Garrick's early versions published in 1751 and in 1763, see Garrick, *Plays*, 4:432–33 note.
36. In the final scene Garrick's Hamlet abruptly predicts Gertrude's death ('*O, may she breathe / An hour of penitence 'ere madness ends her*', 'Garrick', 5.2.313–14) and refers to Ophelia's demise ('*Thy sister's, father's death*', 'Garrick', 5.2.316). As far as the stage business is concerned, the two characters simply exit, and their deaths are never reported.
37. For the period 1751–1800, I personally inspected, along with Garrick's 1772 adaptation already discussed, Hamlet 1761; [1763]; 1779; 1782; Bell 1774 (in

vol. 3, dated '1773'). Charles Beecher Hogan states that these playbooks are virtually 'identical' with the 1751 version (*Shakespeare in the Theatre, 1701–1800: A Record of Performances in London* (Oxford: Clarendon Press, 1952–7), 2:188–9), but the 1761 edition is a Hughes-Wilks text and still cites Wilks as Hamlet in the cast list, though the actor died in 1732.

38. The '*Hic et ubique*' sequence is retained in Hamlet [1763].
39. Hogan, *Shakespeare in the Theatre*, 2:187.
40. Incidentally, Claudius makes this same proposal in Q1 (Allen and Muir 1981, 606).
41. [Anon.], *An Authentic Narrative of Mr. Kemble's Retirement from the Stage* (London: J. Miller, 1817), xxvi.
42. John A. Mills, *Hamlet on Stage: The Great Tradition* (Westport, CT: Greenwood Press, 1985), 52.
43. Hazlitt also criticises Kean's lack of 'general conception' in Shylock (5:179, 180); Richard III (5:184); Othello (5:189); Macbeth (5:207); Romeo (5:208–9); Lear (18:336).
44. *Examiner*, 20 March 1814.
45. As far as the texts are concerned, the reading and theatrical versions were virtually identical: between Hamlet's entrance ('To be, or not to be, that is the question', 3.1.56) and the end of Ophelia's soliloquy ('I have seen what I have seen, see what I see', 3.1.162), Kemble's versions lost only around 4 lines.
46. John Finlay, *Miscellanies* (Dublin: J. Cumming, 1835), 223–4.
47. Cited in Mills, *Hamlet on Stage*, 83. Figure 19 captures a moment just before this famous 'crawl'.
48. Finlay, *Miscellanies*, 226–7.
49. Hawkins, *Life of Kean*, 1:209–10.
50. Leigh Hunt, 'Kean's Performance of Dying Scenes', in Hunt, *Dramatic Essays*, 230.
51. William Wordsworth, *The Prelude* (1805), 10:38–77, in *The Prelude 1799, 1805, 1850*, ed. Jonathan Wordsworth et al., Norton Critical Edition (New York: Norton, 1979). Further references to this edition are given after quotations in the text.
52. The Norton editors suggest that 'the dramatic story' refers to *The Excursion*, which is 'the "dramatic" – or narrative – section of *The Recluse*' (*The Prelude*, 406 note). Wordsworth could also be referring to the 1797 drama prophetically from the viewpoint of 1792. The relations between *The Borderers* and the Revolution have been discussed extensively. See, among others, Reeve Parker, 'Reading Wordsworth's Power: Narrative and Usurpation in *The Borderers*', *ELH* 54 (1987), 299–331, and '"In Some Sort Seeing with My Proper Eyes": Wordsworth and the Spectacles of Paris', *Studies in Romanticism* 2 (1988), 369–90; Alan Liu, *Wordsworth: The Sense of History* (Stanford: Stanford University Press, 1989), 225–310; Marjean D. Purinton, *Romantic Ideology Unmasked: The Mentally Constructed Tyrannies in Dramas of William Wordsworth, Lord Byron, Percy Shelly, and Joanna Baillie* (Newark: University of Delaware Press, 1994), 26–50; and Victoria Myers, 'Justice and

Indeterminacy: Wordsworth's *The Borderers* and the Trials of the 1790s', *Studies in Romanticism* 40 (2001), 427–57.

53. William Wordsworth, *The Borderers*, ed. Robert Osborn, The Cornell Wordsworth (Ithaca: Cornell University Press, 1982), 813, 815. Further references to this edition are given after quotations in the text. The following plot summary is according to the early version (1797–9) of the play.
54. Samuel Taylor Coleridge, *Collected Letters*, ed. Earl Leslie Griggs, 6 vols. (Oxford: Clarendon Press, 1956–71), 1:318 (To William Lisle Bowles, [16 March 1797]). Further references to Coleridge's letters are to this edition and are given after quotations in the text.
55. Samuel Taylor Coleridge, *Poetical Works*, ed. J. C. C. Mays, Bollingen Series, 3 double vols. (1. Poems: reading text; 2. Poems: variorum text; 3. Plays) (Princeton: Princeton University Press, 2001), 3:150 note. Further references to Coleridge's plays and poems are to this edition and are given after quotations in the text.
56. William and Dorothy Wordsworth, *Letters*, ed. Ernest de Selincourt, 2nd edn, rev. Chester Shaver et al., 8 vols. (Oxford: Clarendon Press, 1967–93), 1:189 (To Mary Hutchinson [?], [June, 1797]).
57. The process through which *Christabel* was phased out of the 1800 publication is analysed in Richard Holmes, *Coleridge: Early Visions* (London: Hodder & Stoughton, 1989), 283–6.
58. William Wordsworth, *Lyrical Ballads, and Other Poems, 1797–1800*, ed. James Butler and Karen Green, The Cornell Wordsworth (Ithaca: Cornell University Press, 1992), 791.
59. Ibid., 743.
60. Ibid., 743 note.
61. For the revisions for the period 1815–50, see William Wordsworth, *Prose Works*, ed. W. J. B. Owen and Jane Worthington Smyser, 3 vols. (Oxford: Clarendon Press, 1974), 1:118–59.
62. See Coleridge's letters to William Sotheby (2:811–1213; July 1802) and Robert Southey (2:830; 29 July 1802).
63. *Biographia Literaria*, ed. James Engell and W. Jackson Bate, Bollingen Series, 2 vols. (Princeton: Princeton University Press, 1983), 2:6.
64. Ibid., 2:266.
65. Samuel Taylor Coleridge, *Lectures 1808–1819: On Literature*, ed. R. A. Foakes, Bollingen Series, 2 vols. (Princeton: Princeton University Press, 1987), 1:135.
66. Ibid.
67. Patricia M. Jenkins, *Coleridge's Literary Theory: The Chronology of Its Development, 1790–1818* (Fairfield: Department of English, Fairfield University, 1984), 158. See also Coleridge's letter to Southey (1:533; 30 September [1799]).
68. For a discussion of the relations between Coleridge's theory of imagination and dramatic illusion, see Frederick Burwick, *Illusion and the Drama: Critical Theory of the Enlightenment and Romantic Era* (University Park: Pennsylvania State University Press, 1991), 191–229. Burwick, however, discusses only *Remorse* and not *Osorio* in this context (267–79).

69. The Bollingen editor gives an overview of Coleridge's sources (*Poetical Works*, 3:52–4).
70. Donohue, *Dramatic Character*, 280–312.
71. Stephen Maxfield Parrish, *The Art of the Lyrical Ballads* (Cambridge, MA: Harvard University Press, 1973), 70–9, and Paul Magnuson, *Coleridge and Wordsworth: A Lyrical Dialogue* (Princeton: Princeton University Press, 1988), 51–67.
72. Coleridge noted in a manuscript copy, 'A scene of magic is introduced, in which no single person on the Stage has the least Faith – all tho' in different ways think or know it to be a *Trick* . . .' (*Poetical Works*, 3:158 note).
73. Ibid., 3:158 note.
74. Ibid.
75. Ibid.
76. Ibid., 3:150 note.
77. *Lectures 1808–1819*, 1:539.
78. Ibid., 2:147.
79. 'Dr Johnson's mistaking of the marks of reluctance & procrastination for impetuous horror-striking fiendishness! Of such importance is it to understand the *Germ* of a character.' See Samuel Taylor Coleridge, *Marginalia*, ed. H. J. Jackson and George Whalley, Bollingen Series, 6 vols. (Princeton: Princeton University Press, 1980–2001), 4:855. See also John Payne Collier's record of Coleridge's lecture (*Lectures 1808–1819*, 1:389).
80. Coleridge, *Poetical Works*, 3:150 note.
81. Coleridge, *Marginalia*, 4:854–5.
82. Ibid., 4:855.
83. Samuel Taylor Coleridge, *Aids to Reflection*, ed. John Beer, Bollingen Series (Princeton: Princeton University Press, 1993), 132.
84. Coleridge, *Marginalia*, 4:855.
85. Critics have studied the importance of the theme of remorse in Romantic drama in relation to the gothic tradition (see Bertrand Evans, 'Manfred's Remorse and Dramatic Tradition', *PMLA* 62 (1947), 752–74), and to the trauma of the Revolution (Julie Ann Carlson, *In the Theatre of Romanticism: Coleridge, Nationalism, Women* (Cambridge: Cambridge University Press, 1994), 176–212).
86. See Mays's 'Introduction' (*Poetical Works*, 3:1028–9; 1036–40). See also Coleridge's preface to the play where he acknowledges the contributions of the theatre members (*Poetical Works*, 3:1066–7). Daily progress reports of the production are recorded in Coleridge's *Letters* (3:420–7).
87. Samuel Schoenbaum, 'Dyce's Recollections of Wordsworth, Mrs. Siddons, and Other Notable Persons', *Times Literary Supplement*, 22 January 1971, 101–2.
88. 'The Foster-Mother's Tale' was printed as an appendix when the play was published. 'The Dungeon' is retained in the printed text but marked to be cut in the Drury Lane promptbook. See Carl R. Woodring, 'Two Prompt Copies of Coleridge's *Remorse*', *Bulletin of the New York Public Library* 65 (1961), 229–35 (232).

89. There was confusion over the death of Ordonio. On the opening night, Naomi, instead of Alhadra, stabbed Ordonio, apparently by mistake. For the various revisionary stages of the final scene, see *Poetical Works*, 3:1204–6 and 1207–25 (figures 13–22).
90. The full record of the performances is in *Poetical Works*, 3:1041–8.
91. For the periodical reviews of the performance and the publication of *Remorse*, see J. R. de J. Jackson, ed., *Coleridge: The Critical Heritage*, The Critical Heritage Series, 2 vols. (London: Routledge & Kegan Paul, 1970–91), 1:111–88. Coleridge was pleased with the audience's response ('the Remorse has met with *unexampled* APPLAUSE', 3:429; To Mrs. S. T. Coleridge, [27 January 1813]), but was unhappy about the review articles.
92. See Coleridge's letter to Thomas Poole (3:437, [13 February 1813]).
93. *Poetical Works*, 3:1239 note.
94. See Donohue, *Dramatic Character*, 299.
95. Samuel Taylor Coleridge, *The Table Talk and Omniana*, ed. Coventry Patmore (London: H. Milward, 1917), 213.
96. *Poetical Works*, 3:1066–8.
97. Southey's letter is cited in *Poetical Works*, 3:55.
98. Byron's letter is cited in Coleridge, *Letters*, 4:563 note. In fact, Kean played in *Remorse* in Exeter (5, 17, 22 March 1813), though his part was Alvar, not Ordonio (*Poetical Works*, 3:1044). It apparently had no impact on the London theatrical scene.
99. 'Recollections of Keats', in John Keats, *Poetical Works and Other Writings*, Hamstead Edition, ed. Harry Buxton Forman, rev. Maurice Buxton Forman, 8 vols. (New York: Charles Scribner, 1938–9), 5:325–62 (5:328).
100. John Keats, *Letters, 1814–1821*, ed. by Hyder Edward Rollins, 2 vols. (Cambridge, MA: Harvard University Press, 1958), 2:139 (To Benjamin Bailey, 14 August 1819). Further references to Keats's letters are to this edition and are given after quotations in the text.
101. The relationship between Hazlitt and Keats has been discussed extensively. See, among others, David Bromwich, *Hazlitt: The Mind of a Critic* (New York: Oxford University Press, 1983), 362–401, and Jonathan Bate, *Romantic Imagination*, 157–74.
102. Keats's annotations on *Characters* are reproduced in *Poetical Works* (Hamstead), 5:280–86.
103. John Keats, *Complete Poems*, ed. John Barnard, 3rd edn (Harmondsworth: Penguin, 1988), 529. Further references to the review are to this edition and are given after quotations in the text.
104. See Hazlitt's *Lectures on the English Poets* (*Works*, 5:54–5).
105. In *Lectures on the English Poets*, Hazlitt noted a similar lack of premeditation in Shakespeare's lines themselves ('the dialogues in Shakspeare are carried on without any consciousness of what is to follow, without any appearance of preparation or premeditation', 5:50).
106. Especially relevant is Keats's letter to Benjamin Bailey (22 November 1817), where the poet already claims that men of genius 'have not any individuality,

any determined Character' (1:184). For a comprehensive treatment of the concept, see Walter Jackson Bate, *Negative Capability: The Intuitive Approach in Keats* (Cambridge, MA: Harvard University Press, 1939). The political, as well as philosophical and aesthetic, backgrounds of Keats's poetics are surveyed in Nicholas Roe, *John Keats and the Culture of Dissent* (Oxford: Clarendon Press, 1997), 230–67.
107. Hunt, on the other hand, admired West's *Death on the Pale Horse*. For Hunt's relationship with West, see Ian Jack, *Keats and the Mirror of Art*, 2nd edn (London: Oxford University Press, 1968), 3.
108. For Kean's Wolf Club, see Hawkins, *Life of Kean*, 1:305–14, 417–20. Recent writers emphasise the political implications of Keats's interest in Kean. See, for instance, John Kandl, 'Plebian Gusto, Negative Capability, and the Low Company of "Mr. Kean": Keats' Dramatic Review for the *Champion*', *Nineteenth-Century Prose* 28 (2001), 130–41, and Jonathan Mulrooney, 'Keats in the Company of Kean', *Studies in Romanticism* 42 (2003), 227–50.
109. Cited in Andrew Motion, *Keats* (London: Faber and Faber, 1997), 420.
110. John Middleton Murry, *Keats and Shakespeare: A Study of Keats' Poetic Life from 1816 to 1820* (London: Oxford University Press, 1925), 155, 153.
111. Charles Armitage Brown, 'Life of John Keats', in Hyder Edward Rollins, ed., *The Keats Circle: Letters and Papers ... of the Keats Circle*, 2nd edn (Cambridge, MA: Harvard University Press, 1965), 2:52–97 (2:66).
112. Thomas McFarland, *The Masks of Keats: The Endeavour of a Poet* (Oxford: Oxford University Press, 2000), 171.
113. Rollins, *Keats Circle*, 2:66.
114. Motion, *Keats*, 420.
115. John Keats, *Otho the Great*, 3.1.1–6, in *Poems*, ed. Jack Stillinger (London: Heinemann Educational, 1978). Further references to *Otho* are to this edition and are given after quotations in the text.
116. Keats's sources are studied in C. L. Finney, *The Evolution of Keats's Poetry*, 2 vols. (Cambridge, MA: Harvard University Press, 1936), 2:660–7.
117. Charles Armitage Brown, *Letters*, ed. Jack Stillinger (Cambridge, MA: Harvard University Press, 1966), 48.
118. Ibid., 49.
119. Ibid., 49 note.
120. Coleridge, *Lectures 1808–1819*, 1:539.
121. Colley Cibber, *The Laureat; or, The Right Side of Colley Cibber, Esq.* (London: J. Roberts, 1740), 31.
122. Diderot, *Paradox of Acting*, in Strasberg, *The Paradox of Acting* and *Masks or Faces?*, 11–71 (32–33).
123. Boswell, *Life of Johnson*, 4:243–44.
124. Cited in *Masks or Faces?*, in Strasberg, *The Paradox of Acting* and *Masks or Faces?*, 148.
125. Cavendish's letter is cited in Vickers, *Critical Heritage*, 1:42–44.
126. See Oscar James Campbell, ed., *A Shakespeare Encyclopaedia* (London: Methuen, 1966), ('Shakespeare, Hamnet'). The name of this boy was

mistakenly given as 'Samuel' by George Steevens but was restored to 'Hamnet' by Edmond Malone. See Samuel Schoenbaum, *Shakespeare's Lives*, 2nd edn (Oxford: Clarendon Press, 1991), 94, 126.
127. Keats identifies Hamlet's agony with his own more explicitly in a letter written in 1820 ('Hamlet's heart was full of such Misery as mine is when he said to Ophelia "Go to a Nunnery, go, go!"', 2:312; To Fanny Brawne, August [?] 1820).
128. For the resemblance between the features of Fanny and Auranthe, see John Keats, *Poems*, ed. Miriam Allott (London: Longman, 1970), 609 note.
129. Motion, *Keats*, 422.
130. This letter was so uncharacteristic of the affable Keats that the puzzled Taylor forwarded it to Richard Woodhouse, who commented on Keats's idea of 'pride'. Woodhouse's letter dated 31 August 1819 is cited in Keats, *Letters*, 2:150–3.
131. Rollins, *Keats Circle*, 2:66.
132. Hazlitt's and Northcote's lines are quoted with some omissions from Hazlitt, *Works*, 11:193–5. Other references are given individually. Speech prefixes, spellings, capitalisations and punctuations are standardised.
133. *Idler* in *The Idler and the Adventurer*, ed. John M. Bullitt, W. J. Bate and L. F. Powell, The Yale Edition, 2 vols. (New Haven: Yale University Press, 1958), 2:140 (no. 45, 24 February, 1763).
134. Ibid.

CONCLUSION: KEAN'S FAREWELL

1. For the rumours of Montagu's involvement in the Ode, see Davies, *Life of Garrick*, 2:213–15, and Blunt, *Montagu*, 1:224. The possibility of Burke's authorship of the Jubilee oration is discussed by England in *Garrick's Jubilee* (127–42).
2. See Blunt, *Montagu*, 1:224, for the authorship controversy over Montagu's publication.
3. Reynolds's authorship of *Discourses* is discussed in Frederick Whiley Hilles, *The Literary Career of Sir Joshua Reynolds* (Cambridge: Cambridge University Press, 1936), 134–45. A page from Reynolds's manuscript bearing corrections in Johnson's hand is reproduced on page 135.
4. See [Arthur Murphy], ed., *The Gray's Inn Journal* (London: Faden and Bouquet, 1753–4), 223–27 (no. 38, 15 June 1754). This article is understandably omitted from the 1756 edition.
5. See Johnson, *The Rambler*, ed. W. J. Bate and Albrecht B. Strauss, The Yale Edition, 3 vols. (New Haven: Yale University Press, 1969), 3:228–33 (no. 190, 11 January 1752).
6. Boswell, *Life of Johnson*, 1:356.
7. Robert Donald Spector, *Arthur Murphy* (Boston: Twayne, 1979), 27.
8. See Coleridge's note on Act 2 scene 2 (*Poetical Works*, 3.2:1268–70).
9. This essay was originally titled: 'On Garrick, and Acting; and the Plays of Shakespeare, Considered with Reference ...'. See Jonathan Bate, ed., *The Romantics on Shakespeare* (London: Penguin, 1992), 111–27, 566–7 note.

10. See his *Actors and the Art of Acting* (New York: Grove Press, 1957), 100–2.
11. Roach, *Player's Passion*, 195–217.
12. The following account is adapted from [B. W. Procter], *Life of Edmund Kean*, 2 vols. (London: E. Moxon, 1835), 2:235–46; Hawkins, *Life of Kean*, 2:379–84; J. Fizgerald Molloy, *The Life and Adventures of Edmund Kean*, 2 vols. (London: Ward and Downey, 1888), 2:275–80; H. N. Hillebrand, *Edmund Kean* (New York: Columbia University Press, 1933), 325–7; and Giles Playfair, *The Flash of Lightning: A Portrait of Edmund Kean* (London: Kimber, 1983), 310–16.

Bibliography

The bibliography consists of:
(1) Shakespearean editions, acting versions and adaptations, subdivided into (a) collections and (b) individual plays.
(2) Works by other authors.

(1) SHAKESPEAREAN EDITIONS, ACTING VERSIONS, AND ADAPTATIONS CONSULTED

(a) Collections

F1: *Mr. William Shakespeares Comedies, Histories, & Tragedies*, 1623. (Reprinted in Hinman 1996).

Rowe 1709: *The Works of Mr. William Shakespear*. Ed. N[icholas] Rowe. 6 vols. London: J. Tonson, 1709.

Pope 1723–5: *The Works of Shakespear*. Ed. [Alexander] Pope. 6 vols. London: J. Tonson, 1723–5.

Theobald 1733: *The Works of Shakespeare*. Ed. [Lewis] Theobald. 7 vols. London: A. Betterworth and C. Hitch, 1733.

Hanmer 1744: *The Works of Shakespear*. Ed. T[homas] Hanmer. 6 vols. Oxford: [At the Theatre], 1744.

Warburton 1747: *The Works of Shakespear*. Ed. [William] Warburton. 8 vols. London: J. and P. Knapton and others, 1747.

Johnson 1765: *The Plays of William Shakespeare*. Ed. Sam[uel] Johnson. 8 vols. London: J. and R. Tonson and others, 1765.

Capell [1767–8]: *Mr William Shakespeare his Comedies, Histories, and Tragedies*. Ed. Edward Capell. 10 vols. London: J. and R. Tonson, [1767–8].

Johnson-Steevens 1773: *The Plays of William Shakespeare*. Ed. S[amuel] Johnson and G[eorge] Steevens. 10 vols. London: C. Bathurst and others, 1773.

Bell 1774: *Bell's Edition of Shakespeare's Plays*. Ed. [Francis Gentleman]. 9 vols. London: J. Bell, 1774.

Malone 1790: *The Plays and Poems of William Shakspeare*. Ed. E[dmond] Malone. 10 vols. London: J. Rivington and others, 1790.

Steevens 1802: *The Dramatic Works of Shakspeare*. Ed. George Steevens. 9 vols. London: J. and J. Boydell and others, 1802.
Reed 1803: *The Plays of William Shakspeare*. Ed. Isaac Reed. 21 vols. London: J. Johnson and others, 1803.
Inchbald 1808: *The British Theatre; or, A Collection of Plays*. Ed. [Elizabeth] Inchbald. 25 vols. London: Longman, 1808.
Spencer 1965: *Five Restoration Adaptations of Shakespeare*. Ed. Christopher Spencer. Urbana: University of Illinois Press, 1965.
Shattuck 1974: *John Philip Kemble Promptbooks*. Ed. Charles H. Shattuck. The Folger Facsimile. 11 vols. Charlottesville: University Press of Virginia for the Folger Shakespeare Library, 1974.
Allen and Muir 1981: *Shakespeare's Plays in Quarto: A Facsimile Edition of Copies Primarily from the Henry E. Huntington Library*. Ed. Michael J. B. Allen and Kenneth Muir. Berkeley: University of California Press, 1981.
'Oxford' 1986: *The Complete Works*. Gen eds. Stanley Wells and Gary Taylor. Oxford: Clarendon Press, 1986.
Hinman 1996: *The First Folio of Shakespeare: The Norton Facsimile*. Ed. Charlton Hinman. 2nd edn. New York: Norton, 1996.
'Riverside' 1997: *The Riverside Shakespeare*. Gen ed. G. Blakemore Evans. 2nd edn. Boston: Houghton, 1997.
'Arden' 2001: *The Arden Shakespeare Complete Works*. Gen eds. Richard Proudfoot, Ann Thompson and David Scott Kastan. 2nd edn. London: Arden Shakespeare, 2001.

(b) Individual plays

Hamlet

Hamlet Q1: *The Tragicall Historie of Hamlet, Prince of Denmarke* (1603). (Reprinted in Allen and Muir 1981.)
Hamlet Q2: *The Tragicall Historie of Hamlet, Prince of Denmarke* (1604, [1605]). (Reprinted in Allen and Muir 1981.)
Hamlet 1676: *The Tragedy of Hamlet . . . As It Is Now Acted at His Highness the Duke of York's Theatre*. London: J. Martyn and H. Herringman, 1676.
Hamlet 1703: *The Tragedy of Hamlet . . . As It Is Now Acted by Her Majesties Servants*. London: R. Wellington and E. Rumball, 1703.
Hamlet 1718: *Hamlet . . . As It Is Now Acted by His Majesty's Servants*. London: M. Wellington, 1718.
Hamlet 1761: *Hamlet . . . As It Is Now Acted by His Majesty's Servants*. London: J. and P. Knapton and others, 1761.
Hamlet [1763?]: *Hamlet . . . As It Is Now Acted at the Theatres Royal, in Drury-Lane and Covent-Garden*. London: H. Woodfall and others, [1763?].
Hamlet 1773: *Hamlet, Prince of Denmark . . . Collated with the Old and Modern Editions*. Ed. [Charles Jennens]. London: W. Bowyer and J. Nichols, 1773.

Hamlet 1779: *Hamlet . . . As It Is Acted at the Theatres-Royal, in Drury-Lane and Covent-Garden*. London: Harrison, 1779.
Hamlet 1782: *Hamlet . . . Marked with the Variations in the Manager's Book at the Theatre-Royal in Drury-Lane*. London: C. Burthurst and others, 1782.
Hamlet 1800: *Hamlet . . . Revised by J. P. Kemble . . . As It Is Acted by Their Majesties Servants of the Theatre Royal, Drury Lane*. London: C. Lowndes, 1800.
Hamlet 1804: *Shakspeare's Hamlet . . . Revised by J. P. Kemble . . . As It Is Acted at the Theatre Royal in Covent Garden*. London: R. Ridgway, 1804. (Reprinted in Shattuck 1974, vol. 2)
Hamlet 1814: *Shakspeare's Hamlet . . . Revised by J. P. Kemble . . . As It Is Acted by Their Majesties Servants at the Theatre Royal, Drury Lane*. London: J. Miller, 1814.
Hamlet 1818: *Hamlet . . . As It Is Performed at the Theatres Royal*. Oxberry's New English Drama. London: For the proprietors, 1818.
Hamlet 1877: *Hamlet*. Ed. Horace Howard Furness [the Elder]. New Variorum Edition. 2 vols. Philadelphia: J. B. Lippincott, 1877.
Hamlet 1985: *Hamlet, Prince of Denmark*. Ed. Philip Edwards. New Cambridge Shakespeare. Cambridge: Cambridge University Press, 1985.
Hamlet 2006 (Q2): *Hamlet, Prince of Denmark*. Ed. Ann Thompson and Neil Taylor. Arden 3. London: Arden Shakespeare, 2006.
Hamlet 2006 (Q1, F1): *Hamlet, Prince of Denmark: The Texts of 1603 and 1623*. Ed. Ann Thompson and Neil Taylor. Arden 3. London: Arden Shakespeare, 2006.

King Lear

Lear Q1: *M. William Shak-speare: His True Chronicle Historie of the Life and Death of King Lear and His Three Daughters* (1608). (Reprinted in Allen and Muir 1981.)
Lear 1681: *The History of King Lear. Acted at the Duke's Theatre. Reviv'd with Alterations*. By N[ahum] Tate. London: E. Flesher, 1681.
Lear 1756: *The History of King Lear . . . Revived, with Alterations*. By N[ahum] Tate. London: C. Hitch and others, 1756. [British Library c.119.dd.22: A contemporary prompt copy, with manuscript notes and alterations.]
Lear 1770: *King Lear . . . Collated with the Old and Modern Editions*. Ed. [Charles Jennens]. London. W. White, 1770.
Lear 1786: *King Lear . . . Altered . . . by David Garrick, Esq., Marked with the Variations in the Manager's Book at the Theatre-Royal in Drury Lane*. London: C. Bathurst and others, 1786.
Lear 1808: *Shakspeare's King Lear, (with Nahum Tate's Alterations) . . . Revised by J. P. Kemble . . . As It Is Acted at the Theatre Royal in Covent Garden*. London: For the Theatre, 1808. (Reprinted in Kemble 1974, vol. 5.)
Lear 1815: *Shakspeare's King Lear, (from Nahum Tate's Alterations) . . . Revised by J. P. Kemble . . . As It Is Performed at the Theatres Royal*. London. J. Miller, 1815.
Lear 1820: *King Lear, Altered . . . by N. Tate . . . As It Is Performed at the Theatres Royal*. Oxberry's New English Drama. London: For the proprietors, 1820.
Lear 1880: *King Lear*. Ed. Horace Howard Furness [the Elder]. New Variorum Edition. Philadelphia: J. B. Lippincott, 1880.

Lear 1997: *King Lear*. Ed. R. A. Foakes. Arden 3. Walton-on-Thames: Thomas Nelson, 1997.

Macbeth
Macbeth 1674: *Macbeth . . . As It Is Now Acted at the Duke's Theatre*. [By William Davenant]. London: P. Chetwin, 1674.
Macbeth 1773: *Macbeth . . . Collated with the Old and Modern Editions*. Ed. [Charles Jennens]. London. W. Owen, 1773.
Macbeth 1794a: *Macbeth . . . As Represented by Their Majesties Servants, on Opening the Theatre Royal Drury Lane, on Monday, April 21st. 1794*. London: C. Lowndes, 1794.
Macbeth 1794b: *Macbeth . . . As Represented by Their Majesties Servants, on Opening the Theatre Royal, Drury Lane, Monday, April 21st. 1794*. 2nd edn. London: C. Lowndes, 1794.
Macbeth 1803: *Shakspeare's Macbeth . . . Revised by J. P. Kemble . . . As It Is Acted at the Theatre Royal in Covent Garden*. London: J. Ridgway, 1803. (Reprinted in Shattuck 1974, vol. 5.)
Macbeth 1814: *Shakspeare's Macbeth . . . Revised by J. P. Kemble . . . As It Is Performed at the Theatres Royal*. London: J. Miller, 1814.
Macbeth 1818: *Shakespeare's Macbeth . . . Revised by J. P. Kemble . . . As It Is Acted at the Theatre Royal, Drury Lane*. London: T. Rodwell, 1818.
Macbeth 1915: *Macbeth*. New Variorum Edition. Ed. Horace Howard Furness. 2nd edn. Philadelphia: J. B. Lippincott, 1915.
Macbeth 1997: *Macbeth*. Ed. A. R. Braunmuller. New Cambridge Shakespeare. Cambridge: Cambridge University Press, 1997.

(2) WORKS BY OTHER AUTHORS

Abrams, M. H. 'Belief and Willing Suspension of Disbelief'. *Literature and Belief*. Ed. M. H. Abrams. English Institute Essays 1957. New York: Columbia University Press, 1958, 1–30.
Adams, Hazard. 'Revisiting Reynolds's *Discourses* and Blake's Annotations'. *Blake in His Time*. Ed. Robert N. Essick and Donald Ross Pearce. Bloomington: Indiana University Press, 1978, 128–44.
Adventurer, The. 1753–54. (See also Hawkesworth; Johnson.)
Albrecht, W. P. *Hazlitt and the Creative Imagination*. Lawrence: University of Kansas Press, 1965.
   The Sublime Pleasures of Tragedy: A Study of Critical Theory from Dennis to Keats. Lawrence: University of Kansas Press, 1975.
Altick, Richard D. *Paintings from Books: Art and Literature in Britain, 1760–1900*. Columbus: Ohio University Press, 1985.
Analytical Review, The. 1788–98.
Arac, Jonathan. 'The Media of Sublimity: Johnson and Lamb on *King Lear*'. *Studies in Romanticism* 26 (1987), 209–20.

Archer, William. *Masks or Faces?* In Strasberg, *The Paradox of Acting* and *Masks or Faces?*, 73–226.
Aristotle. *Poetics*. Ed and trans. Stephen Halliwell. Longinus. *On the Sublime*. Trans. W. H. Fyfe. Rev. Donald Russell. Demetrius. *On Style*. Ed. and trans. Doreen C. Innes based on W. Rhys Roberts. Loeb Classical Library. 2nd edn. Cambridge, MA: Harvard University Press, 1995.
Ashfield, Andrew, and Peter de Bolla, eds. *The Sublime: A Reader in British Eighteenth-Century Aesthetic Theory*. Cambridge: Cambridge University Press, 1996.
Asleson, Robyn, ed. *A Passion for Performance: Sarah Siddons and Her Portraitists*. Los Angeles: John Paul Getty Museum, 1999.
Authentic Narrative of Mr. Kemble's Retirement from the Stage, An. London: J. Miller, 1817.
Avery, Emmett L. 'The Shakespeare Ladies Club'. *Shakespeare Quarterly* 7 (1958), 153–8.
    et al., eds. *The London Stage, 1660–1800*. 5 pts. in 11 vols. Carbondale: Southern Illinois University Press, 1960–8.
Aycock, Roy E. 'Shakespearean Criticism in the *Gray's Inn Journal*'. *Yearbook of English Studies* 2 (1972), 68–72.
Babcock, Robert Witbeck. *The Genesis of Shakespeare Idolatory, 1766–1799: A Study in English Criticism of the Late Eignteenth Century*. Chapel Hill: University of North Carolina Press, 1931.
Badawi, M. M. *Coleridge, Critic of Shakespeare*. Cambridge: Cambridge University Press, 1973.
Baer, Marc. *Theatre and Disorder in Late Georgian London*. Oxford: Clarendon Press, 1992.
Baker, Herschel Clay. *John Philip Kemble: The Actor in His Theatre*. Cambridge, MA: Harvard University Press, 1942.
Barbato, Louis R. '*Hamlet* on the Nineteenth Century London Stage: The Kemble, Phelps, and Irving Promptbooks'. *Shakespeare Jahrbuch* 121 (1985), 151–9.
Bartholomeusz, Dennis. *Macbeth and the Players*. London: Cambridge University Press, 1969.
Bate, Jonathan. *Shakespeare and the English Romantic Imagination*. Oxford: Clarendon Press, 1986.
    Shakespearean Constitutions: Politics, Theatre, Criticism, 1730–1830. Oxford: Clarendon Press, 1989.
    ed. *The Romantics on Shakespeare*. London: Penguin, 1992.
    and Russell Jackson, eds. *Shakespeare: An Illustrated Stage History*. New York: Oxford University Press, 1996.
Bate, Walter Jackson. *Negative Capability: The Intuitive Approach in Keats*. Cambridge, MA: Harvard University Press, 1939.
    Samuel Johnson. New York: Harcourt Brace Jovanovich, 1977.
Beaudry, Harry R. *The English Theatre and John Keats*. Salzburg: University of Salzburg, 1973.
Benedetti, Jean. *David Garrick and the Birth of Modern Theatre*. London: Methuen, 2001.

Benjamin, Walter. *Selected Writings*. Trans. Edmund Jephcott et al. Ed. Marcus Bullock and Michael W. Jennings. 4 vols. Cambridge, MA: Belknap Press of Harvard University, 1996–2003.

Bennett, Shelley, and Mark Leonard. '"A Sublime and Masterly Performance": The Making of Sir Joshua Reynolds's *Sarah Siddons as the Tragic Muse*'. In Asleson, ed., *A Passion for Performance*, 97–140.

Berkowitz, Gerald M. *David Garrick: A Reference Guide*. Boston: G. K. Hall, 1980.

Besterman, Theodore, ed. *Voltaire on Shakespeare*. Genève: Institut et Musée Voltaire, 1967.

Blake, William. *Writings*. Ed. G. E. Bentley, Jr. 2 vols. Oxford: Clarendon Press, 1978.

Complete Poems. Ed. W. H. Stevenson. 2nd edn. London: Longman, 1989.

Blakemore, Steven, ed. *Burke and the French Revolution: Bicentennial Essays*. Athens: University of Georgia Press, 1992.

Blunt, Reginald, ed. *Mrs. Montagu, 'Queen of the Blues': Her Letters and Friendships from 1762 to 1800*. 2 vols. London: Constable, [1923].

Boaden, James. *Memoirs of the Life of John Philip Kemble, Esq*. 2 vols. London: Longman and others, 1825.

Memoirs of Mrs. Siddons. 2 vols. London: H. Colburn, 1827.

ed. *The Private Correspondence of David Garrick, with the Most Celebrated Persons of His Time*. 2 vols. London: H. Colburn and R. Bentley, 1831–2.

Boase, T. S. R. 'Illustrations of Shakespeare's Plays in the Seventeenth and Eighteenth Centuries'. *Journal of Warburg and Courtauld Institute* 10 (1947), 83–108.

Bond, Donald F., ed. *The Spectator*. 5 vols. Oxford: Clarendon Press, 1965.

ed. *The Tatler*. 3 vols. Oxford: Clarendon Press, 1987.

Booth, Michael, John Stokes and Susan Bassnett. *Three Tragic Actresses: Siddons, Rachel, Ristori*. New York: Cambridge University Press, 1996.

Boswell, James, the Elder. *Life of Johnson: Together with Boswell's Journal of a Tour to the Hebrides and Johnson's Diary of a Journey into North Wales*. Ed. George Birkbeck Hill. 2nd edn. Rev. L. F. Powell. 6 vols. Oxford: Clarendon Press, 1934, 1950.

Journal of a Tour to the Hebrides with Samuel Johnson. Ed. Frederick A. Pottle and Charles H. Bennett. London: W. Heinemann, 1936.

Botting, Roland B. 'The Textual History of Murphy's *Gray's-Inn Journal*'. *Research Studies of the State College of Washington* 25 (1957), 33–48.

[Boydell, John], ed. *A Catalogue of the Pictures in the Shakespeare Gallery, Pall-Mall*. London: [J. Boydell], 1789.

[ ], ed. *A Collection of Prints, from Pictures Painted for the Purpose of Illustrating the Dramatic Works of Shakspeare, by the Artists of Great Britain*. 2 vols. London: J. and J. Boydell, 1803.

Bratton, J. S. *King Lear*. Plays in Performance. Bristol: Bristol Classical, 1987.

Bristol, Michael D. *Big-Time Shakespeare*. London: Routledge, 1996.

Bromwich, David. *Hazlitt: The Mind of a Critic*. New York: Oxford University Press, 1983.

Brown, Charles Armitage. *Letters*. Ed. Jack Stillinger. Cambridge, MA: Harvard University Press, 1966.
Bryant, Donald C. *Edmund Burke and His Literary Friends*. Washington University Studies (n. s.), Language and Literature. St Louis: Washington University, 1939.
Burke, Edmund. *Four Letters on the Proposals for Peace with the Regicide Directory of France*. Select Works. Ed. E. J. Payne. 2nd edn. 4 vols. Oxford: Clarendon Press, 1878. Vol. 3.
  Correspondence. Ed. Thomas W. Copeland et al. 10 vols. Cambridge: Cambridge University Press; Chicago: Chicago University Press, 1958–78.
  Writings and Speeches. Gen. ed. Paul Langford. 9 vols. (to date). Oxford: Clarendon Press, 1981–.
  Reflections on the Revolution in France. Ed. J. C. D. Clark. Stanford: Stanford University Press, 2001.
Burnim, Kalman A. 'The Significance of Garrick's Letters to Hayman'. *Shakespeare Quarterly* 9 (1958), 149–52.
  David Garrick, Director. Pittsburgh: University of Pittsburgh Press, 1961.
  and Philip H. Highfill, Jr, eds. *John Bell, Patron of British Theatrical Portraiture: A Catalog of the Theatrical Portraits in His Editions of Bell's Shakespeare and Bell's British Theatre*. Carbondale: Southern Illinois University Press, 1998.
Burwick, Frederick. *Illusion and the Drama: Critical Theory of the Enlightenment and Romantic Era*. University Park: Pennsylvania State University Press, 1991.
  'John Boydell's Shakespeare Gallery and the Stage'. *Shakespeare Jahrbuch* 133 (1997), 54–76.
Busse, John. *Mrs Montagu, Queen of the Blues*. London: Gerald Howe, 1928.
Butler, Marilyn, ed. *Burke, Paine, Godwin, and the Revolution Controversy*. Cambridge: Cambridge University Press, 1984.
Campbell, Oscar James, ed. *A Shakespeare Encyclopaedia*. London: Methuen, 1966.
Campbell, Thomas. *Life of Mrs. Siddons*. 2 vols. London: E. Wilson, 1834.
Carlisle, Carol J. 'The Nineteenth-Century Actors *versus* the Closet Critics of Shakespeare'. *Studies in Philology* 51 (1954), 599–615.
  'Hamlet's "Cruelty" in the Nunnery Scene: The Actors' Views'. *Shakespeare Quarterly* 18 (1967), 129–40.
Carlson, Julie Ann. *In the Theatre of Romanticism: Coleridge, Nationalism, Women*. Cambridge: Cambridge University Press, 1994.
Carter, Elizabeth. *Letters . . . to Mrs. Montagu, between the Years 1755 and 1800*. Ed. Montagu Pennington. 3 vols. London: F. C. and J. Rivington, 1817.
Censor, The. 1715–17.
Child, Harold. *The Shakespearean Productions of John Philip Kemble*. London: The Shakespeare Association, 1935.
Cibber, Colley. *Apology for the Life of Mr. Colley Cibber, Comedian*. London: For the author, 1740.
[   ]. *The Laureat; or, The Right Side of Colley Cibber, Esq*. London: J. Roberts, 1740.

Clark, Sandra, ed. *Shakespeare Made Fit: Restoration Adaptations of Shakespeare.* London: Dent, 1997.

Clarke, Norma. *Dr Johnson's Women.* London: Hambledon and London, 2000.

Climenson, Emily J., ed. *Elizabeth Montagu, the Queen of the Blue-Stockings: Her Correspondence from 1720 to 1761.* 2 vols. London: J. Murray, 1906.

Cole, Toby, and Helen Krich Chinoy, eds. *Actors on Acting: The Theories, Techniques, and Practices of the Great Actors of All Times as Told in Their Own Words.* 2nd edn. New York: Crown Publishers, 1970.

Coleridge, Samuel Taylor. *The Table Talk and Omniana.* Ed. Coventry Patmore. London: H. Milward, 1917.

Collected Letters. Ed. Earl Leslie Griggs. 6 vols. Oxford: Clarendon Press, 1956–71.

Notebooks. Ed. Kathleen Coburn et al. 5 double vols. (to date). New York: Routledge & Kegan Paul, 1957–.

Marginalia. Ed. H. J. Jackson and George Whalley. Bollingen Series. 6 vols. Princeton: Princeton University Press, 1980–2001.

Biographia Literaria. Ed. James Engell and W. Jackson Bate. Bollingen Series. 2 vols. Princeton: Princeton University Press, 1983.

Lectures 1808–1819: On Literature. Ed. R. A. Foakes. Bollingen Series. 2 vols. Princeton: Princeton University Press, 1987.

Aids to Reflection. Ed. John Beer. Bollingen Series. Princeton: Princeton University Press, 1993.

Poetical Works. Ed. J. C. C. Mays. Bollingen Series. 3 double vols. (1. Poems: reading text; 2. Poems: variorum text; 3. Plays). Princeton: Princeton University Press, 2001.

Colman, George, the Elder. *Man and Wife; or, The Shakespeare Jubilee.* London: T. Becket and R. Baldwin, 1770.

Conklin, Paul S. *A History of Hamlet Criticism, 1601–1821.* London: Routledge & Kegan Paul, 1947.

Cooke, William. *Memoirs of Charles Macklin, Comedian.* 2nd edn. London: J. Asperne, 1806.

Davies, Thomas. *Memoirs of the Life of David Garrick, Esq.* 2 vols. London: For the author, 1780.

Dramatic Mi[s]cellanies. 3 vols. London: For the author, 1784.

Dawson, Anthony B. *Hamlet.* Shakespeare in Performance. Manchester: Manchester University Press, 1995.

De Bolla, Peter. *The Discourse of the Sublime: Readings in History, Aesthetics and the Subject.* Oxford: B. Blackwell, 1989.

De Bruyn, Frans. 'Theater and Countertheater in Burke's *Reflections on the Revolution in France*'. In Blakemore, ed., *Burke and the French Revolution*, 28–68.

De Grazia, Margreta. *Shakespeare Verbatim: The Reproduction of Authenticity and the 1790 Apparatus.* Oxford: Clarendon Press, 1991.

Deelman, Christian. *The Great Shakespeare Jubilee.* London: Michael Joseph, 1964.

DeMaria, Robert, Jr. *The Life of Samuel Johnson: A Critical Biography.* Cambridge, MA: Basil Blackwell, 1993.

Dennis, John. *Critical Works*. Ed. Edward Niles Hooker. 2 vols. Baltimore: Johns Hopkins University Press, 1939–43.
Desmet, Christy, and Robert Sawyer, eds. *Shakespeare and Appropriation*. London: Routledge, 1999.
Dibdin, Charles. *The Professional Life of Mr. Dibdin, Written by Himself*. 4 vols. London: For the author, 1803.
Diderot, Denis. *The Paradox of Acting*. Trans. Walter Henis Pollock. In Strasberg, *The Paradix of Acting* and *Masks or Faces?*, 11–71.
Dircks, Phyllis T. 'David Garrick, George III, and the Politics of Revision'. *Philological Quarterly* 76 (1997), 289–312.
Dobson, Michael. *The Making of the National Poet: Shakespeare, Adaptation and Authorship, 1660–1769*. Oxford: Clarendon Press, 1992.
  gen. ed. *The Oxford Companion to Shakespeare*. Oxford: Oxford University Press, 2001.
Donohue, Joseph W., Jr. 'Hazlitt's Sense of the Dramatic Actor as Tragic Character'. *SEL* 5 (1965), 703–21.
  'Kemble's Production of *Macbeth* (1794): Some Notes on Scene Painters, Scenery, Special Effects, and Costumes'. *Theatre Notebook* 21 (1967), 63–74.
  'Kemble and Mrs. Siddons in *Macbeth*: The Romantic Approach to Tragic Character'. *Theatre Notebook* 22 (1968), 65–86.
  Dramatic Character in the English Romantic Age. Princeton: Princeton University Press, 1970.
  '*Macbeth* in the Eighteenth Century'. *Theatre Quarterly* 1.3 (1971), 20–24.
  Theatre in the Age of Kean. Oxford: Basil Blackwell, 1975.
Doran, J. *'Their Majesties' Servants'; or, Annals of the English Stage, from Thomas Betterton to Edmund Kean*. 3 vols. 2nd edn. London: W. Allen, 1865.
Doran, Madeleine. 'That Undiscovered Country: A Problem Concerning the Use of the Supernatural in *Hamlet* and *Macbeth*'. *Philological Quarterly* 20 (1941), 413–27.
Downer, Alan S. 'Nature to Advantage Dressed: Eighteenth-Century Acting'. *PMLA* 58 (1943), 1002–37.
Downes, Henry. *Roscius Anglicanus; or, An Historical Review of the Stage*. London: H. Playford, 1708.
Draper, John W. 'Aristotelian Mimesis in Eighteenth-Century England'. *PMLA* 36 (1921), 372–400.
Eagleton, Terry. *The Ideology of the Aesthetic*. Oxford: Basil Blackwell, 1990.
  Sweet Violence: The Idea of the Tragic. Malden, MA: Basil Blackwell, 2003.
Eger, Elizabeth, ed. *Elizabeth Montagu, Bluestocking Feminism: Writings of the Bluestocking Circle, 1738–1785*. London: Pickering and Chatto, 1999.
Elliot, Eugene Clinton. 'Reynolds and Hazlitt'. *Journal of Aesthetic and Art Criticism* 21 (1962), 73–9.
Ende, Stuart A. *Keats and the Sublime*. New Haven: Yale University Press, 1976.
England, Martha Winburn. *Garrick's Jubilee*. Columbus: Ohio State University Press, 1964.

Evans, Bertrand. 'Manfred's Remorse and Dramatic Tradition'. *PMLA* 62 (1947), 752–74.
Evans, G. Blakemore, ed. *Shakespearean Prompt-Books of the Seventeenth Century*. 8 vols. (to date). Charlottesville: Bibliographical Society of the University of Virginia, 1960–.
Ewert, Leonore Helen. 'Elizabeth Montagu to Elizabeth Carter: Literary Gossip and Critical Opinions from the Pens of the Queen of the Blues'. PhD. Claremont Graduate School, 1968.
Examen of the New Comedy, Call'd 'The Suspicious Husband', An. London: J. Roberts, 1747.
Examiner, The. 1808–51.
Fairer, David. 'Authorship Problems in *The Adventurer*'. *RES* 25 (1974), 137–51.
Farley-Hills, David, ed. *Critical Responses to Hamlet 1600–1900*. The Hamlet Collection. 4 vols. New York: AMS, 1997–2006.
Fielding, Henry. *The History of Tom Jones: A Foundling*. Ed. Fredson Bowers and Martin C. Battestin. Wesleyan Edition. 2 vols. Oxford: Clarendon Press, 1974.
Finlay, John. *Miscellanies*. Dublin: J. Cumming, 1835.
Finney, C. L. *The Evolution of Keats's Poetry*. 2 vols. Cambridge, MA: Harvard University Press, 1936.
Fitzgerald, Percy Hetherington. *The Life of David Garrick*. 2 vols. London: Tinsley, 1868.
Foakes, R. A., ed. *Hamlet versus Lear: Cultural Politics and Shakespeare's Art*. Cambridge: Cambridge University Press, 1993.
Foot, Jesse. *The Life of Arthur Murphy, Esq*. London: J. Faulder, 1811.
[Foote, Samuel]. *A Treatise on the Passions*. London: C. Corbet, 1747.
  The Roman and English Comedy Consider'd and Compar'd. London: T. Waller, 1747.
  The Devil Upon Two Sticks. London: T. Cadell, 1778.
Franklin, Colin. *Shakespeare Domesticated: The Eighteenth-Century Editions*. Aldershot: Scolar, 1991.
Friedman, Winifred H. *Boydell's Shakespeare Gallery*. New York: Garland Publishing, 1976.
Furniss, Tom. 'Stripping the Queen: Edmund Burke's Magic Lantern Show'. In Blakemore, ed. *Burke and the French Revolution*, 69–96.
  Edmund Burke's Aesthetic Ideology: Language, Gender, and Political Economy in Revolution. Cambridge: Cambridge University Press, 1993.
Fuseli, Henry. *Life and Writings*. Ed. J. Knowles. 3 vols. London: Colburn and Bentley, 1831
[Garrick, David]. *An Essay on Acting*. London: W. Bickerton, 1744.
[   ]. *The Sick Monkey: A Fable*. London: J. Fletcher, 1765.
  Garrick Attack on Shakespeare. (Folger Shakespeare Library, W. b 460) New York: Folger Shakespeare Library, 1769.
  ('D. G.'). *An Ode upon Dedicating a Building and Erecting a Statue to Shakespeare, at Stratford upon Avon*. London: T. Becket and P. A. de Hondt, 1769.

    Poetical Works. Ed. George Kearsley. 2 vols. London: G. Kearsley, 1785.
    Dramatic Works. 3 vols. London: A. Millar, 1798.
    Diary. Ed. Ryllis Clair Alexander. New York: Oxford University Press, 1928.
    Journal . . . Describing His Visit to France and Italy in 1763. Ed. George Winchester Stone, Jr. New York: Modern Language Association of America, 1939.
    Letters. Ed. David M. Little and George M. Kahrl. 3 vols. London: Oxford University Press, 1963.
    Plays. Ed. Harry William Pedicord and Frederick Louis Bergmann. 7 vols. Carbondale: Southern Illinois University Press, 1980–2.
    et al. *Shakespear's Garland*. Dublin: J. Mitchell, 1769.
[Genest, John]. *Some Account of the English Stage, from the Restoration in 1660 to 1830*. 10 vols. Bath: H. E. Carrington, 1832.
[Gentleman, Francis]. *The Stratford Jubilee: A New Comedy of Two Acts*. London: T. Lowndes and J. Bell, 1769.
[   ]. *The Dramatic Censor*. 2 vols. London: J. Bell and others, 1770.
Gibson-Wood, Carol. *Jonathan Richardson: Art Theorist of the English Enlightenment*. New Haven: Yale University Press for the Paul Mellon Centre for Studies in British Art, 2000.
Gill, Stephen. *William Wordsworth: A Life*. Oxford: Clarendon Press, 1989.
Glick, Claris. 'Hamlet in the English Theater: Acting Texts from Betterton (1676) to Olivier (1963)', *Shakespeare Quarterly* 20 (1969), 17–35.
Gombrich, Ernst. 'Reynolds's Theory and Practice of Imitation'. *Norm and Form: Studies in the Art of the Renaissance*. London: Phaidon, 1966, 129–34.
Gondris, Joanna, ed. *Reading Readings: Essays on Shakespeare Editing in the Eighteenth Century*. Madison: Fairleigh Dickinson University Press, 1998.
Gray, Charles Harold. *Theatrical Criticism in London to 1795*. 1931. New York: B. Blom, 1964.
Gray, Tim, and Paul Hindson. 'Edmund Burke and the French Revolution as Drama'. *History of European Ideas* 14 (1992), 203–11.
Gray's-Inn Journal, The. 1753–54. (See also Arthur Murphy.)
Halstead, William Perdue, ed. *Shakespeare as Spoken: A Collection of 5000 Acting Editions and Promptbooks of Shakespeare*. Monograph Publishing on Demand, Sponsor Series. 12 vols. Ann Arbor: UMI for the American Theatre Association, 1977–8.
Hammelmann, Hanns. *Book Illustrators in Eighteenth-Century England*. Studies in British Art. Ed. T. S. R. Boase. New Haven: Yale University Press for the Paul Mellon Centre for Studies in British Art, 1975.
Hammond, Antony. '"Rather a Heap of Rubbish Than a Structure": The Principles of Restoration Dramatic Adaptation Revisited'. *The Stage in the 18th Century*. Ed. J. D. Browning. New York: Garland Publishing, 1981, 133–48.
Hapgood, Robert, ed. *Hamlet, Prince of Denmark*. Shakespeare in Production. Cambridge: Cambridge University Press, 1999.
Harris, Arthur John. 'Garrick, Colman, and *King Lear*: A Reconsideration'. *Shakespeare Quarterly* 22 (1971), 57–66.

Hassall, Anthony J. 'Fielding and Garrick's *Hamlet*'. *Studies in the Eighteenth Century*. Ed. R. F. Brissenden and J. C. Eade. Canberra: Australian National University, 1979, 147–65.
Hawkesworth, John, et al., eds. *The Adventurer*. 2 vols. London: J. Payne, 1753–4.
Hawkins, Frederick W. *The Life of Edmund Kean*. 2 vols. London: Tinsley, 1869.
Hayden, John O. *The Romantic Reviewers, 1802–1824*. London: Routledge & Kegan Paul, 1969.
Hazlitt, William. *Complete Works*. Ed. P. P. Howe. 21 vols. London: J. M. Dent, 1930–34.
  Letters. Ed. Herschell Moreland Sikes et al. London: Macmillan, 1978.
Hazlitt, W. Carey. *Memoirs of William Hazlitt, with Portions of His Correspondence*. 2 vols. London: R. Bentley, 1867.
Hedgcock, Frank A. *A Cosmopolitan Actor: David Garrick and His French Friends*. London: S. Paul, [1912].
Heller, Janet Ruth. *Coleridge, Lamb, Hazlitt and the Reader of Drama*. Columbia, MO: University of Missouri Press, 1990.
Herrick, Marvin T. *The Poetics of Aristotle in England*. New Haven: Yale University Press, 1930.
Highfill, Philip H., Jr, Kalman A. Burnim and Edward A. Langhans. *A Biographical Dictionary of Actors, Actresses, Musicians, Dancers, Managers, and Other Stage Personnel in London, 1660–1800*. 16 vols. Carbondale: Southern Illinois University Press, 1973–93.
[Hill, Aaron], ed. *The Prompter*. London: J. Peele, 1734–6.
  The Art of Acting. London: J. Osborn, 1746.
Hill, George Birkbeck, ed. *Johnsonian Miscellanies*. 2 vols. Oxford: Clarendon Press, 1897.
[Hill, John]. *The Actor: A Treatise on the Art of Playing*. [An adaptation of Pierre Remond de Sainte-Albine's *Le comédien*] London: R. Griffiths, 1750.
Hillebrand, H. N. *Edmund Kean*. New York: Columbia University Press, 1933.
Hilles, Frederick Whiley. *The Literary Career of Sir Joshua Reynolds*. Cambridge: Cambridge University Press, 1936.
Hindson, Paul, and Tim Gray. *Burke's Dramatic Theory of Politics*. Avebury Series in Philosophy. Aldershot: Avebury, 1988.
Hipple, Walter John, Jr. 'General and Particular in the *Discourses* of Sir Joshua Reynolds: A Study in Method'. *Journal of Aesthetic and Art Criticism* 11 (1953), 231–47.
  The Beautiful, the Sublime, and the Picturesque in Eighteenth-Century British Aesthetic Theory. Carbondale: Southern Illinois University Press, 1957.
Hoagwood, Terence Allan, and Daniel P. Watkins, eds. *British Romantic Drama: Historical and Critical Essays*. Madison: Fairleigh Dickinson University Press, 1998.
Hogan, Charles Beecher. *Shakespeare in the Theatre, 1701–1800: A Record of Performances in London*. Oxford: Clarendon Press, 1952–7.
Holland, Peter, ed. '*Macbeth* and Its Afterlife'. *Shakespeare Survey* (Special Issue) 57 (2004), 1–195.

Holmes, Richard. *Coleridge: Early Visions*. London: Hodder & Stoughton, 1989.
  Coleridge: Darker Reflections. London: HarperCollins, 1998.
Home, Henry, Lord Kames. *Elements of Criticism*. 2nd edn. 3 vols. Edinburgh: A. Millar and others, 1763.
Howard, Jean E., and Marion F. O'Connor, eds. *Shakespeare Reproduced: The Text in History and Ideology*. New York: Methuen, 1987.
Howe, P. P. *The Life of William Hazlitt*. 3rd edn. London: H. Hamilton, 1947.
Huchon, R. *Mrs Montagu, 1720–1800: An Essay*. London: J. Murray, 1907.
Hughes, Leo. *The Drama's Patrons: A Study of the Eighteenth-Century London Audience*. Austin: University of Texas Press, 1971.
Hume, R. D., ed. *The London Theatre World, 1660–1800*. Carbondale: Southern Illinois University Press, 1980.
Hunt, Leigh. *Dramatic Essays*. Ed. William Archer and Robert W. Lowe. London: W. Scott, 1894.
  Dramatic Criticism, 1808–1831. Ed. Lawrene Huston Houtchens and Carolyn Washburn Houtchens. London: G. Cumberlege, 1950.
Idler, The. 1758–60. (See also Johnson.)
Ingleby, C. M., et al., eds. *The Shakspere Allusion-Book: A Collection of Allusions to Shakspere from 1591 to 1700*. The Shakespeare Library. 2 vols. London: Chatto & Windus, 1909.
Jack, Ian. *Keats and the Mirror of Art*. 2nd edn. London: Oxford University Press, 1968.
Jackson, J. R. de J., ed. *Coleridge: The Critical Heritage*. The Critical Heritage Series. 2 vols. London: Routledge & Kegan Paul, 1970–91.
Jacobus, Mary. '"That Great Stage Where Senators Perform": *Macbeth* and the Politics of Romantic Theatre'. *Studies in Romanticism* 22 (1983), 353–87.
Jameson, Anna Brownell. *Characteristics of Women, Moral, Poetical, and Historical*. 2nd edn. 2 vols. London: Sounders and Otley, 1833.
Jenkin, H. C. Fleeming, ed. *Mrs. Siddons as Lady Macbeth and as Queen Katharine*. Papers on Acting, 2nd series. New York: Columbia University Dramatic Museum, 1915.
Jenkins, Patricia Mavis. *Coleridge's Literary Theory: The Chronology of Its Development, 1790–1818*. Fairfield: Department of English, Fairfield University, 1984.
Jewett, William. *Fatal Autonomy: Romantic Drama and the Rhetoric of Agency*. Ithaca: Cornell University Press, 1997.
Johnson, Jeffrey Lawson Laurence. 'Sweeping up Shakespeare's "Rubbish": Garrick's Condensation of Acts IV and V of *Hamlet*'. *Eighteenth-Century Life* 8.3 (1983), 14–25.
Johnson, Samuel, ed. *A Dictionary of the English Language*. 4th edn. 2 vols. London: W. Strahan and others, 1773.
  The Idler and the Adventurer. Ed. John M. Bullitt, W. J. Bate and L. F. Powell. The Yale Edition. 2 vols. New Haven: Yale University Press, 1963.
  Johnson on Shakespeare. Ed. A. Sherbo. The Yale Edition. 2 vols. New Haven: Yale University Press, 1968.

Poems. Ed. E. L. McAdam, Jr. The Yale Edition. New Haven: Yale University Press, 1965.
The Rambler. Ed. W. J. Bate and Albrecht B. Strauss. The Yale Edition. 3 vols. New Haven: Yale University Press, 1969.
Letters. Ed. Bruce Redford. The Hyde Edition. 5 vols. Princeton: Princeton University Press, 1992–4.
Jones, Leonidas M. 'Keats's Theatrical Reviews in the *Champion*'. *Keats-Shelley Journal* 3 (1954), 55–65.
Jones, Stanley. *Hazlitt: A Life from Winterslow to Frith Street*. Oxford: Clarendon Press, 1989.
Joseph, Bertram. *The Tragic Actor*. London: Routledge & Kegan Paul, 1959.
Kahrl, George M., and Dorothy Anderson, eds. *The Garrick Collection of Old English Plays: A Catalogue with an Historical Introduction*. London: British Library Reference Division, 1982.
Kandl, John. 'Plebian Gusto, Negative Capability, and the Low Company of "Mr. Kean": Keats' Dramatic Review for the *Champion*'. *Nineteenth-Century Prose* 28 (2001), 130–41.
Keats, John. *Poetical Works and Other Writings*. Ed. Harry Buxton Forman. Rev. Maurice Buxton Forman. Hamstead Edition. 8 vols. New York: C. Scribner, 1938–39.
Letters, *1814–1821*. Ed. Hyder Edward Rollins. 2 vols. Cambridge, MA: Harvard University Press, 1958.
Poems. Ed. Miriam Allott. London: Longman, 1970.
Poems. Ed. Jack Stillinger. London: Heinemann Educational, 1978.
Complete Poems. Ed. John Barnard. 3rd edn. Harmondsworth: Penguin, 1988.
Kelly, Linda. *The Kemble Era: John Philip Kemble, Sarah Siddons, and the London Stage*. London: Bodley Head, 1980.
Kemble, John Philip ('J. P. K.'). *Macbeth Reconsidered*. London: T. and J. Egerton, 1786.
Macbeth, and King Richard the Third. London: J. Murray, 1817.
Kinnaird, John. 'Hazlitt and the "Design" of Shakespearean Tragedy: A "Character" Critic Reconsidered'. *Shakespeare Quarterly* 28 (1977), 22–39.
William Hazlitt, Critic of Power. New York: Columbia University Press, 1978.
Kliman, Bernice W. *Macbeth*. Shakespeare in Performance. Manchester: Manchester University Press, 1992.
Klingel, Joan E. 'Backstage with Dr. Johnson: "Punch Has No Feelings"'. *Studies in Philology* 77 (1980), 300–18.
Knight, Joseph. *David Garrick*. London: K. Paul, Trench and Trubner, 1894.
Le Brun, Charles. *The Conference ... upon Expression, General and Particular*. Trans. J. Smith. London: J. Smith, E. Cooper and D. Mortier, 1701.
Lee, John. *Shakespeare's* Hamlet *and the Controversies of Self*. Oxford: Clarendon Press, 2000.
Leggatt, Alexander. *King Lear*. Shakespeare in Performance. Manchester: Manchester University Press, 1991.
Lewes, George Henry. *Actors and the Art of Acting*. New York: Grove Press, 1957.

Lichtenberg, Georg Christoph. *Lichtenberg's Visits to England, as Described in His Letters and Diaries*. Trans. Margaret L. Mare and W. H. Quarrell. Oxford: Clarendon Press, 1938.
Liu, Alan. *Wordsworth: The Sense of History*. Stanford: Stanford University Press, 1989.
[Lloyd, Robert]. *The Actor: A Poetical Epistle to Bonnell Thornton, Esq.* London: R. and J. Dodsley, 1760.
Lock, F. P. *Edmund Burke*. 2 vols. Oxford: Clarendon Press, 1998–2006.
London Magazine; or, Gentleman's Monthly Intelligencer, The. 1732–85.
[Longinus, Dionysius]. *On the Sublime*. Trans. William Smith. London: W. Innys and R. Manby, 1739.
  On the Sublime. In Aristotle, *Poetics*; Longinus, *On the Sublime*; Demetrius, *On Style*, 143–307.
Lounsbury, Thomas Raynesford. *Shakespeare and Voltaire*. Shakespearean Wars. London: D. Nutt, 1902.
Lowes, John Livingston. *The Road to Xanadu: A Study in the Ways of the Imagination*. 2nd edn. London: Pan Books, 1978.
Lynch, James J. *Box, Pit, and Gallery: Stage and Society in Johnson's London*. Berkeley: University of California Press, 1953.
McFarland, Thomas. 'The Willing Suspension of Disbelief'. *Shapes of Culture*. Iowa City: University of Iowa Press, 1987, 114–45.
  The Masks of Keats: The Endeavour of a Poet. Oxford: Oxford University Press, 2000.
McIntyre, Ian. *Garrick*. London: Penguin, 1999.
MacMillan, Dougald, ed. *Drury Lane Calendar, 1747–1776*. Oxford: Clarendon Press, 1938.
McPherson, Heather. 'Picturing Tragedy: *Mrs. Siddons as the Tragic Muse* Revisited'. *Eighteenth-Century Studies* 33 (2000), 401–30.
Magnuson, Paul. *Coleridge and Wordsworth: A Lyrical Dialogue*. Princeton: Princeton University Press, 1988.
Maguire, Nancy. 'Nahum Tate's *King Lear*: "The King's Blest Restoration"', in Marsden, ed., *The Appropriation of Shakespeare*, 29–42.
Mahoney, John L. *The Logic of Passion: The Literary Criticism of William Hazlitt*. Salzburg: Salzburg University, 1978.
  'Reynolds's *Discourses on Art*: The Delicate Balance of Neoclassic Aesthetics'. *British Journal of Aesthetics* 18 (1978), 126–36.
Mannings, David, ed. *Sir Joshua Reynolds: A Complete Catalogue of His Paintings*. 2 vols. New Haven: Yale University Press for the Paul Mellon Centre for Studies in British Art, 2000.
Manvell, Roger. *Sarah Siddons: Portrait of an Actress*. London: Heinemann, 1970.
Marsden, Jean I., ed. *The Appropriation of Shakespeare: Post-Renaissance Reconstructions of the Works and the Myth*. Hemel Hempstead: Harvester Wheatsheaf, 1991.
  The Re-Imagined Text: Shakespeare, Adaptation, and Eighteenth-Century Literary Theory. Lexington: University Press of Kentucky, 1995.

Massai, Sonia. 'Tate's Critical "Editing" of His Source-Text(s) for *The History of King Lear*'. *Analytical and Enumerative Bibliography* 9.4 (1995), 168–96.
Merchant, William Moelwyn. *Shakespeare and the Artist*. London: Oxford University Press, 1959.
Mills, John A. *Hamlet on Stage: The Great Tradition*. Westport, CT: Greenwood Press, 1985.
Molloy, J. Fizgerald. *The Life and Adventures of Edmund Kean*. 2 vols. London: Ward and Downey, 1888.
  Sir Joshua and His Circle. 2 vols. London: Hutchinson, 1906.
Monk, Samuel H. *The Sublime: A Study of Critical Theories in XVIII-Century England*. Modern Language Association of America, General Series. New York: Modern Language Association of America, 1935.
[Montagu, Elizabeth]. *An Essay on the Writings and Genius of Shakespear*. London: J. Dodsley and others, 1769.
  Letters. Ed. Matthew Montagu. 4 vols. London: T. Cadell and W. Davies, 1809–13.
Montagu, Jennifer. *The Expression of the Passions: The Origin and Influence of Charles Le Brun's 'Conférence sur l'expression générale et particulière'*. New Haven: Yale University Press, 1994.
Moore, John David. 'Coleridge and the "Modern Jacobinical Drama": *Osorio*, *Remorse*, and the Development of Coleridge's Critique of the Stage, 1797–1816'. *Bulletin of Research in the Humanities* 85 (1982), 443–64.
Morrill, Dorothy I. 'Coleridge's Theory of Dramatic Illusion'. *MLN* 42 (1927), 436–44.
Motion, Andrew. *Keats*. London: Faber and Faber, 1997.
Mowat, Barbara. 'The Form of *Hamlet*'s Fortunes'. *Renaissance Drama* 19 (1988), 97–126.
Mulrooney, Jonathan. 'Keats in the Company of Kean'. *Studies in Romanticism* 42 (2003), 227–50.
[Murphy, Arthur] ('Charles Ranger'), ed. *The Gray's Inn Journal*. London: Faden and Bouquet, 1753–4.
[   ] ('Charles Ranger'), ed. *The Gray's Inn Journal*. 2nd edn. 2 vols. London: P. Vaillant, 1756.
  An Essay on the Life and Genius of Samuel Johnson. London: T. Longman and others, 1792.
  The Life of David Garrick, Esq. 2 vols. London: J. Wright, 1801.
Murry, John Middleton. *Keats and Shakespeare: A Study of Keats' Poetic Life from 1816 to 1820*. London: Oxford University Press, 1925.
Musgrave, William R. '"That Monstrous Fiction": Radical Agency and Aesthetic Ideology in Burke'. *Studies in Romanticism* 36 (1997), 3–26.
Myers, Victoria. 'Justice and Indeterminacy: Wordsworth's *The Borderers* and the Trials of the 1790s'. *Studies in Romanticism* 40 (2001), 427–57.
Nicoll, Allardyce. *The Garrick Stage: Theatres and Audience in the Eighteenth Century*. Ed. Sybil Rosenfeld. Manchester: Manchester University Press, 1980.

Nicolson, Marjorie Hope. *Newton Demands the Muse: Newton's Opticks and the Eighteenth-Century Poets*. Princeton: Princeton University Press, 1946.
Northcote, James. *The Life of Sir Joshua Reynolds*. 2nd edn. 2 vols. London: H. Colburn, 1819.
Odell, George C. D. *Shakespeare from Betterton to Irving*. 2 vols. London: Constable, 1920–1.
Orgel, Stephen. 'The Authentic Shakespeare'. *Representations* 21 (1988), 1–25.
Oulton, W. C. *The History of the Theatres in London*. 2 vols. London: Martin and Bain, 1796.
Oxberry, Catherine Elizabeth, and William Oxberry, eds. *Oxberry's Dramatic Biography and Histrionic Anecdotes*. 5 vols. London: G. Virtue, 1825–26.
Oya, Reiko. 'A Dream of Passion: Representation and Reception of Shakespearean Tragedy in the Age of Garrick to Kean'. PhD. University of London, 2003.
Owen, Felicity, and David Blayney Brown. *Collector of Genius: A Life of Sir George Beaumont*. New Haven: Yale University Press for the Paul Mellon Centre for Studies in British Art, 1988.
Paine, Thomas. *The Rights of Man*. Ed. Henry Collins. Harmondsworth: Penguin, 1969.
Pape, Walter, and Frederick Burwick, eds. *The Boydell Shakespeare Gallery* (Exhibition Catalogue). Bottrop: P. Pomp, 1996.
Park, Roy. *Hazlitt and the Spirit of the Age: Abstraction and Critical Theory*. Oxford: Clarendon Press, 1971.
Parker, G. F. *Johnson's Shakespeare*. Oxford: Clarendon Press, 1989.
Parker, Reeve. 'Reading Wordsworth's Power: Narrative and Usurpation in *The Borderers*'. *ELH* 54 (1987), 299–331.
'"In Some Sort Seeing with My Proper Eyes": Wordsworth and the Spectacles of Paris'. *Studies in Romanticism* 2 (1988), 369–90.
'Osorio's Dark Employments: Tricking Out Coleridgean Tragedy'. *Studies in Romanticism* 33 (1994), 119–60.
Parrish, Stephen Maxfield. *The Art of the Lyrical Ballads*. Cambridge, MA: Harvard University Press, 1973.
Parsons, Clement. *Garrick and His Circle*. 2nd edn. London: Methuen, 1906.
Paulson, Ronald. *Book and Painting: Shakespeare, Milton, and the Bible: Literary Texts and the Emergence of English Painting*. Knoxville: University of Tennessee Press, 1982.
Penny, Nicholas, ed. *Reynolds* (Exhibition Catalogue). London: Royal Academy of Arts, 1986.
Phippen, Francis. *Authentic Memoirs of Edmund Kean*. London: R. Roach, 1814.
[Pickering, Roger]. *Reflections upon Theatrical Expression in Tragedy*. London: W. Johnston, 1755.
Piozzi, Hester Lynch (Thrale). *Dr Johnson by Mrs Thrale: The 'Anecdotes' of Mrs Piozzi in Their Original Form*. Ed. Richard Ingram. London: Chatto & Windus, 1984.
Pittard, Joseph. *Observations on Mr. Garrick's Acting*. London: J. Cooke and J. Coote, 1758.

Pittock, Joan. *The Ascendancy of Taste: The Achievement of Joseph and Thomas Warton*.London: Routledge & Kegan Paul, 1973.
Playfair, Giles. *The Flash of Lightning: A Portrait of Edmund Kean*. London: Kimber, 1983.
Postle, Martin. *Sir Joshua Reynolds: The Subject Pictures*. Cambridge: Cambridge University Press, 1995.
Powell, Nicolas. *Fuseli:* The Nightmare. London: Allen Lane, 1973.
[Procter, B. W.]. *Life of Edmund Kean*. 2 vols. London: E. Moxon, 1835.
Prompter, The. 1734–36. (See also Aaron Hill.)
Public Advertiser, The. 1752–94.
Purinton, Marjean D. *Romantic Ideology Unmasked: The Mentally Constructed Tyrannies in Dramas of William Wordsworth, Lord Byron, Percy Shelly, and Joanna Baillie*. Newark: University of Delaware Press, 1994.
Quarterly Review, The. 1809–
Raddadi, Mongi. *Davenant's Adaptations of Shakespeare*. Acta Universitatis Upsaliensis. Stockholm: Almqvist & Wiksell, 1979.
Rambler, The. 1750–52. (See also Johnson.)
Raysor, Thomas Middleton. 'The Study of Shakespeare's Characters in the Eighteenth Century'. *MLN* 42 (1927), 495–500.
Reid, J. H. C. 'An Edition of Letters of Joseph Warton (1722–1800)'. PhD. University of London, 1988.
[Repton, Henry]. *The Bee; or, A Companion to the Shakespeare Gallery*. London: T. Cadell, [1789].
Reynolds, Joshua. *Works*. Ed. Edmund Malone. 2 vols. London: T. Cadell, Jr. and W. Davies, 1797.
  Discourses on Art. Ed. Robert R. Wark. 3rd edn. New Haven: Yale University Press for the Paul Mellon Centre for Studies in British Art, 1997.
Richardson, Alan. *A Mental Theater: Poetic Drama and Consciousness in the Romantic Age*. University Park: Pennsylvania State University Press, 1988.
Richardson, Jonathan. *Two Discourses*. 2 vols. in 1. London: W. Churchill, 1719.
Richardson, William. *A Philosophical Analysis and Illustration of Some of Shakespeare's Remarkable Characters*. 2nd edn. London: J. Murray, 1774.
Roach, Joseph R. *The Player's Passion: Studies in the Science of Acting*. Newark: University of Delaware Press, 1985.
Robinson, Henry Crabb. *The London Theatre 1811–1866: Selections from the Diary of Henry Crabb Robinson*. Ed. Eluned Brown. London: Society for Theatre Research, 1966.
Robson, William. *The Old Play-Goer*. London: J. Masters, 1846.
Roe, Albert S. 'The Demon behind the Pillow: A Note on Erasmus Darwin and Reynolds'. *Burlington Magazine* 113 (1971), 460–70.
Roe, Nicholas. *Wordsworth and Coleridge: The Radical Years*. Oxford English Monographs. Oxford: Clarendon Press, 1988.
  John Keats and the Culture of Dissent. Oxford: Clarendon Press, 1997.
Rollins, Hyder Edward, ed. *The Keats Circle: Letters and Papers ... of the Keats Circle*. 2nd edn. Cambridge, MA: Harvard University Press, 1965.

Rosenberg, Marvin. *The Masks of King Lear.* Berkeley: University of California Press, 1972.
The Masks of Macbeth. Berkeley: University of California Press, 1978.
'Macbeth and Lady Macbeth in the Eighteenth and Nineteenth Centuries'. *Focus on Macbeth.* Ed. John Russell Brown. London: Routledge & Kegan Paul, 1982, 73–86.
The Masks of Hamlet. Newark: University of Delaware Press, 1992.
Ross, Ian. 'A Bluestocking over the Border: Mrs. Elizabeth Montagu's Aesthetic Adventures in Scotland, 1766'. *Huntington Library Quarterly* 28 (1965), 213–33.
Rulfs, Donald J. 'The Romantic Writers and Edmund Kean'. *Modern Language Quarterly* 11 (1950), 425–37.
Rzepka, Charles J. '*Theatrum Mundi* and Keats' *Otho the Great*: The Self in "Society"'. *Romanticism Past and Present* 8 (1984), 35–50.
Schiff, Gert, ed. *Johann Heinrich Füssli, 1741–1825.* Oeuvrekataloge Schweizer Kunstler. 2 vols. Zurich: Berichthaus, 1973.
Schiller, Friedrich von. *The Ghost-Seer.* Ed. Jeffrey L. Sammons. Trans. Henry G. Bohn. Columbia: Camden, 1992.
Five Plays. Trans. Robert David MacDonald. London: Oberon, 1998.
Schneider, Elizabeth. *The Aesthetics of William Hazlitt: A Study of the Philosophical Basis of His Criticism.* Philadelphia: University of Pennsylvania Press, 1933.
Schoenbaum, Samuel. 'Dyce's Recollections of Wordsworth, Mrs. Siddons, and Other Notable Persons'. *Times Literary Supplement,* 22 January 1971, 101–2.
Shakespeare's Lives. 2nd edn. Oxford: Clarendon Press, 1991.
Shaffer, Elinor S. 'Coleridge's Theory of Aesthetic Interest'. *Journal of Aesthetics and Art Criticism* 27 (1969), 399–408.
Shakespeare Illustrated by an Assemblage of Portraits and Views. 2 vols. London: S. and E. Harding, 1793.
Shapiro, James. 'Shakspur and the Jewbill'. *Shakespeare Survey* 48 (1995), 51–60.
Shattuck, Charles H. *The Shakespeare Promptbooks: A Descriptive Catalogue.* Urbana: University of Illinois Press, 1965.
Sheldon, Esther Keck. *Thomas Sheridan of Smock-Alley, Recording His Life as Actor and Theatre Manager in Both Dublin and London; and Including a Smock-Alley Calendar for the Years of His Management.* Princeton: Princeton University Press, 1967.
Sherbo, Arthur. *Samuel Johnson, Editor of Shakespeare, with an Essay on* The Adventurer. Urbana: University of Illinois Press, 1956.
The Birth of Shakespeare Studies: Commentators from Rowe (1709) to Boswell-Malone (1821). East Lansing: Colleagues, 1986.
Siddons, Henry. *Practical Illustrations of Rhetorical Gesture and Action.* London: R. Phillips, 1807.
Siddons, Sarah. *The Reminiscences of Sarah Kemble Siddons, 1773–1785.* Ed. William Van Lennep. Cambridge: Widener Library, 1942.
Sillars, Stuart. *Painting Shakespeare: The Artist as Critic, 1720–1820.* Cambridge: Cambridge University Press, 2006.

Slote, Bernice. *Keats and the Dramatic Principle*. Lincoln: University of Nebraska Press, 1958.
Smart, Alastair. 'Dramatic Gesture and Expression in the Age of Hogarth and Reynolds'. *Apollo* 82 (1965), 90–7.
Smith, D. N., ed. *Eighteenth-Century Essays on Shakespeare*. 2nd edn. Oxford: Clarendon Press, 1963.
Spectator, The. 1711–14. (See also Bond.)
Spector, Robert Donald. *Arthur Murphy*. Boston: Twayne, 1979.
Spencer, Hazelton. *Shakespeare Improved: The Restoration Versions in Quarto and on the Stage*. Cambridge, MA: Harvard University Press, 1927.
'Seventeenth-Century Cuts in Hamlet's Soliloquies'. *RES* 9 (1933), 257–65.
Sprague, Arthur Colby. *Shakespeare and the Actors: Stage Business in His Plays (1660–1905)*. Cambridge, MA: Harvard University Press, 1944.
Shakespearian Players and Performances. London: A. & C. Black, 1954.
Spurgeon, Caroline Frances Eleanor. *Keats's Shakespeare: A Descriptive Study Based on New Material*. 2nd edn. London: Oxford University Press, 1929.
Stein, Elizabeth P. *David Garrick, Dramatist*. New York: Modern Language Association of America, 1938.
Steiner, George. *The Death of Tragedy*. London: Faber and Faber, 1961.
Stevenson, John Allen. 'Fielding's Mousetrap: Hamlet, Partridge, and the '45'. *SEL* 37 (1997), 553–71.
Stochholm, Johanne M. *Garrick's Folly: The Shakespeare Jubilee of 1769 at Stratford and Drury Lane*. London: Methuen, 1964.
Stone, George Winchester, Jr. 'Garrick's Long Lost Alteration of *Hamlet*'. *PMLA* 49 (1934), 890–921.
'Garrick's Handling of *Macbeth*'. *Studies in Philology* 38 (1941), 609–28.
'Garrick's Production of *King Lear*: A Study in the Temper of the Eighteenth-Century Mind'. *Studies in Philology* 45.1 (1948), 89–104.
'The God of His Idolatry: Garrick's Theory of Acting and Dramatic Composition with Especial Reference to Shakespeare'. *Joseph Quincy Adams Memorial Studies*. Ed. James G. McManaway et al. Washington: Folger Shakespeare Library, 1948, 115–28.
'David Garrick's Significance in the History of Shakespearean Criticism: A Study of the Impact of the Actor upon the Change of Critical Focus during the Eighteenth Century'. *PMLA* 65 (1950), 183–97.
'Shakespeare in the Periodicals, 1700–1740: A Study of the Growth of a Knowledge of the Dramatist in the Eighteenth Century'. *Shakespeare Quarterly* 2 (1951), 221–31; 3 (1952), 313–28.
and George M. Kahrl. *David Garrick: A Critical Biography*. Carbondale: Southern Illinois University Press, 1979.
Strasberg, Lee, ed. Denis Diderot, *The Paradox of Acting*. Trans. Walter Herries Pollock; William Archer. *Masks or Faces?* New York: Hill and Wang, 1957.
Stratman, Carl J. *Britain's Theatrical Periodicals, 1720–1967: A Bibliography*. New York: New York Public Library, 1972.
Tatler, The. 1709–11. (See also Bond.)

Taylor, Gary. *Reinventing Shakespeare: A Cultural History from the Restoration to the Present*. London: Hogarth, 1989.
Taylor, George. '"The Just Delineation of the Passions": Theories of Acting in the Age of Garrick'. *Essays on the Eighteenth-Century English Stage*. Ed. Kenneth Richards and Peter Thomson. London: Methuen, 1972, 51–72.
Thompson, Ann, and Sasha Roberts, eds. *Women Reading Shakespeare, 1660–1900: An Anthology of Criticism*. Manchester: Manchester University Press, 1997.
Tomarken, Edward. *Samuel Johnson on Shakespeare: The Discipline of Criticism*. Athens: University of Georgia Press, 1991.
Town and Country Magazine, The. 1769–91.
Trawick III, Leonard M. 'Hazlitt, Reynolds, and the Ideal'. *Studies in Romanticism* 4 (1965), 240–7.
Tuveson, Earnest Lee. *The Imagination as a Means of Grace: Locke and the Aesthetics of Romanticism*. Berkeley: University of California Press, 1960.
Tytler, Alex[ander] Fraser. *Memoirs of the Life and Writings of the Honourable Henry Home of Kames*. 2 vols. Edinburgh: W. Creech and others, 1807.
Vance, John A. *Joseph and Thomas Warton: An Annotated Biography*. Twayne's English Authors. Boston: Twayne, 1983.
Vickers, Brian, ed. *Shakespeare: The Critical Heritage*. 6 vols. London: Routledge, 1974.
  'The Emergence of Character Criticism, 1774–1800'. *Shakespeare Survey* 34 (1981), 11–21.
  Returning to Shakespeare. London: Routledge, 1989.
Victor, Benjamin. *The History of the Theatres of London and Dublin from the Year 1730 to the Present Time*. 3 vols. London: T. Davies and others, 1761–71.
Walsh, Marcus. 'Eighteenth-Century Editing, "Appropriation", and Interpretation'. *Shakespeare Survey* 51 (1998), 125–39.
Walton, Kendall L. *Mimesis as Make-Believe: On the Foundations of the Representational Arts*. Cambridge, MA: Harvard University Press, 1990.
Ward, Aileen. '"Sr Joshua and His Gang": William Blake and the Royal Academy'. *Huntington Library Quarterly* 52 (1989), 75–95.
Wasserman, Earl R. 'The Sympathetic Imagination in Eighteenth-Century Theories of Acting'. *Journal of English and Germanic Philology* 46 (1947), 264–72.
Waterhouse, Ellis. *Reynolds*. London: Phaidon, 1973.
Watkins, Daniel P. '"In That New World": The Deep Historical Structure of Coleridge's *Osorio*'. *Philological Quarterly* 69 (1990), 495–515.
Weimann, Robert. 'Reception Aesthetics and the Crisis in Literary History'. Trans. Charles Spencer. *Clio* 5 (1975), 3–35.
Weinsheimer, Joel. 'Mrs. Siddons, the Tragic Muse and the Problem of *As*'. *Journal of Aesthetic and Art Criticism* 36 (1978), 317–28.
Weiskel, Thomas. *The Romantic Sublime: Studies in the Structure and Psychology of Transcendence*. Baltimore: Johns Hopkins University Press, 1976.
Wells, Stanley. 'Shakespeare in Hazlitt's Theatre Criticism'. *Shakespeare Survey* 35 (1982), 43–55.

ed. *Shakespeare in the Theatre: An Anthology of Criticism*. Oxford: Clarendon Press, 1997.
and Gary Taylor, eds. *William Shakespeare: A Textual Companion*. Oxford: Clarendon Press, 1987.
and Sarah Stanton, eds. *The Cambridge Companion to Shakespeare on Stage*. Cambridge: Cambridge University Press, 2002.
Wendorf, Richard. *Sir Joshua Reynolds: The Painter in Society*. London: National Portrait Gallery, 1996.
West, Shearer. *The Image of the Actor: Verbal and Visual Representation in the Age of Garrick and Kemble*. New York: St Martin's Press, 1991.
Whale, John, ed. *Edmund Burke's Reflections on the Revolution in France: New Interdisciplinary Essays*. Manchester: Manchester University Press, 2000.
[Whately, Thomas]. *Remarks on Some of the Characters of Shakespeare*. London: T. Payne, 1785.
Wheeler, David. 'Eighteenth-Century Adaptations of Shakespeare and the Example of John Dennis'. *Shakespeare Quarterly* 36 (1985), 438–49.
White, R. S. *Keats as a Reader of Shakespeare*. London: Athlone Press, 1987.
Whitley, W. T. *Artists and Their Friends in England, 1700–1799*. 2 vols. London: Medici Society, 1928.
Wilders, John, ed. *Macbeth*. Shakespeare in Production. Cambridge: Cambridge University Press, 2004.
Wilkshire, Frances M. 'Garrick's Role in the Shakespeare Controversy in France'. *L'âge du théâtre en France/The Age of Theatre in France*. Ed. David Trott and Nicole Boursier. Edmonton: Academic Printing and Pub., 1988, 219–30.
Williamson, Claude C. H., ed. *Readings on the Character of Hamlet, 1661–1947*. London: Allen and Unwin, 1950.
Wilson, Michael S. 'Garrick, Iconic Acting, and the Ideologies of Theatrical Portraiture'. *Word and Image* 6 (1990), 368–94.
Wind, Edgar. 'The Revolution of History Painting'. *Journal of Warburg Institute* 2 (1938), 116–27.
Wood, Carol Gibson. *Jonathan Richardson: Art Theorist of the English Enlightenment*. New Haven: Yale University Press, 2000.
Woodring, Carl R. *Politics in the Poetry of Coleridge*. Madison: University of Wisconsin Press, 1961.
'Two Prompt Copies of Coleridge's *Remorse*'. *Bulletin of the New York Public Library* 65 (1961), 229–35.
Woods, Leigh. *Garrick Claims the Stage: Acting as Social Emblem in Eighteenth-Century England*. Westport, CT: Greenwood Press, 1984.
Wooll, John. *Biographical Memoirs of the Late Revd Joseph Warton, D.D.* London: T. Cadell and W. Davies, 1806.
Wordsworth, William. *Prose Works*. Ed. W. J. B. Owen and Jane Worthington Smyser. 3 vols. Oxford: Clarendon Press, 1974.
The Prelude 1799, 1805, 1850. Ed. Jonathan Wordsworth et al. Norton Critical Edition. New York: Norton, 1979.

The Borderers. Ed. Robert Osborn. The Cornell Wordsworth. Ithaca: Cornell University Press, 1982.
Lyrical Ballads, and Other Poems, 1797–1800. Ed. James Butler and Karen Green. The Cornell Wordsworth. Ithaca: Cornell University Press, 1992.
and Dorothy Wordsworth. *Letters*. Ed. Ernest de Selincourt. 2nd edn. Rev. Chester Shaver et al. 8 vols. Oxford: Clarendon Press, 1967–93.
Yates, Frances A. 'Transformation of Dante's Ugolino'. *Journal of the Warburg and Courtauld Institute* 14 (1951), 92–117.
Zerilli, Linda M. G. 'Text/Woman as Spectacle: Edmund Burke's "French Revolution"'. *The Eighteenth Century* 33 (1992), 47–72.

Index

acting styles
  'conventional' (pre-Garrick) 13–14
  French, compared with English 44–5
  good *vs.* bad 182
  see also under names of performers
Addison, Joseph
  Cato 8, 141
  Pleasures of Imagination 110–11, 112
  see also The Spectator
Akenside, Mark 47
Altick, Richard D. 202
anecdote(s), as source of information 6–7
Antony and Cleopatra 33
'appropriation' 4–6
Archer, William 188
Aristotle 38, 59, 107, 115, 118, 182, 204, 207
Arnauld, Antoine, Abbé 44
Arne, Thomas 49
art criticism 64–6, 181–2
  see also painting; Reynolds, Joshua
audience responses (theories of) 59–63, 150–1
  criticised for vulgarity 108–9
  emotional 34–5, 42
  reflective 34–5
  see also under names of plays/performers

Bacon, Francis
  The Advancement of Learning 123–4, 198
  Essays 205
Bailey, Benjamin 211–12
Barrowby, William 13
Bate, W. Jackson 7
Beauclerk, Topham 37
Beaumont, Francis (and Fletcher, John) 156, 160, 186
Beaumont, Sir George 186
Behn, Aphra 2–3
Bell, G. J. 76–7, 82
Benjamin, Walter 4–5
Betterton, Thomas 174

Blake, William 64, 126, 205
  annotations on Reynolds's *Discourses* 64, 122–5, 126
  'A Pitiful Case' 122
'Bluestockings' 37, 186–8
Blunt, Reginald 195
Boaden, James 67, 72, 105, 141
Boileau(-Despréaux), Nicolas 19, 24
Booth, Junius Brutus 190
Boswell, James(, the Elder) 29, 35–7, 41, 43, 49, 51, 53, 180, 197
Boteler, Thomas 10
Bouhours, Dominique 110
Bowles, William Lisle 151
Boydell, John 87–8, 97
Bratton, J. S. 192
Brawne, Fanny 176–9
Bristol, Michael D. 4
Brown, Charles 164, 168, 169, 170–1, 177, 180
Burges, James Bland
  Riches 163
  see also Massinger, Philip
Burke, Edmund 6, 84, 92, 101, 107–9, 113, 120, 124, 146, 185, 186, 205
  Four Letters on the Proposals for Peace with the Regicide Directory of France 120–1
  'Hints for an Essay on the Drama' 203
  Philosophical Enquiry into the Origin of Our Ideas on the Sublime and the Beautiful 110, 114–16, 123
  Reflections on the Revolution in France 116–20
    factual inaccuracies 117
Burke, Richard 117
Burwick, Frederick 202, 209
Byron, George Gordon, Lord 161

Campbell, Thomas 74, 82
Carey, Ann (Kean's mother) 131–2
Carter, Elizabeth 39–40
catharsis, concept of 59, 118
Cavendish, Margaret 175

238

'character criticism' 171–3, 194
characterisation, in art/drama 127
  see also Keats; Shakespeare; *titles of works*
Chaucer, Geoffrey 127
Cibber, Colley 35, 134, 174
Cibber, Katherine, *née* Shore 35
Clarke, Charles Cowden 161–2
Clarke, Norma 39–40
Coleridge, Hartley 125
Coleridge, Samuel Taylor 167, 175, 210
  commentary on *Hamlet* 129, 138, 149, 156–7, 172
  comments on Kean's acting 136, 142
  literary reviews 153
  literary theatrical theory 64, 150–1, 209
  Biographia Literaria 149, 150
  Christabel 149, 209
  'Critique of *Bertram*' 150
  'Desultory Remarks on the Stage' 150–1
  Osorio (Remorse) see separate main heading
  The Rime of the Ancient Mariner 149
  see also Wordsworth, William
Collier, Jeremy 137, 138
Colman, George (the Elder) 11
  (with David Garrick), *The Clandestine Marriage* 50
  Man and Wife; or, The Shakespeare Jubilee 56
Colson, John, Rev. 28–9
Constable, John 186
Cooke, George Frederick 133
Coriolanus 136, 141
Corneille, Pierre 38–9
  Cinna 38, 39
Correggio, Antonio 165
Cottle, Joseph 148
Cotton, William 88
Cumberland, Richard 14

d'Alembert, Jean le Rond 44
Damiens, Robert Francis 114
Dante (Alighieri), *Inferno* 84–5, 86
Davenant, William
  adaptation of *Hamlet* 138, 146
  adaptation of *Macbeth* 68, 72, 93, 99, 109, 200, 203
Davies, Thomas 35
  Dramatic Miscellanies 199
'de Coverly, Sir Roger' *see The Spectator*
Dennis, John, *The Grounds of Criticism in Poetry* 111
Dibdin, Charles 49
Diderot, Denis 174
  Pardoxe sur le comédien 174, 188
Dilke, Charles Wentworth 164, 166–7
Dobson, Michael 196
Dodsley, Robert (ed.), *Collection of Poems by Several Hands* 1–2

Donohue, Joseph 69, 71, 74, 160
Downer, Alan S. 14
Dryden, John, *Of Dramatick Poesie* 53
Du Bos, Jean-Baptiste 110
D'Urfey, Thomas 2–3

Eliot, T. S. 70
Elliston, Robert William 161
emotion, actors' expression/experience of 173–5
  see also personal tragedy
England, Martha Winburn 50
Euripides 38
  Hippolytos 109, 119
  Iphigenia in Tauris 112
  Orestes 112

Farquhar, George
  The Beaux' Stratagem 20
  The Recruiting Officer 7
Fielding, Henry 24, 127
  The History of Tom Jones, a Foundling 60–3, 65–6, 73, 81–2, 119, 188, 198
Finlay, John 142–3, 144
Fletcher, John *see* Beaumont, Francis
Foote, Samuel 15, 24, 47–8, 57–8, 194, 198
  The Roman and English Comedy Consider'd and Compar'd 194
Forrest, Edwin 83, 190
Fox, Charles James 101
French classical drama 42, 44–6, 151
French Revolution 114, 116–21, 146–7
  relationship with theatre 117–21
Fuseli, Henry 86, 87, 88, 94, 101
  The Death of Cardinal Beaufort 94
  Macbeth Consulting the Vision of an Armed Head 101, 202
  The Nightmare 93–4
  Robin Goodfellow-Puck 88

Garrick, David 1–4, 5, 7, 24, 110
  acting style 13–15, 20, 63, 65, 86, 135, 174, 188, 194
  boyhood/youth 7, 28–9
  comments on own work 14–15
  contemporary commentaries 20, 43, 45–6, 65–6, 84 (*see also under* Johnson)
  as Hamlet 15, 60–3, 81–2, 86, 142, 144, 207
  performance text 138–9, 207–8
  as King Lear 6, 15–19, 20, 34–5, 86, 174
    audience responses 18–19, 28
    contemporary commentaries 8–10, 13, 15
    modifications to text 11–12, 15–16, 192–3
    sources 16–18
    suggestions for illustrations 16, 194
    treatment of mad scenes 16–18, 28

Garrick, David (cont.)
  as Macbeth 48, 67, 68, 83, 99, 199, 203
    performance text 72, 79, 93, 109
  media relations 47–8, 50–1, 52, 186, 196
  memorial statue 186
  (mock) self-criticism 48
  staging of Stratford Jubilee 46–7
    criticisms of 47
  'The Dream' 54
  An Essay on Acting 48
  'Jubilee Ode' 47, 48–9, 185
    publication 51–5
  The Jubilee (stage entertainment) 56–8, 105
  The Sick Monkey: A Fable 48
  see also Johnson, Samuel; Montagu, Elizabeth
Garrick, Eva Maria Violetta (David's wife) 48, 144, 207
Garrick, George (David's brother) 7
Garrick, Peter, Capt. (David's father) 28–9
genius, opposing views of 123–5, 126
Gentleman, Francis 47
George III 165
Gibbon, Edward 84, 101
Goldsmith, Oliver 84
Gombrich, Ernst 206
gothic stories/elements 153, 160
Gravelot, H. François 94
Gray, Charles Harold 20
Gray, Thomas 47
Gray, Tim 117
Grimm, Friedrich Melchior 171
'gusto,' concept of 163–4

Hamlet 3, 6, 15, 65, 81, 113, 127, 132, 173–4, 198
  characterisation 135, 156–7, 172
  eighteenth/nineteenth-century commentaries 68, 129–31
  relationship with later dramas 152, 154, 157, 170
  variant texts 137–41, 207
  see also Garrick, David; Kean, Edmund; Kemble, John Philip
Hanmer, Thomas 94
Harris, Arthur John 11
Hassall, Anthony J. 198
Hawkesworth, John 19, 24
Haydon, B. R. 163
Hayman, Francis 16, 194
Hazlitt, John 125
Hazlitt, William 6
  art criticism 126–7, 165
  literary criticism 125, 138, 162–3, 165, 175–6, 211
  as painter 125
  theatre reviews/commentaries 133–5, 136–7, 141–2, 143–4, 145–6, 206, 208
  Boswell Redivivus 180–3

Characters of Shakespear's Plays 127–31, 134, 145, 206
  comments on Reynolds 126
  A View of the English Stage 206
Henry IV (Parts 1/2) 38, 40
Henry VI Part 2 83–4, 88–97
Hill, Aaron 14
Hill, John 28, 194
Hindson, Paul 117
Hogan, Charles Beecher 207–8
Homer 44
Hone, William 165
Hughes, John 138
Hume, David 117
Hunt, Edward 2–3
Hunt, Leigh 144, 162, 165, 166, 212
Hutchinson, Sara 159

ideas, exchange of, processes/pitfalls 185–8
imagination, theories of 110–13
imitation *see* genius
inspiration *see* genius

Jacobite Rebellion (1745) 198
Jago, Richard, Rev. 47
Jameson, Anna Brownell 77
Jeffrey, Francis 169
Jenkins, Patricia 151
Jennens, Charles 16
Johnson, Samuel 1–2, 7, 19, 20, 24, 29–37, 39–41, 45, 59, 74, 87, 109–10, 127, 128, 151, 174–5, 181–2, 185–6, 210
  commentary on *Hamlet* 138, 140, 156
  commentary on *Macbeth* 68, 69–70, 73, 77–8, 110, 200
  comments on Garrick's acting 35–7, 84, 86, 174, 175
  comments on Voltaire 40
  criticisms 128–9
  edition of Shakespeare 10, 24, 28, 29–32, 75
    Garrick not mentioned in 29, 31–2, 33–4, 35–6, 43
    Preface 32–5, 39, 53–4, 175
  relationship with Garrick 29, 35–7, 53
  and the Stratford Jubilee 53–4, 197
  Dictionary 128
  Prologue (for Garrick's opening, 1747) 1–3, 7, 53
Jonson, Ben 2, 53, 156
Jubilee *see* Stratford Jubilee
Julius Caesar 38, 39, 43–4, 195

Kames, Lord (Henry Home), *Elements of Criticism* 33–4, 41–3, 110
  criticisms of 41
Kean, Aaron (Edmund's ?father) 131–2

Kean, Charles (Edmund's son) 188–90
Kean, Edmund 3–4, 6, 48, 161, 179–80, 207, 211
    acting style 132–3, 136, 169–70, 174–5
    boyhood/early career 131–2
    comeback appearances 163–4
    compared with Kemble 135–7
    contemporary commentaries 208 (*see also* Hazlitt; Keats)
    farewell appearance (as Othello) 188–90
    as Hamlet 134–5, 137, 141–6
        criticisms 145
        performance text 146, 207
    physical appearance 136, 162
    as Shylock 132–3, 188
    social life 166, 188
Kean, Edmund, Sr. (Edmund's ?father) 131–2
Kean, Moses (Edmund's uncle) 131–2, 142, 175
Keate, George 47
Keats, John 161, 186–8
    biographical details 168, 176–9, 184, 213
    boyhood/personality 161–2
    comments on Kean 162, 167–8, 181, 182, 212
    literary theory 164–8, 176–7, 211–12
    'La Belle Dame Sans Merci' 180
    'The Cap and Bells; or, the Jealousies' 180
    Endymion 181
    The Eve of St Agnes 183
    King Stephen (unfinished) 184
    Lamia 180
    Otho the Great see separate main heading
Keats, Tom 162, 176
Kemble, Charles 137
Kemble, John Philip 3–4, 6, 133, 148, 161
    acting style 132, 135–6, 141
    compared with Kean 135–7
    as Hamlet 137, 141, 142, 144, 145
        performance text 139–41, 146, 207, 208
    and *Macbeth* (play/role) 59, 67–9
        audience responses 82
        contemporary commentaries 86–7
        performance style 72
        performance text 72–3, 93, 200
        staging 79–80, 81–2, 83, 131
        visual effects 79–80
    Macbeth Reconsidered 68–9, 70–3, 75
    physical appearance 135
    stage career 67
Kenrick, William 47
King, Thomas 50–1, 56
King John 42–3
King Lear 5–6, 36, 42, 129, 132
    eighteenth/nineteenth-century commentaries 8–10, 19–28, 29–32, 41, 68, 165
    modified by Garrick 11–12, 15–16, 192–3
    modified by Tate 10–11

in performance *see under* Garrick
source texts 192
Kinnaird, John 206
Klingel, Joan E. 36
Knowles, Sheridan 83

Lacy, James 1
Lamb, Charles 125, 186
Le Brun, Charles 86, 201
Lekain (Henri-Louis Caïn), 'the French Garrick' 44–5
Lewes, G.H. 188
Locke, John 26, 115
    Essay on Human Understanding 123
Longinus, *On the Sublime* 64, 111–13, 114–15
Loughborough, Lord 120
Louis XV of France 114
Louis XVI of France 114, 116–17, 119–20
Lowell, Amy 169
Lownes, L. 199
Lucan (Marcus Annaeus Lucanus), *Pharsalia* 197
Lucretius (T. Lucretius Carus) 19

Macbeth 6, 35, 38, 39, 42–3, 116, 132, 135, 147, 152, 170
    characterisation 68–77
    eighteenth-century commentaries 68, 108, 110, 112–13, 199, 200
    hallucinatory elements 80, 200
    textual modifications 68, 200
    treatment of witches 77–80
    see also Kemble, John Philip; Siddons, Sarah
Macklin, Charles 13, 47
Macready, William Charles 190
Mahomet Mussulmo 2–3
Malone, Edmond 115–16, 213
Marie-Antoinette, Queen 114, 116–17, 119–20, 205
Marlowe, Christopher, *Tamburlaine* 8
Marxist analysis 4–5
Mason, William 47, 92
Massinger, Philip 156, 160
    City Madam (Riches) 163
    The Duke of Milan 178
    A New Way to Pay Old Debts 136–7
Maturin, C.R., *Bertram* 150
Mays, J.C.C. 157
McFarland, Thomas 169
The Merchant of Venice 132–3, 188
metanoia (repentance) 156–7
Meyerhold, Vsevolod Emilevich 188
Michelangelo (Buonarotti) 64–5, 67, 86, 105, 107, 122, 124–5, 186, 201, 203
Middleton, Thomas, *The Witch* 68

Mills, John A. 141
Milton, John 111
　Paradise Lost 74, 107
　'On Shakespeare' 49
Molé, Jean-Baptiste 45
Montagu, Edward 51
Montagu, Elizabeth 41–6, 185, 195
　Essay on the Writings and Genius of Shakespear 37–41, 51–2, 54, 78–9, 109–10, 175, 185
　Keats's criticisms of 186–8
　relationship with Garrick 51–2
　relationship with Johnson 40
　visit to France 43–6
Morgan, Macnamara 186
Much Ado About Nothing 58, 170, 171
Murphy, Arthur (Charles Ranger) 47, 52, 185–6
　articles on Lear 8–10, 16–18, 24–8, 30
　reponses 26–7, 30–1

nature, imitation of 127, 128–31
'Negative Capability,' concept of 164–8, 179
Newton, Isaac 123
Northcote, James 84–6, 87, 88, 92–3, 99–101, 180–3
　The Death of the Earl of Argyll 183
Norton, Thomas, and Thomas Sackville, Gorboduc 44

Odell, George C. D. 5
Offely, Mr 7
Old Price riots (1809) 67
O'Neill, Eliza 133
Osorio (Remorse) (Coleridge) 6, 146, 148–9, 151–61, 186, 210, 211
　audience responses 211
　Coleridge's comments on 155–6, 159–60
　commercial success 159
　demands on actors 160
　problems of performance 154–5
　published version 210
　revisions 157–9
　sources/influences 151–2
Othello 41, 43–4, 132, 135, 163–4, 188–90
Otho the Great (Keats) 6, 162, 168–73, 176, 177–80
　autobiographical basis 177–9
　characterisation 172–3
　critical commentary 169
　dramatic failings 171, 179, 180
　Keats's comments on 179, 181–3, 213
　method of composition 169–70
　production plans 179–80
　(rejected) ideas for enlivenment 170–1
Oxberry, William 137

Paine, Thomas, The Rights of Man 116
painting, analogy with theatre 65–6, 84–7, 150–1, 152, 180–3
Park, Roy 206
Pennington, Mrs 74
Penny, Nicholas 85–6
performance styles, theories/preferences in 41
　see also names of actors
personal tragedy, role in development of performance 16–18, 74, 132, 174–5, 177–9, 188–90
Philips, Ambrose, The Distrest Mother (after Racine) 59–61
Phillips, Thomas 103–5
Pierino da Vinci 86, 201
Piozzi, Hester Lynch (Thrale) 36, 37, 74
Plato 65, 205
Polygnotus 182
Pope, Alexander 81, 127–8
Poussin, Nicolas 65
Pratt, Samuel Jackson 186
Price, Richard, Rev. 118, 119
Pritchard, Hannah 35, 67, 74, 83

Quin, James 14, 135, 194

Racine, Jean, Andromaque 59
Rae, Alexander 161
Ranger, Charles see Murphy, Arthur
Raphael (Raffaello Sanzio) 64, 65, 93, 124–5, 165, 181, 186
　The Miracle of Bolsena 182
Rembrandt van Rijn 181
Remorse see Osorio
remorse, as theme of tragedy 146, 157–9, 210
Repton, Henry ('the Bee') 202
Reynolds, J. H. 179
Reynolds, Joshua 6, 32, 37, 84, 87, 109–10, 125, 128, 129, 141, 181–2, 203, 205, 206
　cenotaph 186
　contemporary criticisms 122–5, 126–7
　Count Ugolino and His Children 84–7, 88, 180, 182
　The Death of Cardinal Beaufort 83–4, 87–97
　　critical responses 92–4, 99–101, 202
　Discourses 63–7, 93, 107, 122–5, 126–7, 185
　Macbeth and the Witches 87, 97–101
　　critical responses 99
　Puck 87–8
　　critical responses 88
　Sarah Siddons as the Tragic Muse 67, 101–7
　　critical responses 103, 105
　　modifications 106–7
　Self Portrait as a Figure of Horror 107

Richard III 1, 68, 133–4, 135, 150, 152, 163, 164, 170, 182
  characterisation, compared with *Macbeth* 69, 70, 71–2
Richardson, Jonathan, *Two Discourses* 86, 201
Richardson, William, *A Philosophical Analysis and Illustration of Some of Shakespeare's Remarkable Characters* 128, 138
Roach, Joseph 14
Rogers, Samuel 103
Romeo and Juliet 57, 135
Rousseau, Jean-Jacques 117–18
Rowe, Nicholas 9, 20, 75, 94, 110, 111, 197
  The Fair Penitent 14
Rubens, Peter Paul 129

Sackville, Thomas *see* Norton, Thomas
Schiller, Friedrich von
  The Ghost-Seer 151–2, 157
  The Robbers 148, 151–2, 157
Schlegel, August Wilhelm 128
Schneider, Elizabeth 206
Scott, Walter 79–80, 86–7, 131
Shackleton, Richard 108, 113
Shaftesbury, 3rd Earl of 71
Shakespeare, Hamnet 176, 212–13
Shakespeare, William
  (alleged) decline following 2
  characterisation 127–31, 133–5, 156–7, 171–2, 175–6
  collection of paintings taken from 87–101, 202
  commemoration *see* Stratford Jubilee
  eighteenth-century commentaries 1–2, 30, 32–5, 43–6, 52–5, 211
  influence on later writers 152, 160, 170, 171
  innovations in performance *see under names of performers*
  language 163
  modern commentaries 4–6
  national importance 4
  personal life 176
  political basis of productions/adaptations 5
  satire on critics 50–1
  see also titles of works
Shakespeare Ladies' Club, The 197
Sherbo, Arthur 30, 33–4
Sheridan, Richard Brinsley 101, 108, 148, 155
Sheridan, Thomas 47, 108, 203
Siddons, Sarah 3–4, 6, 58, 101, 107, 127, 133, 135–6, 148, 161, 174
  as Lady Macbeth 59, 67–9, 82–3, 131, 201
    audience responses 75
    debut in role 73–4
    sources for performance 74

'Remarks on the Character of Lady Macbeth' 68–9, 73–4
  stage appearance as 'Tragic Muse' 105–6 (*see also* Reynolds)
  stage career 67–8
Sillars, Stuart 202
Smith, Horace 166
Smith, William 'Gentleman' (actor) 67
Smith, William (Greek scholar) 111–13
Sophocles 20, 38
  Oedipus Coloneus 42
  Polyxena 113
Southey, Robert 151, 161
The Spectator, review of Garrick's *Hamlet* 59–61, 63, 119
Spencer, Hazleton 5
Stanislavski, Konstantin 188
Steevens, George 47, 52, 75, 87, 138, 140, 213
Stevenson, John Allen 198
Sticotti, Antoine-Fabio 188
Stillinger, Jack 171
Stone, George Winchester (Jr) 11, 194
Stratford Jubilee (1769) 43, 46–7, 48–51, 196
  administrative/financial difficulties 55–6, 186
  aftermath 51–8
  audience responses 49–50, 51
  criticisms 47
  (satirical) counterblasts 50–1, 52, 57–8
  local people's responses 55
  merchandising 197
  order of performance 196–7
Stuart, Daniel 155
Stubbes, George 137–8
sublime, the, theories of 111–16, 124–5

tabula rasa theory 124
Tate, Nahum, adaptation of *King Lear* 5–6, 13, 192
  dedicatory letter 6
  divergences from Shakespeare 10–11, 30
  further modified by Garrick 11–12
  preferred to Shakespeare 29–30
  vocabulary 15
Taylor, Gary 4
Taylor, John 179
The Tempest 43–4
Thistlewood, Arthur 175
Thrale, Mrs *See* Piozzi, Hester Lynch (Thrale)
three unities *see* unities
Tidswell, Miss 132
Tighe, G. 18
Titian (Tiziano Vecelli) 181
tragedy, definitions 172, 207

unities (of time/place/action), observance of 32–4, 38, 41, 171

verisimilitude 41–3, 65–6
    Johnsonian theory of 32–5
Vesey, Elizabeth 44
Vickers, Brian 5, 194
Victor, Benjamin 51, 55
Villani, Giovanni 86
Voltaire (François-Marie Arouet) 38–41, 44, 45, 50, 53, 54–5, 110, 195, 196
    Mahomet 44–5
    L'Orphelin de la Chine 38

Wallack, James 157
Walmesley, Gilbert 7, 28–9
Walpole, Horace 54
Warton, Joseph 47, 185
    articles on *Lear* 8, 19–24, 28, 193
        contemporary commentaries 24–8, 30–1
        inconsistencies between essays 22–4
    'The Enthusiast; or, The Lover of Nature' 52
Watson, Caroline 97
Watson, Robert, *History of the reign of Philip the second, King of Spain* 151

Weimann, Robert 4
Wells, Stanley 206
West, Benjamin, *Death on the Pale Horse* 165, 212
Whately, Thomas, *Remarks on Some of the Characters of Shakespeare* 69–72, 73, 128
White, George 85, 86
Wilks, Robert 138
Williams, Raymond 4
'willing suspension of disbelief' 150
The Winter's Tale 129
Woodhouse, Richard 167
Woodmason, James 101
Wordsworth, Dorothy 148
Wordsworth, William 125, 164, 167–8, 182, 186
    relationship with Coleridge 148–50
    The Borderers 147–9, 152, 172, 208–9
    The Excursion 163
    Prelude 146–7
    The Ruined Cottage 148
    (with Coleridge), *Lyrical Ballads* 148–51
Wyndham, Wadham 101

Young, Charles 190

Zeuxis 182

OHIO UNIVERSITY LIBRARY

Please return this book as soon as you have finished with it. In order to avoid a fine it must be returned by the latest date stamped below. All books are subject to recall after two weeks or immediately if needed for reserve.

CF